TH

THE
AL QAEDA
READER

EDITED AND TRANSLATED BY

RAYMOND IBRAHIM

INTRODUCTION BY

VICTOR DAVIS HANSON

BROADWAY BOOKS

NEW YORK

PUBLISHED BY BROADWAY BOOKS

A hardcover edition of this book has been published
simultaneously by Doubleday.

Published in the United States by Broadway Books, an imprint of
The Doubleday Broadway Publishing Group, a division of
Random House, Inc., New York.
www.broadwaybooks.com

BROADWAY BOOKS and its logo, a letter B bisected on the diagonal,
are trademarks of Random House, Inc.

LIBRARY OF CONGRESS CATALOGING-IN-PUBLICATION DATA
The Al Qaeda reader / edited and translated by Raymond Ibrahim ;
introduction by Victor Davis Hanson.—1st ed.
p. cm.
Summary: "Gathers together the essential texts and documents
that trace the origin, history, and evolution of the ideas of
al-Qaeda founders Ayman al-Zawahiri and Osama bin Laden"—
Provided by publisher.
Includes bibliographical references.
1. Qaida (Organization) 2. Zawāhirī, Ayman. 3. Bin Laden,
Osama, 1957– . 4. Jihad. 5. Islam and politics. 6. Terrorism—
Religious aspects—Islam. 7. War on Terrorism, 2001– .
8. United States—Relations—Islamic countries. 9. Islamic
countries—Relations—United States. I. Ibrahim, Raymond.
II. Zawāhirī, Ayman. III. Bin Laden, Osama, 1957– .
HV6433.I742Q33 2007
363.325—dc22   2006029721

ISBN: 978-0-7679-2262-3

PRINTED IN THE UNITED STATES OF AMERICA

1 3 5 7 9 10 8 6 4 2

FIRST PAPERBACK EDITION

TO MY SON, ALEXANDER,

AND FOR ALETHEIA

CONTENTS

PREFACE

The tragedy of September 11, 2001, has influenced many. It altered my academic interests away from the ancient and medieval Mediterranean—a landscape of long-ago Mesopotamians, Egyptians, Greeks, Romans, Byzantines, Arabs, and Turks—and led me to strictly focus on the contemporary Arab-Islamic world. Like many others, after 9/11 I desired to learn what precisely was the motivation—and inspiration—of radical Islamic groups such as al-Qaeda, who had formally declared war on the United States.

To make a long story short, in 2002 I applied to and was accepted by Georgetown University's Center for Contemporary Arab Studies— a leading institution in Islamic studies located in Washington, D.C. Soon thereafter, I also landed an internship at the Near East section of the Library of Congress—where the largest collection of Arabic books in the United States is housed. When, happily, the internship evolved into a permanent, full-time position—and considering the exigencies of newly married life and fatherhood—I took a leave of absence from my formal academic studies in order to focus on more practical work.

Finding myself in the world's largest library, and working in the division that houses all Arabic materials—where thousands of new books, serials, microfilms, etc., arrive yearly from the little-known publishing houses of the Arab world, many dealing with radical Islam—I was, admittedly, like the proverbial child in a well-stocked toy store.

Arabic books dealing with radical Islam, al-Qaeda, or terrorism passing through my hands—and these were many—naturally were perused. It was with some shock that I discovered that a good number of these contained not only hitherto unknown excerpts or quotes by al-Qaeda, but entire treatises and even whole books written by them. Thus I came to discover that a good number of these had never been translated into English, much less disseminated to the general public.

Further striking, most of their writings and speeches neatly fit into two genres—religious exegesis, meant to motivate and instruct Muslims, and propagandist speeches, aimed at demoralizing the West and inciting Muslims to action.

Out of that examination of such a disparate group of writings, this present book of translated documents was conceived and the idea of its publication accepted.

This volume is presented to the public for educational and didactic purposes—for Americans to know and comprehend their enemy, an essential prerequisite throughout history for victory. This volume of translations, taken as a whole, proves once and for all that, despite the propaganda of al-Qaeda and its sympathizers, radical Islam's war with the West is not finite and limited to political grievances—real or imagined—but is existential, transcending time and space and deeply rooted in faith.

Furthermore, censoring political speeches and writings—particularly in the United States in the era of its struggle of ideas against absolutism—might only encourage the belief that such statements by al-Qaeda must be true, hence the need to silence them. In fact, bin Laden has used this very argument to win widespread agreement in the Arab world. On October 10, 2001, for example, the White House advised television networks to censor bin Laden broadcasts, citing the possibility of coded messages to other terrorist cells. Less than two weeks later, bin Laden, in an interview on the al-Jazeera television network, had this to say about it:

> The values of this Western civilization under the leadership
> of America have been destroyed. Those awesome symbolic

[twin] towers that spoke of liberty, human rights, and
humanity have been destroyed. They have gone up in smoke.
The proof came when the U.S. government pressured the
media not to run our statements that are not longer than a
very few minutes. . . . They forgot all about fair and objective
reporting and reporting the other side of the issue. I tell you
freedom and human rights in America are doomed.[1]

The publication of this book proves otherwise.

Raymond Ibrahim
Washington, D.C., October 2006

ACKNOWLEDGMENTS

I first wish to thank my former professor and M.A. thesis chair, Victor Davis Hanson, currently a Senior Fellow at the Hoover Institution, Stanford University. It was to him that I first took my initial ideas about these translations, and it was he who referred me to his literary agents Glen Hartley and Lynn Chu of Writer's Representatives—who, in their turn, took my proposal to editor-at-large Adam Bellow of Doubleday. To all of them, I offer my gratitude—first for their wisdom in appreciating the importance of such an endeavor, but also for their courage, especially Doubleday, in supporting what proved to be a controversial project years before its materialization.

My thanks to Mary-Jane Deeb, Chief of the African and Middle Eastern Division of the Library of Congress (and subsequently my boss) for first giving me, a then unemployed graduate student, the opportunity to work at the Library of Congress—an experience that has thus far proven to be both intrinsically and instrumentally rewarding.

I thank my father and mother for all their support, and for first instilling in me a curiosity toward language as well as a special interest in Arabic and our ancestral homeland of Egypt.

Finally, my thanks are due to my wife, who, since the start of this project, has had to endure her husband's (sometimes excessive) linguistic, philological, and historical attempts at unraveling the philosophy of radical Islam.

NOTE ON TEXT
AND TRANSLATION

The translations included in this volume come from various sources. The four documents that form the Theology section were originally posted on the Internet by many Islamist Web sites (which were subsequently shut down) but are still found separately in a number of Arabic books. For those interested in sourcing original Arabic copies, there is one particular title that conveniently contains all four, called (in translation), *Alliance of Terrorism: The Al-Qaeda Organization*.[1] Most of the selections of the Propaganda section were translated directly from video- and audiotapes and transcripts found on the Internet—especially from the al-Jazeera Web site (http://www.aljazeera.net) and MEMRI (the Middle East Media Research Institute: http://www.memri.org). Both of these organizations should be commended for the important services they render.

An anonymous French wit is credited with saying that translations are like wives—either beautiful or faithful, seldom both. Translating from such unrelated languages as Arabic and English—from Semitic to Germanic—makes such a slander somewhat appreciable. Still, I have tried to dispel this cynical rumor by trying to wed both virtues in the forthcoming translations. On those occasions, however, where a choice had to be made between fidelity and aesthetics, I always opted for the former, even if less-than-fluid English was the result. In short, since this volume is presented for didactical and not literary purposes, priority has always been given to capturing precise meaning, with style and idiomatic usage coming second.

In order to appeal to a broad readership, certain measures were taken to ensure that the translation is as "user-friendly" as possible. Here pedantry gave way to accessibility. The most common and familiar name spellings were used, even if they are not as phonetically accurate as more updated versions. For example, *al-Qur'an* and *Salah ad-Din* are here spelled *Koran* and *Saladin*. Diacritics have been avoided as well as the inverted apostrophe representing the Arabic letter 'ayn, since such markings usually serve to make an already strange word that much more bewildering for the general English reader. In most cases, the Arabic *hamza* (represented by an apostrophe and pronounced as a glottal stop) is retained: its appearance is generally widespread, and without it many words become unrecognizable. The unpronounced *h* in words ending in the Arabic *ta-marbuta* (e.g., *sharia* instead of *shariah*) has been omitted. Since Arabic singulars often morph into nearly unrecognizable plurals, the latter have been anglicized by merely adding an "s" (e.g., *hadiths* instead of *ahadith*, *fatwas* instead of *fatawa*), except for words that have recognizable singulars and plurals, in which case both have been preserved (e.g., *mujahid* and *mujahidin*). ("Scholar" is here used for the singular of *ulema: Alim* is rarely seen in English, and at any rate, it is the plural *ulema* that bears an important connotation, that of "consensus.") All dates have been rendered according to the Gregorian calendar.

The customary religious formulas always uttered after pronouncing the names of Allah, Muhammad, his Companions, or deceased and pious Muslims—e.g., "prayers and peace be upon him," "Allah have mercy on him," "Allah be pleased with him"—have not been reproduced: such repetitiveness interrupts flow and reading comprehension, not to mention is not easily translatable. This decision was not taken lightly, as the religiosity that permeates the original Arabic becomes lost in translation. Yet here fluidity was chosen at the expense of rigid literalism.

Like all languages, Arabic possesses certain idiosyncrasies, which, if carried over in English, would result in extremely cumbersome sentences. One of these is the fact that the typical Arabic sentence, especially in these writings, can often be as long as the typical English paragraph, punctuated by numerous commas and conjunctions. I have eliminated this feature, producing shorter sentences, usually by treating the Arabic comma as an English period, semicolon, colon, or hyphen, depending on context.

Deciding which Arabic words were to be left untranslated due to their unique natures and which were to be translated has been a thorny issue. Usually one transliterates only those words that possess such intrinsic value that to translate them is to do them injustice. The problem, however, is where one draws the line—an inevitably subjective endeavor and an arbitrary decision. My method was therefore to transliterate only those words that have become or are becoming commonplace in the media and to provide a critical glossary of such terms, while translating the rest, with explanatory footnotes as needed.

Since *Allah* not only denotes "The Deity" in Islam but is also a proper name, the Arabic *Allah* instead of the more generic *God* has been used throughout.

The theological writings—especially al-Zawahiri's three treatises—contain many *hadiths* and quotations from the early *ulema*. The original versions of these treatises probably contained the proper citations, but they have been edited out in the Arabic editions surveyed. This is normal and should not lead the reader to suppose that al-Qaeda may have willfully manipulated or misquoted some *hadiths* in pursuit of a particular agenda. A high-profile organization such as al-Qaeda cannot afford to engage in such fraudulence, which would be quickly exposed and used to discredit them in the eyes of their intended audience, the Muslim world. At any rate, citing the *hadith* by compiler only (e.g., "Bukhari's *hadith*") is common, which is probably why the editors of the Arabic versions omitted them. (There is an atmosphere of honesty among Muslims where Islamic texts are concerned. In fact, most of the Koranic verses in these texts also did not contain citations, but these have been provided in brackets.)

It became clear early on that using one standard English translation for the many Koranic verses quoted in the text would not be feasible: whenever a verse is evoked and then commented upon, the particular aspect in context being stressed by the commentator (whether al-Qaeda or the *ulema*) would not be clear by relying on one particular translation. Therefore, the method used for translating Koranic verses was to compare the most authoritative English versions (e.g., Pickthall, Dawood, Ali, Shakir) in juxtaposition to the original Arabic, revising as necessary, always with an eye to context. Having said that, English readers are encouraged to look up any given verse in any translation they prefer.

CRITICAL GLOSSARY
OF ARABIC TERMS

❧

Dhimmis: Non-Muslims living under Islamic rule. In exchange for voluntarily paying the *jizya* and accepting "second-class" status by obeying several social restrictions, Christians, Jews, and other "People of the Book" are guaranteed protection from a Muslim state under *sharia* law. The neologism *dhimmitude* denotes non-Muslim (usually Western) appeasement of Muslims.

Emir: Prince or military commander.

Fatwa: A legal opinion or decree issued by a recognized authority and derived from Islam's roots of jurisprudence (*usul al-fiqh*).

Hadith: Traditions of the words and deeds of Muhammad, which supplement and provide context for the Koran. All traditional schools of Sunni jurisprudence (*madhhabs*) regard the *hadith* as an extremely important source for determining the *sunna* and by extension the *sharia*. There are six authoritative collections, compiled by Bukhari, Muslim, Abu Dawud, al-Tirmidhi, al-Nasa'i, and Ibn Maja. The collections of Bukhari and Muslim especially are considered second only to the Koran in authority.

Imam: Title for a religious leader, especially for one of the founders of the four *madhhabs*. Also a prayer leader. (In Shi'a Islam, *imam* denotes a divinely appointed and infallible ruler whose word is law.)

Islam: Verbal imperative meaning "Submit" (to Allah). Monotheistic religion begun in seventh-century Arabia by the Prophet Muhammad and adhered to by some 1.2 billion people worldwide.

Jahiliyya: "Ignorance." Historically, the period of pre-Islamic Arabia when most Arabs were pagans and idolators. In contemporary usage, it refers to any condition, society, or person that does not live in accordance with Islam and its *sharia*.

Jihad: To "strive" or "struggle." In the Koran and *hadith, jihad* primarily means warfare in the service of Islam, or "holy war." A secondary meaning, upheld especially by Sufis, holds that the "greater" *jihad* is an internal struggle between a person and his vices.

Jizya: Under *sharia* law, a special tax paid by non-Muslims (*dhimmis*) living in Islamic states, founded on Koran 9:29 and the *hadith*. In classical juridical writings, *jizya* is often used to connote the social restrictions placed on *dhimmis*.

Madhhab: Literally, "road followed" or "ideology." *Madhhabs* are Islamic schools of thought and religious jurisprudence. There are currently four universally recognized schools of jurisprudence in Sunni Islam: Malaki, Shafi'i, Hanbali, and Hanafi, all named after their founders. They all agree over the fundamentals of the faith and differ primarily over finer points of jurisprudence and methodology.

Mufti: An Islamic scholar from the class of *ulema* specialized in *sharia* law and capable of issuing legal opinions (*fatwas*).

Mujahid (pl. *mujahidin*): A Muslim "holy warrior." Etymologically related to the word *jihad*, a *mujahid* is one who wages *jihad. Mujahidin* are generally referred to as "jihadists" in English.

Al-Qaeda: The "base." Name of infamous radical Islamic terrorist organization headed by Osama bin Laden and Ayman al-Zawahiri, responsible for the 9/11 strikes on U.S. soil. Al-Qaeda members often refer to their organization as the "base of *jihad*" (*Qaedat al-Jihad*).

Sharia: The "way." Drawn mostly from commandments, prohibitions, and precedents found in the Koran and *sunna*, the *sharia* is a comprehensive body of laws governing Islamic society. Understood to be Allah's Law, and often translated as "Divine Law," the *sharia* covers everyday issues such as politics, economics, finances, business and contractual laws, dress codes, dietary laws, familial obligations, and sexual ethics.

Sheikh: Honorific title generally meaning a revered or wise elder, but also an authoritative scholar of Islam.

Sultan: The "power-wielder." In contemporary usage, connotes an authority figure who rules through force.

Sunna: The words, habits, and practices of Muhammad, as transmitted by reliable witnesses and recorded in the *hadith*. Much of *sharia* law is based on the *sunna*, since it is believed that upholding Muhammad's practices and habits is the perfect form of Islam. Sunnis, who make up almost 90 percent of all Muslims, are therefore the "people of tradition."

Taqiyya: "To fear." Based primarily on Koran 3:28 and 16:106, *taqiyya* is an Islamic doctrine allowing Muslims to dissemble their true beliefs when fearing persecution. Based on certain *hadiths*, some *ulema* expand the meaning of *taqiyya* to also permit general lying in order to advance any cause beneficial to Islam.

Tawhid: The affirmation of the oneness or unity of Allah, sometimes translated as "monotheism." *Tawhid* is the belief that Allah has no partners or associates in any way, shape, or form. Traditional Islam holds that most religions (especially Christianity and Judaism) express this basic truth but have been perverted through the belief or practice that there is something else—whether a person (e.g., Jesus) or concept (e.g., democracy)—that is equal to or sovereign with Allah. It is enshrined in the Muslim profession of faith: "There is no god but Allah . . ."

Ulema: "The learned ones," all the past and present scholars who have made it their business to know and study every aspect of Islam. As guardians and interpreters of the *sharia*, the *ulema* have traditionally held a prominent place in Muslim society. The consensus of the *umma*—which in reality translates into the consensus of the *ulema*—is second only to the Koran and *sunna* in authority and is generally seen as binding on the entire *umma*. Their backing is therefore often sought (or bought) by the governments of Muslim countries, as they confer religious legitimacy.

Umma: The international "community" or "nation" of Muslims that transcends ethnic, linguistic, and political definition.

IMPORTANT FIGURES IN ISLAM

The following list provides brief biographies of famous *ulema* cited and quoted by al-Qaeda in their texts and speeches. They are listed by their most common names.

Abu Dawud (817–888). Compiler of one of the six canonical collections of *hadith* known as *Sunan Abu Dawud*.

Abu Hanifa (699–767). Great scholar and jurist. Founder of the Hanifi school of jurisprudence, one of Sunni Islam's four universally recognized *madhhabs*.

Ahmad ibn Hanbal (780–855). Great scholar and jurist, often referred to by his first name only. Founder of the Hanbali school of jurisprudence, one of Sunni Islam's four universally recognized *madhhabs*, famous for its rigid literalism. Compiler of a vast collection of *hadith* known as *Musnad Ahmad*.

Ahmad Shakir (b. 1892). *Hadith* scholar who studied and taught at Egypt's al-Azhar university, one of Sunni Islam's most authoritative institutions.

al-Awza'i (707–774). Founder of one of the earliest schools of laws that was eventually subsumed by the Maliki *madhhab*. Nonetheless, as one of Islam's "pious ancestors," his views are often still recognized and debated.

Bukhari (810–870). Compiler of the most authoritative collection of *hadith* in Sunni Islam, known as *Sahih Bukhari* or "Bukhari's authentic [*hadith*]." His nine-volume collection is second in authority only to the Koran.

Ibn al-Arabi (1076–1148). Maliki jurist from Andulisia (modern-day Spain). Produced an authoritative commentary on the *hadith* collection of al-Tirmidhi.

Ibn Hajar al-Asqalani (1372–1449). Historian and scholar. Wrote *Al-Fath al-Bari*, an eighteen-volume commentary on Sahih Bukhari, commonly considered the final authority on the matter.

Ibn Hazam (994–1069). Muslim philosopher and scholar born in Andulisia. Wrote hundreds of authoritative books and treatises.

Ibn Ishaq (704–767). Wrote the earliest biography of Muhammad, known as *The Life of the Prophet*.

Ibn Kathir (1301–1373). Student of Ibn Taymiyya and Ibn Qayyim. Renowned for his great memory of the Koran and *hadith* and overall erudition. Wrote many theological books, the most famous of which is his voluminous *Tafsir* (exegesis of the Koran). Considered to be a summary of all previous commentaries, Kathir's *Tafsir*, known for juxtaposing *hadiths* to their corresponding Koranic verses, is one of the most celebrated and authoritative commentaries of the Koran in the Islamic world today.

Ibn Qayyim (1292–1350). Close student and spiritual successor of Ibn Taymiyya. Like his master, he authored many works still considered authoritative today. Renowned for his great knowledge in all branches of Islamic science. Mentor of Ibn Kathir.

Ibn Qudama (1147–1223). Hanbali scholar and author of *Al-Mughni*, a primary manual on Hanbali jurisprudence.

Ibn Taymiyya (1263–1328). Hanbali scholar and jurist revered for his encyclopedic knowledge and piety who lived in the chaotic times of the Mongol invasions. Prolific author and issuer of numerous *fatwas*. Famous for preaching *jihad* against the Mongol invaders. Taught that emulating the first three generations of Islam was the ideal way of living. Sporadically jailed by the Mamluks and finally died in prison for his outspokenness. Greatly influenced many other important *ulema*, such as Ibn Qayyim, Ibn Kathir, and Abd al-Wahhab, as well as modern-day fundamentalists and radicals. Known by the honorific *Sheikh al-Islam* ("learned elder of Islam").

al-Jassas (d. 981). Scholar and author of the *Ahkam al-Koran*.

Malik ibn Anas (715–796). Great scholar and jurist. Founder of the Maliki school of jurisprudence, one of Sunni Islam's four universally recognized *madhhabs*. Compiler of an authoritative collection of *hadiths* known as *Al-Muwatta*.

al-Mawdudi (1903–1979). Influential Muslim scholar and prolific writer. Founder of Pakistan's Jamaat e Islami ("Islamic Assembly"). Along with Egypt's Sayyid Qutb, thought to be one of Islamic fundamentalism's founding fathers.

Muhammad bin Ibrahim (d. 2002). Jurist and former grand *mufti* of Saudi Arabia.

Muslim (821–875). Compiler of the second most authoritative collection of *hadiths* in Sunni Islam, known as *Sahih Muslim* or "Muslim's authentic [*hadith*]." He and Bukhari are collectively known as *al-Sahihan* ("the authentic two").

al-Nawwawi (1233–1277). Famous Shafi'i jurist, known for his exceptional knowledge of the *hadith* and author of one of the most authoritative law books, *The Path of the Students*.

al-Qurtubi (d. 1273). Cordoban-born Maliki scholar and author of a highly acclaimed twenty-volume exegesis of the Koran.

Sayyid Qutb (1906–1966). Ideologue of the Muslim Brotherhood in Egypt. Wrote many books and pamphlets, the most famous of which is his monumental *In the Shade of the Koran*, a Koranic exegesis written while he was imprisoned. Heavily emphasized the concept of militant *jihad*. Considered to be one of the founding fathers of modern-day Islamic fundamentalism. Executed by the Egyptian government.

al-Shafi'i (767–820). Great scholar and jurist. Known as the "architect" of Islamic law. Pupil of Malik and founder of the Shafi'i school of jurisprudence, one of Sunni Islam's four universally recognized *madhhabs*.

al-Shawkani (1760–1834). Former Shi'a who embraced traditional Sunnism. Devised a strict system of legal analysis based on traditional Sunni thought still influential today.

al-Tabari (838–923). Great historian and scholar. Famous for his thirty-eight-volume history and thirty-volume *Tafsir* ("exegesis") of the Koran. Both are still standard and authoritative works in the field of Islam.

al-Tirmidhi (824–892). Compiler of one of the six canonical collections of *hadiths* known as *Sunan al-Tirmidhi*.

INTRODUCTION

BY VICTOR DAVIS HANSON,
SENIOR FELLOW, THE HOOVER INSTITUTION,
STANFORD UNIVERSITY

Are the al-Qaeda terrorists really engaged in a war to destroy Western culture? Or are they simply an unsophisticated, ragtag group of radical fundamentalists who are little more than petty criminals that got lucky on September 11?

In the years following the attacks on New York and Washington, and the subsequent invasions of Afghanistan and Iraq, that debate still rages in the West. It is framed largely between those who wish to mobilize the military to defeat an all-embracing ideology of existential enemies and, on the other hand, those who see largely sporadic and uncoordinated attacks, predicated on local, unrelated grievances such as the Palestinian question, Chechnya, the Balkans, or Kashmir. So the former see war, the latter the criminal justice system, as the proper tool against Islamic fundamentalist terror. But all too often this controversy hinges not on the terrorists' real capability but rather on the very motives and methods that we ourselves impute to bin Laden and his al-Qaeda operatives.

Instead, we should keep quiet and listen. Raymond Ibrahim—through these published translations from the Arabic of much of what Osama bin Laden and his ideological mentor, Dr. Ayman Zawahiri, have written or spoken—now allows us the opportunity to hear from the terrorists directly. And we should recall that there is ample precedent to make us worried, since most megalomaniacs are usually candid about their aims well in advance—perhaps because their rantings unfortunately are rarely taken seriously. Hitler's *Mein Kampf* outlined both a world war and a holocaust—and was ignored. To read Mao's *Little Red Book* is to understand the logic of the carnage of the Cultural Revolution. The mess of present-day Libya was outlined well in advance in Col. Mu'ammar Gadhafi's *Green Book*. In the same fashion, the architects of al-Qaeda explain to us why they are at war and what they have in store for us.

What, then, are their expressed motives? Are we hated because of our support for Israel? Are the problems related to America's general policies in the Middle East? The answer is yes to all that—but far more still, as dozens of grievances sprout from nearly every page. Osama bin Laden and Dr. Zawahiri are aggrieved over Afghanistan, Bosnia, Chechnya, East Timor, Iraq, Kosovo, Lebanon, the Philippines, Somalia, Saudi Arabia, and Spain (Andalusia). Sometimes the hurt stems from unkind treatment received from leaders as diverse as the Queen of England, George Bush Sr., and Bill Clinton.

Indeed, the pretexts seem to steadily multiply and constantly metamorphose throughout their communiqués. When American troops leave Saudi Arabia or the United Nations' blockade of Saddam's Iraq is lifted, then fresh edicts and new threats immediately follow. The net effect is to accept that bin Laden and Zawahiri—like all fascists who seek state power to implement an all-encompassing reactionary ideology—have not so much an identifiable and specific gripe, but rather total and general hatred of the influence of liberal Western civilization.

The source of such elemental loathing in these texts proves to be lost honor, humiliation, attendant envy, and the ensuing fear that the Islamists' "authority will pass away." Al-Qaeda is fueled by such existential fury, it appears, because the purer and more devout Muslim world is now seen as weak and impotent. And this paradox, bin Laden and Zawahiri further assert, is a result of the perfidy of Arab leaders who have allowed the West to obtain superior weapons, plunder their wealth, and water down their ancient religion.

The culprits deserving of righteous justice in these texts also turn out to be legion: America the all-powerful world cop, Israel the Zionist crusader state encroaching on Holy Lands, decadent Westerners who practice amoral sex and promulgate a crass global culture, turncoat Arab dictators who profit with the infidels, and Muslim moderates who reinterpret the Koran to fit blasphemous Western liberal pieties.

Still, Islam's vulnerability to the Crusaders and their henchmen in the Middle East remains perplexing to al-Qaeda because the world of Islam has so many assets. Oil, of course, is mentioned often, but not as much as the advantages of a more zealous and committed population—and a religion, that if properly practiced, sanctions *jihad* against Jews, Christians, Americans, and Europeans.

So Muslims are told not to despair: al-Qaeda offers to an Islamic street humiliated by the West both practical redress and psychological assurance that the United States and its minions are headed for a fall. With enough determined *jihadists*, craven and decadent Westerners will cave and then be given a choice: convert to Islam, leave all Muslim lands, or pay sufficient tribute and homage. All methods are sanctioned by Allah: murdering civilians ("It is permissible to slay the human shield without any disagreement"); collateral killing of Muslims, since "the intended target is always the infidel"; and free rein for Muslims "to kill the Americans and seize their money, wherever and whenever they find them."

There is also another, more controversial, revelation from these translated texts. Bin Laden and Zawahiri take much of their critique of the West from the West itself. To conclude that is not to imply McCarthyism about dissent at home, but again simply to be empirical and to read the terrorists firsthand. For all their bragging about interviews with *Time* and CNN, bin Laden and Zawahiri remain parochial men of the seventh century, without much experience outside the Middle East, and now in hiding in the desolate badlands along the Pakistani border. Yet, despite their isolation, and thanks to global communications, they offer precise advice about American books we should read—William Blum's *Rogue State* about the evils of American imperialism is a favorite. Their description of George W. Bush reading "a little girl's story about a goat" to children while the

World Trade Center falls is lifted directly from Michael Moore's *Fahrenheit 9/11*—as are frequent references to "the lies of George Bush" and Dick Cheney's Halliburton.

Even advocates of American campaign reform will find their echoes here ("rich and wealthy people, who hold sway in parties, and fund their election campaigns with their gifts," and who "swell the bank accounts of the White House gang"). Often, al-Qaeda's complaints against the United States read like those leveled by atheistic and socialist Europeans: the United States "refused to sign the Kyoto agreement" and excused itself from the International criminal court. Furthermore, America pollutes the world's skies and seas. That we ended World War II with an atomic bomb is likewise a constant source of complaint.

Two other themes characterize much of what bin Laden and Zawahiri say and write in these texts—and these revelations offer us both a warning and a hope. Al-Qaeda hates democracy of all types ("It rebels against and prevents the *sharia* of Allah from becoming established law"). True, bin Laden and Zawahiri complain that Arab regimes are not consensual. But by that critique they mean that they are not yet absolutely theocratic governments, in which all Muslims without debate naturally must consent to *sharia* law under the auspices of fundamentalists such as bin Laden and Dr. Zawahiri. Relatively secular strongmen such as Saddam Hussein and Hosni Mubarak are not nearly the threat of Hamid Karzai and the newly elected government in Iraq. Their new Afghanistan and Iraq pose an existential danger to al-Qaeda should Muslims—especially women—ever be free to choose their own governance and, indeed, way of life.

Second, the terrorists insist that history is on their side. Vietnam, Lebanon, and Somalia prove that the United States eventually will weaken, give up the war, and leave—given that as infidels we love life, while they, as true believers (in a sensual Paradise to come) worship death. For the United States to stay on in Afghanistan and Iraq, then, and to ensure consensual governments may well be al-Qaeda's worst nightmare.

The Al Qaeda Reader is arranged in two parts: formal theology and popular propaganda. And while the reader may find the latter political rants—usually transcripts from televised interviews, taped communiqués, and radio broadcasts—the more timely, the longer written religious treatises, many of them hitherto unknown, ultimately are the more instructive and disturbing. They are written mostly by Dr. Zawahiri and offer a cobbled-together summary of what al-Qaeda stands for and plans for the West.

Ibrahim does not enter into Islamic exegesis; he simply presents the words of al-Qaeda's leaders about the Koran, and lets others decide the validity of various interpretations by bin Laden, who brags that "our Prophet . . . did not remain more than three months in Medina without raiding or sending a raiding party into the lands of the infidels to beat down their strongholds and seize their possessions, their lives, and their women."

Nor are these two terrorists in any sense systematic thinkers who outline a logical belief system. Bin Laden and Zawahiri ramble about America ("You brought AIDS as a Satanic invention"); they dissimulate in what they call "war through treachery." Falsehoods appear on every page ("You steal our . . . oil at paltry prices"). Some transcripts are direct warnings and addresses to America and its leaders; others are ad hoc messages and rants. Still others are obscure treatises that debate the minutiae of *sharia* law. Yet always is the reminder for Muslims to have nothing to do with unbelievers ("No believer will love an infidel; and whoever does love an infidel is not a believer"). Through all the exhortation, of course, is the underlying command to avoid the hated Jew at all costs.

Raymond Ibrahim works as a researcher and technician in the Near East section of the African and Middle Eastern division of the Library of Congress in Washington, D.C. It was there that he discovered in the archives many of these disparate texts—the tracts on theology for the most part had never before been translated into English nor even was their existence widely known outside of the Middle East. He alone is responsible for their present collection, organization, and translation from Arabic. Ibrahim himself was born to Egyptian Coptic parents, and he grew up in the United States both speaking colloquial Arabic and studying more formal written Arabic texts. He has been a frequent visitor to the Middle East, and is currently on leave from graduate work at Georgetown University.

By formal training he is a historian of the ancient Middle East; in this regard, I became familiar with Mr. Ibrahim when I had him as a student of philology in several of my advanced classical Greek courses at California State University, Fresno. In addition, I served as a reader of his master's thesis dealing with early Byzantine and Islamic interaction and conflict. His notes, glossary, and foreword reveal that he is both a historian and a linguist.

A final note: Controversy arises over the wisdom of disseminating the work of the al-Qaeda leadership, especially at a time of war, when much of the electronic media has facilitated the propaganda campaign of bin Laden and Zawahiri. In that context, is it wise to give such terrorists an even wider audience in the West, especially when they are media savvy and seek political concessions from an American public that after September 11 is by now terrified of suicide bombings, airplane hijackings, beheadings, kidnappings, and roadside explosions?

The answer would be clearly no—if the intent or result of Raymond Ibrahim's translations were to be to romanticize or even sensationalize the cult of these two mass murderers. Instead, the revelations from these texts serve as a wake-up call to an often naïve and therapeutic West that believes enemies are to be understood rather than defeated, and their threats explained away as empty rhetoric rather than braced for as the bitter truth.

Do not confuse Ibrahim's dispassionate presentation with otherworldliness; as an American who grew up in a household that had fled religious discrimination in Egypt, he is deeply concerned about the aims of Islamic fundamentalists and the ability of such terrorists to enact their agenda outlined on these pages. He has done us a great service—at some risk to his person—in revealing the full intention and motives of al-Qaeda "to kill the Americans and their allies, civilians and military." But it is now up to America to use that gift for its own defense.

FOREWORD

❧

On September 11, 2001, nineteen men under the leadership of the radical Islamist organization al-Qaeda hijacked four American planes, crashing two into the World Trade Center towers, one into the Pentagon, and one into a rural Pennsylvania field. Along with the hijackers themselves, some three thousand U.S. citizens were killed. Why would these men commit such a heinous act? A host of reasons have been offered from academics and politicians, apologists and polemicists, secularists and theists, pointing to Islam itself, righteous anger against biased U.S. policies, material want, even envy and sexual frustration. Within this ongoing debate, however, al-Qaeda's own words have often been overlooked or dismissed.

This volume is meant to fill that gap. Only the words of Osama bin Laden (the leader of al-Qaeda) and Dr. Ayman al-Zawahiri (his second in command) have been included. Zawahiri's treatises make up the bulk of this book: as his writings attest, Zawahiri, a fifty-five-year-old Egyptian pediatrician who has engaged in radical activities since the age of fourteen, is al-Qaeda's primary ideologue and theoretician.[1]

By now, people in the West are vaguely familiar with some of al-Qaeda's messages. Every so often, the images of bin Laden and Zawahiri surface, usually on the Arabic satellite station al-Jazeera, condemning the West. These speeches are then translated and posted on the Internet (which is fast becoming al-Qaeda's primary conduit for spreading its messages). Though both men have delivered many such messages to the West, their theme is always the same: al-Qaeda is merely retaliating for all the injustices the West, and the United States in particular, has brought upon Muslims.

Largely absent from the Western hemisphere, however, are al-Qaeda's theological treatises, which justify and glorify violence and hatred toward the West within an Islamic framework. Written for Muslim audiences, they are rarely translated into English or disseminated to a non-Muslim public. This is unfortunate, since they reveal much more about al-Qaeda's ideology than the more famous political speeches.

In these theological tracts, al-Qaeda gives Muslims reasons why they should hate and fight the West that differ from those they give in their political speeches. In the latter, bin Laden and Zawahiri insist that they are waging a "Defensive *Jihad*" against an oppressive West. When discussing the tenets of Islam, however, they argue to Muslims that Muslims should battle the West because it is the infidel, or the "Great Satan."

In order to give the English reader a comprehensive understanding of al-Qaeda's ideology as well as its grievances, this volume brings together both the propagandistic writings and speeches intended for the West as well as the more important and theological writings intended for Muslims. In certain respects, these two genres agree over certain grievances: that the West is oppressive and unjust toward Islam, heedlessly or out of malice spilling the blood of innocent Muslims all around the world; that the West supports ruthless and dictatorial regimes in the Islamic world; that the West is responsible for the Israeli occupation of Palestine; that the West has killed 1 million Iraqi children; and so on.

The two parts of this book, "Theology" and "Propaganda," complement each other and take steps toward solving the al-Qaeda conundrum. They give both the religious and the "official" reasons for al-Qaeda and its supporters' war on the United States. More important, when juxtaposed, they reveal some startling contradictions and inconsistencies.

PART I. THEOLOGY

The first part of the volume consists of four never-before-translated documents (one essay and three treatises), providing the English reader with the religious justifications for al-Qaeda's radical world-view.

Three of these documents, by Ayman al-Zawahiri, are fashioned as *fatwas*[2]—that is, legal decrees derived from the sources of Islamic jurisprudence. The term *fatwa* applied here, however, is somewhat misleading. A *fatwa* generally concerns a question not clearly addressed by the sources of Islamic jurisprudence. They are, therefore, not so much *fatwas* but treatises, for they develop themes well established in Islamic thinking; Zawahiri uses the *fatwa* form to remind the Muslim *umma* of their obligations. Only the questions of martyrdom and the killing of innocents in the third treatise are not universally agreed on in Islam, and thus can be considered a *fatwa*.

The first document, "Moderate Islam Is a Prostration to the West," is an essay authorized or written by Osama bin Laden. It must be regarded as one of al-Qaeda's most important documents. In it, moderate Muslims are condemned for trying to peacefully coexist or even hold dialogue with non-Muslims. "Offensive *Jihad*"—once thought to have been relegated to the dustbin of history—is defended as not only legitimate but obligatory. Muslims are exhorted to always hate, discriminate, humiliate, and debase non-Muslims. This essay contradicts the message of "reciprocity" that al-Qaeda uses in its propaganda meant for Western consumption, implying that bin Laden's war is a total war that is not susceptible to olive branches or negotiation with the enemy.

The first treatise, "Loyalty and Enmity," urges Muslims to be loyal to Islam and each other at all times while maintaining hostility and hatred toward non-Muslims. Muslims are advised to be loyal to each other even when they disagree while displaying enmity for non-Muslims even if the latter are kind and just dealing. When Muslims are strong and capable, they are instructed to wage Offensive *Jihad* in order to bring the light of Islam to the infidels; but when they are weak and incapable, they are to dissemble in front of the infidels and act like their friends while maintaining contempt for them in their hearts. The Koran itself is quite clear regarding this enmity: "You have a good example in Abraham and those who followed him, for they said to their people, 'We disown you and the idols which you worship besides Allah. We renounce you: enmity and hate shall reign between us until you believe in Allah alone' " (60:4). And: "O you who have believed! do not take the Jews and the Christians for friends; they are but friends of each other; and whoever among you takes them for a friend, then surely he is one of them" (5:51). And: "You shall find none who believe in Allah and the Last Day on friendly terms with those who oppose Allah and His Messenger—even if they be their fathers, their sons, their brothers, or their nearest kindred" (58:22).

The second treatise, "*Sharia* and Democracy," outlines the obligation of Muslims to establish and uphold *sharia* law while condemning all other forms of governance—especially democracy, which is depicted in Islam as paganism. This belief is not subject to question; rather, it is fundamental to Islam itself. Islam is a meticulous way of life based on Allah's law (*sharia*), not merely a profession of faith limited to the Five Pillars of Islam (i.e., profession, prayer, fasting, alms, and pilgrimaging). Every form of man-made governance—democracy, monarchy, communism, etc.—is anathema to Islam, since the power to legislate is Allah's alone. Though the enforcement of *sharia* law would seem to concern Muslims alone, it is in fact the basis of the animosity between Islam and the infidel world. Offensive *Jihad*, *dhimmitude*, and enmity for infidels—all these are based on the *sharia*. Therefore, any Muslim who upholds *sharia* law—which is the very definition of a Muslim, that is, "one who submits [to the Laws of] Allah"—must acknowledge its divine authority.

The third treatise, "*Jihad*, Martyrdom, and the Killing of Innocents," establishes that *jihad* in the service of making Allah's word supreme is a fundamental pillar of Islam. Zawahiri argues that suicide bombers (whom he calls "martyrs") are the greatest of *jihad*'s holy warriors (*mujahidin*). Next Zawahiri takes up the controversial issue of killing those whose blood is forbidden from being shed—women, children, Muslims, and *dhimmis*—during a *jihad* or raid, such as 9/11. This is perhaps the most legalistic document in the "Theology" section. In it Zawahiri legitimizes suicide bombings as well as the killing of innocents—two contestable and far from agreed upon issues in Islam.

PART II. PROPAGANDA

The second part of this volume presents al-Qaeda's messages directed to the world at large, particularly the West. These messages tend to be much less revealing than their theological counterparts: wholly propagandistic[3] in nature, they were issued with the express purpose of demoralizing the West while inciting the *umma*. Here, although there is discussion of Defensive *Jihad* (which, due to the adjective "defensive," makes *jihad* palatable to more universal, not just Muslim, sensibilities), there is no mention of Offensive *Jihad*, enmity for infidels, the enforcement of *dhimmitude*, or Islam and the West. Instead, this section focuses on enumerating the many injustices the West has visited upon Islam.

The style and length of these messages contrast sharply with their theological counterparts. Formulated to maximize their impact on the intended audience, they are much shorter and to the point than Zawahiri's comprehensive and scholarly—perhaps labyrinthine and pedantic—treatises. Most of these messages to the West are also delivered in video. The image and voice of a healthy, dignified, determined, and armed bin Laden or Zawahiri (more of the latter lately) is meant to discourage the West just as it is meant to awe and motivate would-be sympathizers around the globe. It is a tactic of psychological warfare. Concise and focused, each message gives al-Qaeda the opportunity to enumerate the many sins of the West. Only the most pertinent or revealing ones have been included in this volume. Those left out—the vast majority—repeat, sometimes verbatim, the same complaints. To read one is therefore to read them all.

These messages portray a world where the United States wages unjust and cruel wars solely to serve the avaricious interests of a few—usually American and Jewish elites—not to bring about justice or freedom. Thus blood is being spilled in Iraq simply to secure Israel and oil. America also expresses the "old Crusader hatred" and seeks to finish what European Crusaders started almost a millennium ago when Jerusalem was (temporarily) annexed from the Muslims. The West is accused of being the sole support for the dictatorial secular regimes that govern Muslim countries. Nonetheless, these messages emphasize, al-Qaeda and its affiliates are winning the war in Afghanistan, Iraq, and around the world. Terrorist acts are justified because they retaliate for previous terrorist acts committed by the United States and its proxies (which, according to bin Laden and Zawahiri, are legion).

Al-Qaeda says that violence is just retribution for Western injustice and that Islam authorizes this position. Practically every message issued by al-Qaeda to the West revolves around the theme of "reciprocal treatment." When speaking to the West in general, bin Laden states, "Why should fear, killing, destruction, displacement, orphaning, and widowing continue to be our lot, while security, stability, and happiness is yours? This is injustice. The time to settle accounts has arrived: just as you kill, so shall you be killed; just as you bomb, so shall you be bombed. Expect more to come." The attacks of 9/11 are presented as payback for U.S. complicity in Israel's invasion of Beirut, when Arab skyscrapers were demolished with their Muslim inhabitants still inside.

Thus al-Qaeda's actions can be summarized through the simple syllogism, "an eye for an eye"—which all people, not just Muslims, can appreciate. Yet secular actors in the Arab world do not all agree; some governments are quite friendly to the West, and many individuals favor Western culture and tastes. Even Saddam Hussein, the secularist and onetime ally of the United States, directed his ire more at his own people, including radical Islamists, than at Westerners.

Al-Qaeda plays less on anger at the West for specific grievances in most of its literature than on religious sentiments inherent in Islamic doctrine. The propaganda messages are clearly designed for a Western audience, which by nature is more receptive to concise—and emotional—arguments. Al-Qaeda's theological treatises are lengthy and bland, propped up by a convoluted theological apparatus. But to understand al-Qaeda, one must have a basic understanding of Islamic jurisprudence and how the *sharia* is articulated, since these treatises are concerned with the all-important question of what is and is not legitimate, obligatory, and forbidden in Islam.

DETERMINING RIGHT AND WRONG IN ISLAM

In Sunni Islam, every law, practice, or ideology must ultimately be traced back to *usul al-fiqh*, or the "roots of jurisprudence." These are, in order of authority, the Koran, the *sunna* (example) of the Prophet, the process of analogy, and the consensus of the *umma*, especially the *ulema*. Based on all of these, the *sharia*—commonly known as Islamic law—is established. This is important to understand since al-Qaeda's theological arguments are wholly grounded in Islam's "roots of jurisprudence."

The Koran is the foundation of Islam. The words of the Koran are understood to be inspired by Allah (much as Christians and Jews believe the Bible to be inspired by God). Traditional Islam teaches that the words themselves have been relayed verbatim from an uncreated and eternal slab in heaven that contains the same words, letter for letter—also in Arabic, which is understood to be the celestial language. Due to the Koran's status as *the* word of Allah, all of its commandments are understood to transcend time and space; thus they are binding once and for all. Most Muslims reject arguments suggesting that the commandments contained in the Koran apply only to the seventh century and thus need to be "reinterpreted" to suit today's realities. Needless to say, any commandment or prohibition found in the Koran—and there are many—are to be taken literally and become divine foundations of *sharia* law. For example, the Koran expressly forbids the eating of swine (5:3); to this day, pork is forbidden to Muslims without exception.

After the Koran, the *sunna* of the Prophet arbitrates, based on the Koranic verse "Truly, you have in the Messenger of Allah an excellent example" (33:21). Ultimately, the importance of the *sunna* arises from the function of Muhammad as the founder of Islam—hence the authoritative if not inspired nature of his words and deeds. The word *sunna* can mean "example," "pattern," or "custom." Based on the *hadith*, which contains thousands upon thousands of statements and deeds attributed to Muhammad, examples, patterns, and customs emerge. Depending then on the authenticity of any particular *hadith* (there are six collections of *hadiths* in Sunni Islam that are considered authentic), these *sunnas* go on to become codified as part of the *sharia*.

Named after this second important root of jurisprudence, Sunni Muslims, who make up nearly 90 percent of the world's 1.2 billion Muslims, are extremely concerned with the words and deeds of Muhammad and strive to follow his example—often quite literally: the highly respected scholar Ibn Hanbal, founder of one of the four Sunni schools of jurisprudence, would not eat watermelons simply because he found no instances of Muhammad eating any in the *hadiths*.

Much like the famous Christian acronym WWJD ("What would Jesus do?"), what Muhammad would do in any given situation is crucially important for Sunnis. This is important to remember when reading the four theological translations, full as they are with *hadiths* depicting the Prophet's *sunna*.

The third root of jurisprudence, which is really a method, is analogy (*qiyas*). Here an example should suffice. Based on the Koran and *sunna*, wine is forbidden to Muslims. However, neither the Koran nor the *sunna* expressly outlaws the consumption of beer—no doubt because it was generally unknown in seventh-century Arabia. Through the process of analogy, then, beer as well as all other forms of alcohol become forbidden under Islamic law. The reasoning is as follows: since the Koran and *sunna* obviously forbade wine because of its alcoholic, and thus intoxicating or harmful, qualities, clearly all other forms of alcohol must likewise be prohibited. (Zawahiri utilizes this legitimate method of interpretation to justify suicide bombings in his treatise "*Jihad*, Martyrdom, and the Killing of Innocents.")

The fourth and final[4] source of jurisprudence is *ijma*, or the consensus of the *umma*. If a question is not addressed by the Koran or *sunna*, and if there is no way to derive an analogy from either, the decision then rests with the majority's opinion, based on the *hadith* "My community will never be in agreement over an error." This should not, however, be confused with democracy, since consensus is called upon only as a last resort when the Koran and *sunna* are silent or ambiguous on an issue. In other words, consensus can never supersede or abrogate the authority of the Koran or *sunna*, although it may be needed to interpret both. Moreover, generally it is the consensus of the *ulema* who are learned in *sharia* law that ultimately bears any weight. Rulings based on the consensus of Muslim *ulema* are therefore generally seen as binding.

The *sharia*, then, is completely founded on these four sources of jurisprudence. Indeed, based on the Koran, *sunna*, analogy, and consensus, every conceivable act committed in this life is judged as being either obligatory, recommended, neutral, disliked, or forbidden. Such is the comprehensiveness—or totalitarianism—of the *sharia*. (The concept of separation between religion and state is therefore completely alien to Islam.) Thus al-Qaeda constantly strives to ground its theological arguments in these four sources of jurisprudence. It is the only way their arguments can find legitimacy within the Muslim *umma*. It has become common practice to accuse al-Qaeda of not having the necessary religious credentials to issue *fatwas* or even comment on *sharia* law, thereby discounting the importance of the group's writings. Such an argument, however, is ineffective, since any Muslim—even the Grand *Mufti* himself—must always ground his legal decisions in the roots of jurisprudence. And al-Qaeda leaders, well aware of their lack of official credentials, make up for this by constantly evoking the authoritative words of others—Allah (through the Koran), the Prophet (through the *hadith*), and the *ulema*—to validate their arguments.

Zawahiri's writings especially are grounded in Islam's roots of jurisprudence; in fact, of the many thousands of words translated here from his three treatises, well more than half are direct quotations from the Koran, the *sunna* of Muhammad, and the consensus and conclusions of the *ulema*.[5]

When Adolf Hitler wrote *Mein Kampf* (which ironically is translated in Arabic to *Jihadi*, or "my *jihad*"), he did not hesitate to portray his ultimate worldview. Yet, though the world was well aware of his book, it was not taken seriously—no doubt because many did not think that Hitler had the means to realize his wild visions of Teutonic domination. History proved otherwise, and millions died as a result of the world's indifference to Hitler's straightforward words. This book provides the world with al-Qaeda's ultimate vision. The same mistake should not be made twice.

AL-QAEDA'S DECLARATION OF WAR
AGAINST AMERICANS

❧

Praise be to Allah, who revealed the Book [Koran], controls the clouds, defeats factionalism, and says in His Book: "Then, when the sacred months have passed, slay the idolaters wherever you find them—seize them, besiege them, and be ready to ambush them" [9:5]. And prayers and peace be upon our Prophet, Muhammad bin Abdullah, who said: "I have been sent with the sword between my hands to ensure that no one but Allah is worshipped—Allah who put my livelihood under the shadow of my spear and who inflicts humiliation and scorn on those who disobey my commandments."

Never since Allah made the Arabian Peninsula flat, created its desert, and encircled it with seas has it been stormed by any force like the Crusader hordes that have spread in it like locusts, consuming its wealth and polluting its fertility. All this is happening at a time in which nations are attacking Muslims in unison—as if fighting over a plate of food! In face of this critical situation and lack of support, we are all obliged to discuss current events, as well as reach an agreement on how [best] to settle the matter.

No one argues today about three well-established facts, known to everyone; we enumerate them as a reminder, so that the one remembering may remember.

1. For over seven years America has been occupying the lands of Islam in its holiest of places, the Arabian Peninsula—plundering its riches, dictating to its rulers, humiliating its people, terrorizing its neighbors, and turning its bases in the Peninsula into a spearhead with which it fights the neighboring Muslim peoples.

While some people may have argued in the past over the realities of the occupation, all the people of the Peninsula now acknowledge it. There is no clearer evidence than America's ceaseless aggression against the Iraqi people—all launched right from the Peninsula, though its rulers collectively refuse having their land used for this end. But they have been subdued.

2. Despite the awful devastation inflicted on the Iraqi people at the hands of the Crusader-Jewish alliance, and despite the astronomical number of deaths—which has exceeded 1 million—despite all this, the Americans attempt once again to repeat the horrific massacres, as if the protracted sanctions imposed after the brutal war, or the fragmentation and devastation, was not enough for them.

So now here they come [again] to annihilate what is left of this people and humiliate their Muslim neighbors.[6]

3. Now if the Americans' purposes behind these wars are religious and economic, so too are they also to serve the Jews' petty state [Israel], diverting attention from its occupation of Jerusalem and the murder of Muslims there. There is no better evidence of this than their eagerness to destroy Iraq, the strongest neighboring Arab state, and their endeavor to fragment all the states of the region—such as Iraq, Saudi Arabia, Egypt, and Sudan—into mini–paper states, whose disunion and weakness will guarantee Israel's survival and the continuation of the brutal Crusader occupation of the Peninsula.

All these crimes and sins committed by the Americans are a clear declaration of war on Allah, His Messenger, and the Muslims. *Ulema* throughout Islamic history are unanimously agreed that the *jihad* is an individual duty whenever the enemy tears into the lands of the Muslims. This was related by Imam bin Qudama in *al-Mughni*; Imam al-Kisa'i in *al-Bada'i*; al-Qurtubi in his commentary; and the Sheikh of Islam [Ibn Taymiyya] in his chronicles, where he states: "As for defensive warfare, this is the greatest way to defend sanctity and religion.

This is an obligation consensually agreed to [by the *ulema*]. After faith, there is nothing more sacred than repulsing the enemy who attacks religion and life."

On that basis, and in compliance with Allah's order, we hereby issue the following decree to all Muslims:

The ruling to kill the Americans and their allies—civilians and military—is an individual obligation incumbent upon every Muslim who can do it and in any country—this until the Aqsa Mosque [Jerusalem] and the Holy Mosque [Mecca] are liberated from their grip, and until their armies withdraw from all the lands of Islam, defeated, shattered, and unable to threaten any Muslim. This is in accordance with the Word of the Most High—"[F]ight the pagans all together as they fight you all together" [9:36] and the Word of the Most High, "Fight them until there is no more tumult or oppression, and [all] religion belongs to Allah" [8:39].

And the Most High said: "And why should you not fight in the cause of Allah and on behalf of those oppressed men, women, and children who cry out, Lord! Rescue us from this town and its oppressors. Give us from Your Presence some protecting friend! Give us from Your Presence some defender!" [4:75].

By Allah's leave we call upon every Muslim who believes in Allah and wishes to be rewarded to comply with Allah's order to kill the Americans and seize their money wherever and whenever they find them. We also call on Muslim *ulema*, leaders, youths, and soldiers to launch the raid on the Devil's army—the Americans—and whoever allies with them from the supporters of Satan, and to rout those behind them so that they may learn [a lesson].

Allah Most High said: "O you who have believed! Respond to Allah and the Messenger whenever He calls you to that which gives you life. And know that Allah comes between a man and his heart, and that it is He to whom you shall [all] be gathered" [8:24].

Allah Most High said: "O you who have believed! What is the matter with you? When you are asked to go forth in the cause of Allah, you cling so heavily to the earth! Do you prefer the life of this world to the Hereafter? But little is the comfort of this life, in comparison to the Hereafter. Unless you go forth [and fight], He will punish you with a grievous torment, and put others in your place. But He you cannot harm in the least; for Allah has power over all things" [9:38–39].

Allah Most High said: "So do not lose heart, nor fall into despair. Have faith and you shall triumph" [3:139].

Sheikh Osama bin Muhammad bin Laden
Ayman al-Zawahiri, Commander of the *Jihad* Group in Egypt
Abu Yasir Rifa'i Ahmad Taha, Egyptian Islamic Group[7]
Sheikh Mir Hamza, Secretary of the Organization of Islamic *ulema* in
  Pakistan
Fazlur Rahman, Commander of the *Jihad* Movement in Bangladesh

This statement is more commonly known as The World Islamic Front's Declaration to wage *Jihad* Against the Jews and Crusaders, issued February 23, 1998, in the Arabic newspaper *Al-Quds Al-Arabi.*

PART I

THEOLOGY

The following essay, authorized or written by Osama bin Laden himself,[1] serves as a perfect introduction to the three treatises—"Loyalty
and Enmity," "*Sharia* and Democracy," and "*Jihad*, Martyrdom, and
the Killing of Innocents"—that make up the Theology section of this
volume. The assertion is repeatedly made that the root problem between the Islamic world and the West revolves around these issues:
"The Islam preached by the advocates of interreligious dialogue [i.e.,
"moderate" Muslims] does not contain [the doctrine of] Loyalty and
Enmity; nor does it contain [Offensive] *Jihad*; nor boundaries established by the *sharia*—since it is these very doctrines that worry the
West most. . . . Indeed, the essence of our problem with the West revolves around these principles" (see pp. 25, 30).

On the surface, this polemic has a political agenda—to show how
malicious and militant the "Crusaders" are to Islam, and how impotent
and craven the Saudi leadership is in response. To do this, the essay
quotes from both the American letter and the Saudi response. In reality, however, the American letter is not as aggressive as al-Qaeda makes
it to be; many tolerant—even apologetic—statements such as the following are (for obvious reasons) never quoted in al-Qaeda's essay:

> We recognize that at times our nation has acted with arro-
> gance and ignorance toward other societies. . . . For many peo-
> ple, including many Americans and a number of signatories to
> this letter, some values sometimes seen in America are unat-
> tractive and harmful. Consumerism as a way of life. The no-
> tion of freedom as no rules. The weakening of marriage and

family life. Plus an enormous entertainment and communications apparatus that relentlessly glorifies such ideas and beams them, whether they are welcome or not, into nearly every corner of the globe. . . . We pledge to do all we can to guard against the harmful temptations—especially those of arrogance and jingoism—to which nations at war so often seem to yield. . . . We wish especially to reach out to our brothers and sisters in Muslim societies. We say to you forthrightly: We are not enemies, but friends. We must not be enemies.

Nor is the Saudi letter as "prostrating" as one would expect from the outraged tone of al-Qaeda; consider, for instance, the following Saudi assertions:

The United States, in spite of its efforts in establishing the United Nations with its Universal Declaration of Human Rights and other similar institutions, is among the most antagonistic nations to the objectives of these institutions and to the values of justice and truth. This is clearly visible in America's stance on the Palestinian issue and its unwavering support for the Zionist occupation of Palestinian land and its justification of all the Zionist practices that run contrary to the resolutions passed by the United Nations. It is clearly visible in how America provides Israel with the most advanced weapons that they turn against women, children, and old men, and with which they topple people's homes. . . . In the West, instigating conflict stems from considering and protecting national—if not partisan—interests, even at the expense of the rights of others. The truth is that this policy is what creates a dangerous threat to national security, not only for the West but for the entire world, not to mention the tragic and inhuman conditions that it produces.

Ultimately, what make this al-Qaeda document extremely important are the doctrinal arguments that al-Qaeda relies on to refute the Saudi response. Even though a particular event—the publication of the Saudis' "How We Can Coexist"—triggered this essay, al-Qaeda's condemnation of the Saudi position is perhaps best viewed as "Radical Islam's" condemnation of "Moderate Islam." Indeed, al-Qaeda's main gripe throughout the entire essay has to do with the principles of moderate Islam, which the Saudis claim to uphold in their letter (thereby "prostrating" themselves to appease the West). So while this essay is ostensibly little more than an irate letter from one group of Muslims to another, on a more transcendent level it is a doctrinal denunciation of the very concept of moderate Islam. (This is a critical matter, since moderate Islam is often seen as essential for peace between Islam and the rest of the world.) Al-Qaeda's argument is that "radical" Islam *is* Islam—without exception.[2]

Moreover, since this essay was written as an open letter to the Saudis (that is, for Islamic eyes only), it is refreshingly, if not alarmingly, honest and straightforward. As such, many doctrinal issues that the practitioners of moderate Islam deny or shy away from—Offensive *Jihad* in order to establish Islamic rule around the globe, enforced discrimination against infidels (*dhimmitude*), the doctrine of Loyalty and Enmity—are all expounded without reserve, based on the authoritative sources of Islam: the Koran and *sunna* of the Muslim Prophet. Indeed, the tone best describing al-Qaeda's essay is one of outrage and amazement—that the Saudis would even contemplate abolishing such "fundamentals" of the faith as Offensive *Jihad* and hatred toward non-Muslims all in order to peacefully coexist with the West.

To remedy this, al-Qaeda went on to write their own response to the American letter "What We're Fighting For," titled "Why We Are Fighting You." Interestingly, that essay does not mention those many Islamic doctrines delineated in al-Qaeda's declaration to the Saudis that intrinsically require Muslims to attack non-Muslims—and which al-Qaeda mocked the Saudis for not mentioning. For instance, when speaking to the Saudis, bin Laden writes:

There are only three choices in Islam: either willing submission; or payment of the *jizya*, thereby physical, though not spiritual, submission to the authority of Islam; or the sword—for it is not right to let him [an infidel] live. The matter is summed up for every person alive: either submit, or live under the suzerainty of Islam, or die. Thus it behooves the [Saudi] signatories to clarify this matter to the West— otherwise they will be like those who believe in part of the Book while rejecting the rest.

Yet when speaking to the West directly, bin Laden portrays Islam only as a "religion of showing kindness to others, establishing justice between them, granting them their rights, and defending the oppressed and the persecuted." Curiously, he neglects to mention the aforementioned three options that he chided the Saudis for failing to state to the infidels. Instead, he "altruistically" invites Americans to embrace Islam.

In fact, just like the Saudi response to the Americans, al-Qaeda's letter to the Americans ultimately relies on humanitarian, political, and even emotional arguments as to why al-Qaeda has declared war on the United States (e.g., self-defense, biased U.S. support for Israel, U.S. support for oppressive, dictatorial regimes, unjust war in Iraq, etc.). Even the opening Koranic verse puts everything into a defensive context: "Permission to fight is given to those who are attacked, for they have been wronged and surely Allah is able to give them victory" [22:39]. However, at no time does al-Qaeda's letter to the Americans clarify that the terrorist organization's aggression is ultimately rooted in what they understand to be principles intrinsic to Islam.

In the spirit of debate, the American intellectuals had responded to the Saudis' "How We Can Coexist," with another letter that, among other things, praised their willingness to even correspond:

We know that your decision to write to us at all, as well as some of the comments in your letter, have caused some in your country [e.g., al-Qaeda] to criticize you publicly. We appreciate the spirit of civility and the desire for mutual understanding which are reflected in your letter. In that same spirit, and with that same desire, we wish to continue the conversation.

This second American letter to the Saudis, published months after al-Qaeda's scathing criticism of "How We Can Coexist," received only silence from the Saudi establishment. Regarding this silence, one of the sixty U.S. signatories of both American letters, David Blankenhorn, writes:

> Even the Saudi government seemed upset by this citizen-to-citizen exchange. When my colleagues and I wrote back to the Saudis several months ago, and our [second] letter was published in Arabic in *Al-Hayat*, the pan-Arab newspaper based in London, the Saudi authorities censored the letter, preventing that issue of *Al-Hayat* from even entering the country. What should this tell us?[3]

"MODERATE ISLAM IS A
PROSTRATION TO THE WEST"[4]

⚜

Praise be to Allah, who said: "Say, 'O People of the Book [Christians and Jews], let us reach an agreement: that we worship none beside Allah, nor assign partners to Him, nor take each other as masters in place of Allah.' If they refuse, say: 'Bear witness that we have submitted [become Muslim]' " [3:64].

And prayers and peace be upon His Prophet, who said: "Curse of Allah be upon the Jews and Christians! they took the tombs of their prophets as places of worship."

At a time when Muslims are being drained daily of their blood, honor, possessions, and lands all over the world, at the hands of the hateful Christians, led by that leader of international infidelity, America, a declaration from the [Saudi] intellectuals has appeared. [This declaration] is the epitome of cowardice and defeatism—and disingenuousness, for it presents a few truths while abandoning the majority. This message from the intellectuals, titled "How We Can Coexist"?!—which has truly grieved us—is a response to a message issued by the Crusader intellectuals and priests, titled "What We're Fighting For." And after Islam was made manifest in glory during its first centuries, its adherents are now possessed as slaves by the infidels all around the world. So at this time, a message comes out to us today from the descendants of the original forebears, assuming that we urgently need to find a way to live in peace with the Crusader[s]—but there is no power or ability save in Allah![5]

I take issue against this declaration on many counts and mean to reveal its many faults. I do not claim to pause at every error, for these far exceed what I focus on. Nonetheless, I do take issue with a number of them. Whatever I do rightly is from Allah; whatever I err in is from myself and Satan.

SUMMARY OF THE DECLARATION

The declaration came at a most inopportune time. Indeed, we had expected from ones such as these a speech to incite the zeal of the men of the Islamic *umma* to defend their religion, way of life, and blood—which the Jews and Crusaders spill all around the world. But instead of us finding messages empowering the world's helpless through all legitimate [Islamic] means, we find that they have lost their way and issued a statement that, in short, consists of entreaties and supplications to the West, urging them to converse with us—and this, after they first acknowledge their [the West's] values and ideologies in their entirety, while shying away from evoking the truths valued by the religion [Islam] and its foundations. The declaration is proof of defeatism from its very name alone, "How We Can Coexist"—as if one of the foundations of our religion is how to coexist with infidels!! And if they had clarified to the West how the Muslim is to coexist with the infidel, based on [Koranic] verses and *hadiths*, then it would have been a blessed enterprise. But instead, its [the declaration's] starting point of coexisting with the West is to approve of their ideologies and do whatever gains their favor.

But what's even more startling is that this defeatist declaration came as a response to a harsh and blunt declaration issued by sixty Crusaders under the title "What We're Fighting For." Of course, there is nothing amazing about Crusaders striking and attacking a religion that today ranks first in the world by way of number of adherents and proselytes.[6] But what does amaze us from some who claim to adhere to Islam is that when the infidels attack and ridicule their religion, openly advertising it as a "Crusade" against Islam, we suddenly find them responding by saying that they do not crave war but instead they desire coexistence, universal peace, and justice. Surely there is no power or ability save in Allah!

Among other things, the Crusaders asserted in their declaration the following: "In the name of universal human morality, and fully conscious of the restrictions and requirements of a just war, we support our government's, and our society's, decision to use force of arms against them [terrorists]."

They said: "[W]ith one voice we say solemnly that it is crucial for our nation and its allies to win this war. We fight to defend ourselves, but we also believe that we fight to defend those universal principles of human rights and human dignity that are the best hope for mankind." They said concerning the Islamic movements [specifically al-Qaeda] against which they support the continuation of their government's war: "[It] openly professes its desire and increasingly demonstrates its ability to use murder to advance its objectives." Then they said regarding al-Qaeda and the various *mujahidin* groups, which were the focus of their dialogue: "[T]his movement now possesses not only the openly stated desire, but also the capacity and expertise—including possible access to, and willingness to use, chemical, biological, and nuclear weapons—to wreak massive, horrific devastation on its intended target."[7] So while the Crusaders call their nation and the nations of the Crusader alliance to continue their war against Islam, which [U.S. president George W.] Bush initiated by his announcement—"This is a Crusade"[8]—is it not depressing and dishonorable for the intellectuals to respond to them by saying, We have a common cause with you, we condemn terrorism and the operations of September [11], and we desire to treat [Islamic] extremism in order to stave off war between our people, to live in security and universal peace? Does this not count as a defeat? Is it not a perversion of the Islam of Muhammad? How stand they concerning the Most High's Word: "O you who have believed! whoever among you renounces his faith, Allah will establish another people [in his stead] whom He will love and who will love Him, humble with the believers, mighty against the infidels, and fighting in the cause of Allah, fearless of those who cast blame. Such is the grace of Allah: He bestows it on whom He will. Allah encompasses all and is all knowing" [5:54]. The statements of the declaration try to ostracize the *mujahidin*, disavow their deeds, and hold them in contempt. Conversely, its expressions toward the Crusaders are full of humility, entreaties, and prostrations. It repudiates Offensive *Jihad*[9] and frantically seeks for any shred of evidence to agree with the whims of the Crusaders. There is no ability or power save in Allah.

THE OTHER FACE OF THE DECLARATION

Nor does this defeatist declaration merely grossly distort our religion, but it possesses another aspect—the dialogue between religions or conferences seeking to unify all religions. Nor were those who represent Islam at these conferences to discuss the foundations of the religion [Islam] or its particulars that separate it from other religions. Instead, they focused on matters secondary to every religion, such as repudiating injustice, the ban on suicide, being kind to people, justice, and other matters connected to Islam but that do not conflict [with] other religions. As to what distinguishes Islam from other faiths, this they shy away from mentioning or calling attention to. Even more, they efface it, fearing lest the wrath of the West fall upon us. The Islam preached by the advocates of interreligious dialogue does not contain [the doctrine of] Loyalty and Enmity; nor does it contain [Offensive] *Jihad*; nor boundaries established by the *sharia*—since it is these very doctrines that worry the West most. And the West already possesses certain knowledge that these fundamentals are the point of conflict with Muslims and not the other principles.

Hindus burn women along with their husbands when the latter die. Buddhists sell and buy women as a commodity and part of commerce; the woman is obliged to worship her husband as well as her idols. As for women in communism, they are available for all, both far and near, and no one has possessions. Indeed, there are many laws and principles inherent to these nations that contradict nature. So if the Americans claim to battle those who oppose freedom and justice, then first they should battle these other nations—not the Islamic *umma*, which possesses well-gauged justice and freedom, the likes of which can never be found in other religions.

But instead, the declaration of the intellectuals came supporting the United Nations and their humanistic articles, which revolve around three principles: equality, freedom, and justice. Nor do they mean equality, freedom, and justice as was revealed by the Prophet Muhammad. No, they mean the West's despicable notions, which we see today in America and Europe, and which have made the people like cattle. Verily, Allah described them well: "They are like cattle—indeed! they are more misguided, for they are heedless" [7:179]. So if the declaration is in earnest to wipe out the fundamentals of the faith in order to hold dialogue with the West, that's their own initiative—not the initiative of Islam. This will become apparent in the following sections.

NO EXCUSE FOR THE SIGNATORIES

Some may say that they wrote this declaration humbly pleading the West in order to show them that there are Muslims who repudiate violence and support intercivilizational dialogue—all this in order to alleviate pressure off Muslims who experience calamities at the hands of the Americans. So they wrote what they wrote not in agreement but by way of the Most High's Word: "Let believers not take for friends and allies infidels rather than believers: and whoever does this shall have no relationship left with Allah—unless you but guard yourselves against them, taking precautions. But Allah cautions you [to fear] Himself. For the final goal is to Allah" [3:28]. And by way of the Prophet's dealings, when he contemplated giving the tribe of Ghatafan a third of the produce of Medina in order for them to withdraw from the fighting arena.[10]

In truth, attributing good intentions to this degree does not comport with Islamic legal evidence, for Allah said: "[U]nless you but guard yourselves against them, taking precautions" [3:28]. This applies not to them but to the coerced, and even coercion has its limits.

Indeed, none of the conditions [of coercion] apply in the least bit to them, for they were not forced to issue such a declaration. And when one is forced, he is to reply in a manner that barely satisfies his enemy—not expound at great length. Though preventing injustices from befalling Muslims has legal paths, this declaration is not one of them.[11]

As to those who stress the Prophet's dealings with Ghatafan, this had to do with the temporal realities of the Prophet that have nothing to do with them [the intellectuals]. The Prophet is the Imam [leader] of the Muslims, while these represent none other than themselves, not the Muslims. Thus they are of no worth or weight—neither with their governments, nor with the international policy makers, nor even with the local media. Were the two situations similar to each other, then we would have searched for the [Islamic] precedent.

So we say to those who make excuses and justify them, and those who depict the signatories as only defending the Muslims, all you have to do is ask, especially of those who signed: Where are your declarations, denunciations, and repudiations regarding the slaughter befalling Muslims in Palestine, Afghanistan, Iraq, the Philippines, Indonesia, Chechnya, Eritrea, Kashmir—or how about Gujarat, where just twenty days ago one thousand Muslims were burned alive?[12] Or at the very least, where are your declarations whereby you can console these wretched peoples, calling them to patience? Or where are your declarations whereby you look for solutions to the complicated problems facing Muslims and that need to be addressed by you? Where are your declarations whereby you describe the true criminal and his associates in terrorism? Where are your declarations regarding the Muslims held captive between the hands of the Crusaders? Or is lying low in prostration more important than all of this?

We have a good opinion of some of those who rendered their signatures, especially those well-known for their learning and piety. And we say that they signed not because they actually read the declaration, but only knew a summary of its purport. And some of them have admitted that their names were included without their knowledge, while others have said that they trusted the other signatories and so fell in with them without reading the declaration. All in all, however, there is no excuse for those who rendered their signature with the rest, nor can they justify themselves unless they write another declaration making known their opinions and how they oppose this defeatist declaration—especially insofar as doctrinal matters go.

WHAT IS MEANT BY THE DECLARATION

When we read the declaration, we find that, in a word, it utterly contradicts the *sharia*, especially its very foundations. Moreover, it is built upon Western conceptions, which themselves rest upon the most loathsome, secular principles, whose basis is the United Nations and its satellites. It also advocates a dialogue among civilizations lest they clash. This is an infidel notion imported from the West verbatim. Then there are flat-out lies directed against the Muslims and that suggest that this their religion agrees with much that is from the West. In fact, the dangerous features delivered in this declaration against the Muslim's creed are limitless. So we ask: Since the declaration is directed to the West, in a language none but they can understand, why not write the declaration in English and send it to them alone, instead of disseminating it among Muslims? Why disseminate the declaration between Muslims, allowing it to enter their homes and fall into the hands of the laity, if it is directed to the West? Could the purpose of this declaration be to adulterate and pervert the beliefs of the Muslims through defeatist notions such as these? Or is this a call to the West, inviting them to Islam? Or is this meant to clarify the principles of Islam for them?

The reader will be able to answer these questions by closely examining the declaration's expressions; and perhaps we'll be able to point things out that will help clarify.

IGNORANCE OR PLAY-ACTING?

What's notable from the language and purport of the message is that it contains statements evincing that its author is attempting to depict the West to the reader as being ignorant of our beliefs and the fundamentals of our religion. Thus they [intellectuals] need to hold dialogue in order to demonstrate the truth, foundation, and principles of our faith—which happen to "agree" with the West. But the poor wretch has forgotten, or has chosen to forget, that the West has colonized Muslim lands for decades, and that it is responsible for abolishing legitimate Islamic education in exchange for secular education, whose influence we still suffer from to this very day in Muslim countries. The wretch has forgotten that the West, since the days of colonization, has been able to learn every last, important detail about Islam. The poor boy has forgotten that the West has established centers focused exclusively on learning and teaching the affairs of Muslims—ideologically, theologically, legislatively, and sociologically. In fact, when the Orientalists[13] entered the lands of Islam, they produced immense studies about our religion. And the most famous of these products of Western research of Islam—used to this day by Muslim *ulema* [themselves]—is the concordance indexing the words of the *hadith*,[14] wherein a group of Orientalists cataloged all of the Prophet's discourses. Then they proceeded to index them in order to comprehend the nature of the religion and derive themes from it in order to wage war against the faith. So despite all this, here come these characters suggesting that our problem with the West has to do with the West misunderstanding Islam—thus the need for verifications and dialogues in order that they might understand our religion. But woe to such useless intellectualism, which cannot comprehend even the most obvious!

WHERE ARE THE ORIGINS OF THE FAITH?

Just like the declaration summed up the problem between us and the Crusading infidels as a lack of understanding from the West toward our religion and its principles, so too does the declaration try hard time and time again to find shared aspects between the Muslims and the Crusaders. Nor does it stop at this intellectual and methodical madness, but it goes even much further when it perverts the very foundations [of Islam]. For the declaration is completely flawed when it comes to the teachings of our religion—that is, faith in Allah alone, all the prophets, and emulation of Muhammad; upholding the doctrine of Loyalty and Enmity; repudiating all enslavement save to Allah alone, and rejecting all idolatry and false worship; and [Offensive] *Jihad* in the path of Allah Most High. Indeed, the essence of our problem with the West revolves around these principles. Thus when the Prophet wrote to the Christians calling them to Islam, he sent them the Word of Allah Most High: "Say, 'O People of the Book, let us reach an agreement . . .'" Nor did he stop there, and say "So that we might find 'shared commonalities' between us regarding justice, freedom, and values," but he completed the verse by saying " 'that we will worship none beside Allah, nor assign partners to Him, nor take each other as masters in place of Allah.' If they refuse, say: 'Bear witness that we have submitted [become Muslim]' " [3:64]. Can the writers of the declaration be frank with the Crusaders with this verse—in its entirety?

The West is hostile to us on account of Loyalty and Enmity, and [Offensive] *Jihad*. So how can the writers of the declaration address those infidels who attack our faith by word and deed with such trivial matters that have nothing to do with the heart of the conflict? What the West desires is that we abandon [the doctrine of] Loyalty and Enmity, and abandon [Offensive] *Jihad*. This is the very essence of their request and desire of us. Do the intellectuals, then, think it's actually possible for Muslims to abandon these two commandments simply to coexist with the West?

Is the atmosphere for understanding found in this declaration based on the *sharia*, or are they merely expressing their own points of view in an attempt to create an atmosphere of shared understandings to be upheld by the governments and institutions? Are the intellectuals unaware that the "Muslim" [secular] governments and the Western governments are in league to strike the essence of Islam and religiosity in the Islamic world, striving to secularize the people, and [initiating a] separation of religion and state? And how can [secular] governments who wage war on the very essence of Islam have in mind what is good for Muslims? We don't get it—is this naivete, ignorance, or are they merely trying to dupe Muslims? The truth is that the [secular] governments' war today is over the very essence of piety and Islam, and the separation of religion from politics. This is clear, not needing too much explanation. Colonialism has withdrawn from our abode but has left behind henchmen to execute its will. So how can the intellectuals imagine that the governments would adopt any proposal that would benefit the Muslims? And every proposal that can possibly benefit the governments contradicts the *sharia*: we know this by examination, experience, and trial.

As for this atmosphere of shared understandings, what evidence is there for Muslims to strive for this? What did the Prophet, the Companions after him, and the righteous forebears do? Did they wage *jihad* against the infidels, attacking them all over the earth, in order to place them under the suzerainty of Islam in great humility and submission? Or did they send messages to discover "shared understandings" between themselves and the infidels in order that they may reach an understanding whereby universal peace, security, and natural relations would spread—in such a satanic manner as this? The *sharia* provides a true and just path, securing Muslims, and providing peace to the world. If Muslims wished it thus, all they need do is follow it. The West of a surety knows this path and battles us because of it.

NO TO HOSTILITIES AND STRUGGLE!!

The intellectuals said in the[ir] declaration: "At this critical juncture in history, we call to all freethinkers to hold a serious dialogue in order to effect a better understanding between both parties, moving our peoples far away from the circle of hostility and struggle, ushering in a brighter future for our posterity, who expect much of us."

And they said: "It's imperative that we bid all to legitimate talks, presented to the world, under the umbrella of justice, morality, and rights, ushering in legislations creating peace and prosperity for the world."

And they said: "Nor should we be ignorant of the fact that an abundance of power, in all its manifestations, is not enough to defend." They said: "History has taught us that guarantees of safety are not ensured by power alone. Surety achieved through force alone bears with it the seeds of failure and disappointment, accompanied by decline—with anger and grievances from one party, and haughtiness and pride from the other. However, when guarantees are built upon justice, their chances for success are greater."

Surely there is no power save through Allah alone! We never thought that such words would ever appear from those who consider themselves adherents of this religion. Such expressions, and more like them, would lead the reader to believe that those who wrote them are Western intellectuals, not Muslims! Those previous expressions are true *only* by tearing down the wall of enmity from the infidels. They are also expressions true *only* by rejecting *jihad*—especially Offensive *Jihad*. The problem, however, is that Offensive *Jihad* is an established and basic tenet of this religion. It is a religious duty rejected only by the most deluded. So how can they call off this religious obligation [Offensive *Jihad*], while imploring the West to understandings and talks "under the umbrella of justice, morality, and rights"? The essence of all this comes from right inside the halls of the United Nations, instead of the Divine foundations that are built upon hating the infidels, repudiating them with tongue and teeth till they embrace Islam or pay the *jizya* with willing submission and humility. And no matter how much we criticize the aforementioned comments [of the declaration], still we will never be able to give it its just due, by way of its evils and underhanded dealings against our religion.

How can it [the declaration] describe the way of the Prophet and the way of the Companions after him as failures? The Prophet was "sent in the final hours with the sword, so that none is worshipped but Allah alone, partnerless." [Muhammad's] provision has been provided under the shadow of his spear, and humiliation and contempt are upon whoever opposes his command.[15] Why else did the sword come as an important pillar, enslaving mankind to their Master [Allah]? A review of the course of action of the Prophet and his Companions after him makes clear the abomination of their statements. And no matter if they say we mean this or that, their words are clear, not requiring any explanation. Nor are we under any obligation to understand what's meant. What follows will clarify.

Muslims, and especially the learned among them, should spread *sharia* law to the world—that and nothing else. Not laws under the "umbrella of justice, morality, and rights" as understood by the masses. No, the *sharia* of Islam is the foundation. And the most important issue in Islam is the *tawhid* of Allah, the Exalted, the Most High. And whoever openly and clearly repudiates these issues, we consign him to the infidels.

And whoever told you, O you intellectuals, that power is not enough to defend? The Crusading West was incapable of protecting itself if not for power—and this, after sacrificing 300 million lives in all its wars. It suffices us that the consensus reached among the *ulema* has concluded that protection of the possession of this religion is effected through the rite of *jihad* alone. Thus the defense of Muslims is [ensured] through *jihad*—not dialogue and coexistence. And know that the standard of *jihad* shall never fail or diminish, till the Day of Judgment. It is our *only* option for glory, as has been continuously demonstrated in the [Islamic] texts.[16]

DISTORTIONS AND DECEPTIONS

The signatories said in their declaration: "Islam teaches that the Christians are closer to the Muslims than the rest. History acknowledges that the Prophet of Islam sent off several of his Companions in the early years of Islam to one of the Christian kings of Ethiopia."

And they said: "The Prophet Muhammad wrote messages to the Christian Roman [Byzantine] Emperor, and to the king of the Christian Copts; and these messages were found to be kind and hospitable. Moreover, the Glorious Koran declares that the Christians, out of all other religious groups outside of Islam, are the best to get along with, as Spoken: 'You will discover that the most implacable men in their enmity to the believers are the Jews and pagans; and you will discover that the closest in affection to the believers are those who say, "We are Christians' " [5:82].

That the above statements exist in truth, there is no doubt; but that the words are true, only deception and disingenuousness can make it so. How does one go about evoking these insignificant expressions, while abandoning dozens of texts wherein the Christians are cursed, and their blasphemies and treacheries enumerated? Though these expressions came in truth, they lead to falsehood. Could it be that these words mean that there is good in them [Christians], acknowledged by Islam, and, based on that, it is possible for us to coexist with them? Such would be a vain injunction. The good in them has to do with minor particulars, which are definitely not grounds for living with them, nor debating with them, nor "dialoguing" with them, as they call it. First of all, they distort the Messiah and they reject Muhammad. Thus they do not practice the true religion. They neither hold on to their religion, nor are they content with Muhammad's religion. So according to what, exactly, are they to be praised, and according to what are we to reach an understanding? When the Sheikh of Islam [Ibn Taymiyya] debated the Christians in his book *The True Response* or Ibn al-Qayyim, in his book *Guiding the Confused*, and others among the *ulema*—they all desired but one thing: to prove to the Christians that they are blasphemers in regard to their prophet, Jesus, and blasphemers in regard to Muhammad; and that their religion is a deviation, and that Allah will never accept either purity or justice except through Submission [Islam]. So whoever possesses such attributes, but in reality is not pious, or merely practices a religion created by popes—such a one, what use is it trying to reach an understanding and living with him?

And why mention the verse as evidence of the closeness between

Christians and Muslims, but not conclude the verse? It says: "That is because there are priests and monks among them, and they are not arrogant" [5:82]. Nor does it include the follow-up verses. The verse, then, came describing them as being closer [to Muslims] than the Jews and pagans. But if we say the moon is closer [to us] than the sun, that does not prove that the moon is actually "close" to us. It is a relative matter. Moreover, the verse following this verse clarifies who in fact are closer in affection to those who believed among them: "And if they [Christians] listen to that which was revealed to the Messenger, you will see their eyes swell with tears as they recognize the truth. They say: 'Our lord, we believe! Count us among the witnesses [i.e., Muslims]' " [5:83]. This demonstrates that what's meant by those who are "close" to Islam are those among the Christians who ended up believing, since the following verse can be declared only by a believer [i.e., a convert to Islam]. So say the exegetes. Indeed, a number among the learned, such as the Judge Abu Ya'la and others, have said that the doctrines of the Christians are much more heinous than the doctrines of the Jews. This then is the meaning of their closeness: they believed in Jesus, but when Muhammad came they, hearkening to him, discovered the truth and believed. Therefore, their "closeness" does not apply to all Christians—or then even the Americans would be described as such![17]

When the Prophet sent out messages to the Christian kings, he did not write this verse in order to implore them, but he wrote the Word of the Most High: "Say, 'O People of the Book, let us reach an agreement: that we will worship none beside Allah, nor assign partners to Him, nor take each other as masters in place of Allah' . . . " [3:64].

Likewise, why don't the intellectuals mention the Word of the Most High that does apply to the West whom they address: "Infidels are those who say: 'Allah is One of three' [i.e., the Trinity] . . ." [5:73]. And the verse: "Infidels are those who say Allah is the Messiah [Jesus], son of Mary" [5:17]. Why not mention this Word of the Most High? "Fight those among the People of the Book [Christians and Jews] who do not believe in Allah nor the Last Day, who do not forbid what Allah and His Messenger have forbidden [i.e., embrace *sharia* law], and who do not embrace the religion of truth [Islam], until they pay the *jizya* with willing submissiveness and feel themselves utterly subdued" [9:29]. Why not evoke the words of the Prophet, which agree with it: "Curse of Allah be upon the Jews and Christians! they took the tombs of their prophets as places of worship." Thus it is final. In fact, passages such as these and others are abundant; and they do not comport with expressions of prostrations, defeatism. The purpose of the declaration then is an exercise in disingenuousness and an attempt to dupe the [Islamic] *umma*. They depict our religion in an incomplete manner that nullifies it—especially by abolishing the denunciation of the infidels and the objects of their worship as well as *jihad* in the path of Allah.

Moreover, Muslim hostilities vis-à-vis the nations do not revolve around a particular nation's name or its history; instead, it depends on the harm [inflicted] by this or that nation against Islam and Muslims. Whenever the idolaters are in a weaker position to harm Islam or Muslims than the Christians, then it is incumbent to fight the Christians, while postponing the battle against the idolaters, despite the fact that they are described as being a more formidable enemy.[18] And every rational individual today is aware that Crusading America, backed by Britain, Germany, France, Canada, and Australia, poses a greater danger and greater animosity to the Muslims than do Japan, both Koreas, China, and others.

Also, why do the infidels in America associate [themselves] with the Christ—peace be upon him? For the word "Christians" is completely unfounded; instead, Allah and his Messenger named them "Nazarenes."[19] So why abandon the name applied by Allah and his Messenger in favor of the one that they apply to themselves, thereby implicating Jesus with falsehood, while we sanction their falsehood by drawing close to them and appeasing them? It is truly amazing, for whenever the conversation turns to the Christians and idolaters, you will find gentle expressions and lovely pronouncements. But then whenever the conversation turns toward the *mujahidin*, see and be amazed at the censure, scandal, slander, characterizations of extremism and terrorism, etc.! Thus it's only right that we ask: Who are they loyal to? And whom do they hold enmity for?

A CHALLENGE IN ITS PLACE!!

They said in their declaration: "Thus we say in all earnestness and plainly that we can open a mature dialogue around every issue that the West submits, ever cognizant that we share a number of understandings, moral values, rights, and ideas with the West, which, if fostered, can create a better [world] for all concerned. In other words, we possess similar goals. Nonetheless, we, just like you [the West], possess our own governing principles and priorities, and our own cultural assumptions."

Easy does it! Slow down! Why such closeness to the West, with these friendly and placating words? Whoever reads the beginning of the declaration thinks you [intellectuals] to be up to this challenge. But you accomplish this through infernal expressions, whereby you conceal truth with falsehood, trivializing the fundamentals of the faith—thereby making yourselves "credible" and "men of challenge"! So spare us this affirmation, earnestness, and plainness. And regarding which shared understandings, exactly, is it possible that we agree with the immoral West? The secular West, which does not practice any religion—this the intellectuals claim we hold things in common with! What commonalities, if our foundations contradict, rendering useless the shared extremities—if they even exist? For practically everything valued by the immoral West is condemned under *sharia* law. And the few things that we do agree over—such as forthrightness and keeping promises, etc.—these are peripheral matters, not the heart of the problem between us. They claim that, if possible, we should discuss every issue the West submits, so that things go better with us all. Yet the issues most prominent in the West revolve around secularism, homosexuality, sexuality, and atheism. So what shared aspects are we to advance dialogue over in order to make for "a better place for us all"? And what shared religious goals—which are the heart of the matter—will allow us to agree with the West?

ALLAH SAYS THAT THEY ARE LIKE CATTLE, AND THEY CLAIM THEY ARE SACRED!!

They said in their declaration: "Man, from his very makeup, is a sacred creation. Thus it is impermissible to transgress against him, no matter what his color, race, or religion. Allah Most High said: 'We have honored the children of Adam [mankind] . . .' [17:70]." "No matter what his color, race, or religion"—such beautiful expressions, just as found in treaties of the Organization of Non-Aligned States that deserve commendation by way of further development by the Saudi intellectuals, who have begun to incessantly repeat the concepts found in national charters.

Now, then, how can you speak about Allah without knowledge? Who told you that transgression against man is impermissible—if he is an infidel? What about Offensive *Jihad*? Allah Exalted, the Most High, said: "Fight them! Allah will torment them with your hands" [9:14]. And He said: "Then, when the sacred months have passed, slay the idolaters wherever you find them—seize them, besiege them, and make ready to ambush them! But if they repent afterward, and perform the prayer and pay the alms [i.e., submit to Islam], then release them. For Allah is truly All-Forgiving, Merciful" [9:5]. Indeed, these expressions of yours are built upon the principle of equality, as found in the charters of the United Nations, which do not distinguish [among] people, neither by way of religion nor race nor sex. Islam improves; it is not improved. For the Muslim, even if he was a slave, is a million times more superior than an infidel lord. Allah Most High said: "Do not marry infidel women until they believe. For a believing slave-girl is much better than an idolatress—even if the latter pleases you. And do not give your women in marriage to infidels until they believe.[20] For a believing slave is much better than an idolater—even if the latter pleases you. They [idolaters] invite [people] to the Fire but Allah invites to Paradise, and forgiveness by His grace. He makes clear His revelations to mankind, so that they may be mindful" [2:221]. There is no comparison between the invitation to Fire and the invitation to Paradise. And though your falsehoods were geared toward abolishing *jihad*, you have also abolished the fundamentals differentiating between Muslims and infidels. This is a much more critical matter than what you tried to demonstrate in your declaration.

While the declaration addresses the infidel Crusading West, it takes disingenuousness, lies, and delusion on the part of Muslims to address infidels with verses applying to the human race that have nothing to do with the West, without [the verses'] conclusions. So where's the rest of the verse, which will clarify the way Allah Most High has honored all of mankind, as found in this verse: "We have honored the children of Adam, and carried them on land and sea, provided them with good things and preferred them greatly over many of those We have created" [17:70]. The meaning of "preferred," per this verse, then, is [that mankind is] a "more excellent creation," [provided with] ease of movement through land and sea, and provision of good things, just as Ibn Kathir said in his commentary on this verse. So why present this verse without clarification, describing infidels as being [intrinsically] "sacred"? The West understands "sacred" as meaning respect and the preservation of man-made rights. So, [mankind's] superiority vis-à-vis creation as found in the verse is portrayed by them as evidence that it is imperative to hold sacred the Western infidel and preserve his man-made rights. But whenever the human race is tied up with infidelity, legally [per the *sharia*] and logically, one should evoke only those verses that apply to such as are addressed [the West], who are, in fact, described by Allah as being like unto cows, except even more astray. He said: "And we have created for Hell multitudes of jinn and men. They have hearts but do not comprehend; they have eyes but do not see; they have ears but do not hear. They are like cows—nay! They are even more misguided. Such are the heedless ones" [7:179]. He also said: "Or do you suppose that most of them hear or comprehend? They are but like cows. Indeed! even more wayward" [25:44]. And He said: "Infidels are those who say: 'Allah is One of three' [i.e., the Trinity] . . ." [5:73]. And He said: "Infidels are those who say Allah is the Messiah, son of Mary" [5:17]. And other verses that reveal the truth about them.

Someone will say, There is no place for these verses in the declaration where the verse dealing with the honor of man is mentioned. But we say that the positioning of the verse came in the declaration intentionally to support [the notion that there are] shared understandings between the signatories and the West. And the signatories claim that they are speaking in the name of religion. But it is great error to posit that the religion honors mankind. And "mankind" as presented in the declaration represents none other than the Western peoples—otherwise, there would have been no purpose for positing the verse between the shared understandings between the signatories and the Crusaders. But the religion can never possibly honor the Western man who rejects Allah Almighty. Indeed, He describes him as a cow; and He has cursed him and prepared the everlasting Fire for him. This is what the intellectuals should be mindful of mentioning at this juncture of the declaration.

WHY DRESS UP TRUTH WITH FALSEHOOD?!

They said in their declaration: "It is not permitted to coerce anyone regarding his religion. Allah Most High said: 'There is no compulsion in religion' [2:256]." Thus Islam itself does not comport with coercion.

This is a distortion of truth with falsehood. The conflict with the Crusaders has nothing to do with the beliefs of the heart—there is no ambiguity there. For the verse prohibits forcing people to change the faith of their hearts. The reasons for this verse's revelation, which have been articulated by the exegetes, help elucidate this matter.

But once again, why do the intellectuals take the first part of the verse while neglecting [to mention] its end, which is: "There is no compulsion in religion. True guidance is now distinct from error. He that renounces idolatry [or Satan] and believes in Allah shall grasp a firm handle that will never break. Allah is All-Hearing, All-Knowing"

[2:256]. Why not clarify what "renounces idolatry [or Satan]" means to the West? Therefore, just as our religion contains no coercion, so too does it stress renouncing idolatry, and faith in Allah, in the manner of Abraham—peace upon him. Thus what they make the first part of the verse [say] does not agree with its conclusion.

Furthermore, a number of exegetes, including Ibn Kathir, have said that this verse has been abrogated by the Word of Allah Most High. "You [desert-dwellers] shall be called upon to battle a mighty nation unless they submit [i.e., embrace Islam]" [48:16]. And the verse: "O you who believe! fight the infidels who dwell around you, and let them see how ruthless you can be. Know that Allah is with the righteous" [9:123]. And the verse: "O Prophet! Wage war against the infidels and hypocrites and be ruthless. Their abode is hell—an evil fate!" [9:73]. Thus the [matter of] abrogation is conveyed by those who think that the ban has to do with forcefully placing them under the authority of the religion. But those who believe that [the ban] revolves around the beliefs of the heart find no contradiction between the verses.[21]

But what's more important, and what the debate truly revolves around, and what the signatories shy away from mentioning, is the word of the Messenger as has been relayed by Ahmad and others from Ibn Omar: "I have been sent in the final hours with the sword, so that none is worshipped but Allah alone, partnerless. My provision has been provided under the shadow of my spear, and humiliation and contempt is upon whoever opposes my command. Whoever imitates a people is of them." And his saying in the two authentic [accounts of Bukhari and Muslim] as relayed by Ibn Omar: "I have been commanded to battle mankind until they declare that there is no god but Allah and that Muhammad is the Messenger of Allah. [Let them] uphold prayer and render alms; if they do so, they safeguard their blood and possessions from me, except for Islam's due, and their fate is with Allah." He also said, per Berida as found in Muslim and Ahmad: "Whenever the Messenger of Allah appointed someone as leader of an army or detachment, he would especially exhort him to fear Allah and be good to the Muslims with him. Then he would say: 'Attack in the name of Allah and in the path of Allah do battle with whoever rejects Allah. Attack!—but do not embezzle [the spoils], nor behave treacherously, nor mutilate [the dead], nor kill the children. If you happen upon your idolatrous enemies, call them to three courses of action. If they respond to any one of these, accept it and stay yourself from them. [1] Call them to Islam: If they respond [i.e., convert], accept this and cease fighting them. . . . [2] If they refuse to accept Islam, demand of them the *jizya*: If they respond, accept it and cease fighting them. [3] But if they refuse, seek the aid of Allah and fight them." Thus our talks with the infidel West and our conflict with them ultimately revolve around one issue—one that demands our total support, with power and determination, with one voice—and it is: Does Islam, or does it not, force people by the power of the sword to submit to its authority corporeally if not spiritually? Yes. There are only three choices in Islam: either willing submission; or payment of the *jizya*, through physical though not spiritual, submission to the authority of Islam; or the sword—for it is not right to let him [an infidel] live. The matter is summed up for every person alive: Either submit, or live under the suzerainty of Islam, or die. And it behooves the signatories to clarify this matter to the West—otherwise they will be like those who believe in part of the Book while rejecting the rest. But instead they concoct something that has no connection to the struggle, dressing it up and presenting it as Islam. Yet the verse does not support what they wish and mean regarding this matter. The West avenges itself against Islam for giving infidels but three options: Islam, *jizya*, or the sword. Now, then, you intellectuals: Are these options a part of the faith or not? This is what the debates truly revolve around—so stop evading and dissembling the truth with lies!

THE EXCEPTION HAS BECOME THE RULE
AND THE RULE HAS BEEN ABOLISHED

They said in their declaration: "The heart of the relationship between Muslims and non-Muslims is justice, kindness, and charity—this is the equity that Allah loves and has commanded us with. Allah Most High said: 'Allah does not forbid you from being kind and equitable to those who have not fought you nor driven you out of your homes. Allah loves the equitable' [60:8]." The meanings have been so twisted that Islam has now become something we can no longer recognize! For now, pillars and fundamentals have appeared that we supposed were branches of the faith—not its very essence. As to the relationship between Muslims and infidels, this is summarized by the Most High's Word: "You have a good example in Abraham and those with him. They said to their people: 'We disown you and what you worship besides Allah. We renounce you. Enmity and hate shall forever reign between us—till you believe in Allah alone' " [60:4]. So there is an enmity, evidenced by fierce hostility, and an internal hate from the heart. And this fierce hostility—that is, battle—ceases only if the infidel submits to the authority of Islam, or if his blood is forbidden from being shed [a *dhimmi*], or if the Muslims are [at that point in time] weak and incapable [of spreading *sharia* law to the world]. But if the hate at any time extinguishes from the hearts, this is great apostasy; the one who does this [extinguishes the hate from his heart] will stand excuseless before Allah. Allah Almighty's Word to His Prophet recounts in summation the true relationship: "O Prophet! Wage war against the infidels and hypocrites and be ruthless. Their abode is hell—an evil fate!" [9:73]. Such, then, is the basis and foundation of the relationship between the infidel and the Muslim. Battle, animosity, and hatred—directed from the Muslim to the infidel—is the foundation of our religion. And we consider this a justice and kindness to them. The West perceives fighting, enmity, and hatred all for the sake of the religion as unjust, hostile, and evil. But who's understanding is right—our notions of justice and righteousness, or theirs?

So through the use of one verse, the intellectuals claim they have evidence that supports Western—not the *sharia*'s—notions of how we are to deal with one another—culminating with kindness, charity, and justice as found in the Word of the Most High: "Allah does not forbid you from being kind and equitable to those who have not

fought you nor driven you out of your homes. Allah loves the equitable" [60:8]. This is speaking on behalf of Allah without knowledge.
What this verse offers are exceptions to the rule, which concerns kins-
men—not the people of war [enemies who refuse Islam]. How can
[they] make the exception to the rule the rule itself while disregarding
and abolishing the rule?! Why not say that the fundamental relationship between the Muslim and the infidel is based on enmity and hatred, in the pattern of Abraham? Either way, the *ulema* have said that
this verse—which the intellectuals have made the cornerstone [of
their declaration]—has been abrogated by the verses of the sword,[22]
which reply to the intellectuals who scurry to coexist with the West,
since "Allah does not forbid you from being kind and equitable to
those who have not fought you"—but this is followed by: "But Allah
forbids from befriending those who fought you because of your religion, and driven you out from your homes or abetted others to drive
you out. They who befriend them are indeed the evildoers" [60:9]. So
how can you contradict the prohibition of Allah Exalted, the Most
High? You hurry to pay homage to those who fight us and evict us
from our homes; wanting to be kind to them, to live with them, to
agree upon common grounds—what! Do you not fear that you are
among the evildoers?

WHAT "UNDERSTANDINGS" ARE YOU TALKING ABOUT?

They said in their declaration: "Justice between people is their right,
while oppression between them is forbidden—no matter what their
religion, color, or nationality is. Allah Most High said: 'And when you
speak, be just—even if it affects your own kinsman' " [6:152].

   This declaration is indeed full of expressions and notions nebulous and ambiguous, knowing no bounds and inarticulate. It
continuously repeats that it rejects religious, racial, and national distinctions, to assure the West of its prostrations to it—a principle feature of the declaration. Yet based on those expressions regarding
justice and oppression in the previous paragraph, and the nondiffer-

entiation between colors, religions, and nationalities, we are well aware that this mode of speech is found verbatim in the charter of the [UN] Security Council regarding the Council's need to lift up oppression from the peoples.

Moreover, what does the word "justice" here mean? This conversation is with the West. And the West believes that "justice" means that we grant them the freedom to do as they wish and call to bondage whom they wish. They imagine "justice" grants them sexual freedom, grants them the authority to do all things—for surely justice can never hinder their freedom! This is why their conniving Bush has named this Crusader war "the defense for freedom."[23] In other words, they believe America represents freedom, while it . . . [text ends]

PERVERSITY

As for the word "oppression," those addressed take it to mean being placed under the authority of Islam by the sword, as the Prophet did with the infidels. They think that something that denies them [the freedom] to pursue obscenities, atheism and blasphemy, and idolatry is an "oppression." They think that an attack launched against their ground, as in an Offensive *Jihad*, is an "injustice." And so forth.

Then come the [intellectuals] declaring that justice is a right while oppression is forbidden. If they mean justice and oppression, as understood by those addressed—and they [intellectuals] are the ones who chose the language to prove that there are shared understandings between them—then this is a great calamity, and a blasphemous conversation. But if they mean oppression and justice as understood in Islam, well, that is nothing less than what the Crusaders are waging their war over. Indeed, the wars they visit upon Muslims are waged solely because they disagree with us over what constitutes justice and oppression. Justice is freeing slaves from being enslaved to other slaves in order to worship the Lord of mankind; from the chaos of religions to the righteousness of Islam; from the narrow confines of the world to the broad possibilities of this world and the Hereafter. As for oppression, the only oppression is to forsake them in their infidelity, and not use *jihad* as a means to make them enter into the faith—as the Prophet did with them.

AMAZING! THE CRUSADING CAMPAIGN CONTAINS BLESSINGS FOR THE PEOPLE!!

They said in their declaration: "They [many principles of Islam] agree—insofar as they coincide—with a number of principles expounded by the American intellectuals in their declaration; and we believe that such agreements make for a solid platform for us to hold dialogue that will contain blessings for all mankind."

Here the intellectuals establish that an exchange with the Crusaders [writers of the American declaration]—who called Bush to continue his Crusading campaign—that such an exchange affords dialogue and contains blessings for the people, though the essence of their ["Crusaders"] declaration revolved around assertions such as when they said, "In the name of universal human morality, and fully conscious of the restrictions and requirements of a just war, we support our government's, and our society's, decision to use force of arms against them." Such was the declaration of the Crusaders that was met by the declaration of the intellectuals who prostrated low on the ground, saying, Your exchange resembles a common ground for dialogue and blessings for the people. The appropriate and most suitable response from the intellectuals' declaration to the Crusaders [should have been] that we will rise up individually and collectively in order to support *jihad* and the *mujahidin*, and we will support and increase martyrdom operations. It is incumbent upon us to respond to them by transferring the battle from the military realm to the political and economic realms, and the cultural, intellectual, and social realms, and all of life's realms. For such an exchange leads to nothing but evil for all humanity, imposing blasphemy and infidelity and obliterating Islam. O you intellectuals! the good of the people is found in Islam; and Islam is spread with the sword alone, just as the

Prophet was sent forth with the sword. So how can the signatories decide that the good of the people is found in an exchange with the Crusaders, who call for Islam's destruction? And everything they evoked in the declaration—freedom, justice, mercy, and rights—is in complete accordance with the notions of the infidels, not the notions of Islam.

YOU HAVE ABSOLUTELY NO RIGHT EXCEPT TO SPEAK ON YOUR OWN BEHALF

They said in their declaration: "To many in the Islamic world and elsewhere, the attacks of September [11] are neither legitimate nor welcome, due to all the values, principles, and moral standards that we have learned from Islam."

They said: "Nor is it logical to assume that those who attacked the United States on September 11th do not feel a sort of personal justification for what they did due to American policies all over the world. And though we do not hold the view that they were justified in striking civilian targets, still it is necessary to recognize that some sort of causative relationship exists between American policy and what happened."

Really, this declaration failed the expectations of many, particularly the pious. And even though it failed expectations and perturbs the soul, still, what's more painful than its publication is that such mockery, deception, and prostration is published in the name of all Muslims, especially [those] in the land of the Two Holy Sites [Saudi Arabia]. The signatories have absolutely no right to talk in the name of the Muslims living in the land of the Two Holy Sites, as they portray in their declaration. And the greatest calumny is that these signatories do not know the foundations of the creed of the forefathers. Instead they were trained in general matters, and their degrees are in the natural sciences—which do not justify them to speak on matters related to *sharia* law and on behalf of the *umma* in its entirety.

So the expressions in the past two sections culminate into a sort of repugnant bowing to the infidels—and that it goes out under our name vexes us greatly. Moreover, the signatories confirm—by lying—that many in the Islamic world did not welcome the attack of September [11]. This is the furthest thing from the truth. Indeed, happiness and joy have not entered many a Muslim home in decades as it did after what befell the Crusaders, thanks to these blessed strikes—and we implore Allah for more like them. And if the media only focused on a mere slice [of the Muslim populace] exhibiting their disapproval [over 9/11], well, the media is in the habit of showing what the [secular Muslim] governments wish—who themselves are the ones who were grieved over what befell the[ir] masters.

Moreover, how can they ascribe the reason for not welcoming [the attacks of 9/11], among those few, to "all the values, principles, and moral standards that we have learned from Islam"? If these are the reasons, then why didn't we see a separate examination based on the *sharia*—instead of politics—from one of the signatories expounding on these reasons through the [Islamically] legal evidence, and not "logic" and "reason"? Instead they referenced nothing but a draft written by one or two [people], full of corruptions, and then claimed it to be accurate.

DID YOU INSTRUCT YOURSELVES?

They said in their declaration: "Why must we ignore this history, permitting a superficial and premature reading of events?! Nor is that all: the laws of regulation that Islam delivers establish a stable life for both those who believe in it and those who do not."

Again, persisting to abolish the differences between Muslims and non-Muslims! And why don't these signatories permit themselves to read both ancient and modern history? When the king of the Copts of Egypt tried improving relations with the Prophet by dignifying his messenger and sending him back on a beast of burden laden with clothing, and a slave-girl [one of Muhammad's future wives, Mariam], did such niceties prevent the Companions from raiding the Coptic realms, forcefully placing them under Islamic rule?[24]

Moreover, have the signatories never heard of the Crusades, launched by the European church against the lands of Islam, devastating both land and life? Have the signatories never heard of British, French, Belgian, and Italian colonization of the lands of the Muslims? Are the signatories unaware that colonization is still under way, though in an indirect manner? Why do you ignore history and talk to the scourgers [Westerners] by way of this defeatist declaration? If you are incapable of speaking the truth and together with the *mujahidin* confronting the tyrannical foe, then be silent and distort not the image of Islam, sullying its universally binding principles, mutilating its texts, and turning the struggle from absolutes to trivialities. Would that you would stop hindering the Muslims from confronting the enemy alongside the *mujahidin*!

THE CALL TO BRING ISLAM AND CHRISTIANITY CLOSER!!

They said in their declaration: "One of the established notions in our faith today is that the Eastern nations [such as] Japan and China are more alien in their understandings from the Islamic world than the peoples of the West. There are many more bridges connecting the Islamic world to the West than with these Eastern nations, as well as mutually beneficial relationships and common interests [between the Islamic world and West]. It should be assumed that the West perceives that it is in their best interest to have balance and stability in the Islamic world. It should also appreciate that Islamic lands have provided much for them—especially in regard to the West's economic structure. The West is the primary beneficiary from a strong Islamic economy."

They said: "The disagreement between us and American society is not over values of justice or the choice of freedoms. In our view, values are of two kinds: [1] basic human values shared by all people, values that are in accord with the innate nature of the human being and that our religion calls us to; and [2] values particular to a specific people, who choose those values and give precedence to them. But it's not for us to compel them to abandon these [values], since our religion teaches us that there is no coercion in religion. It goes without saying that a number of those values are social preferences that are drawn from their given environment. Likewise, we do not accept others to compel us to change our particular values or to deny us the right to live by them. We see it as our right—as it is the right of every people—to clarify to others what we believe and our values in order to foster better understanding between the peoples of the world, thereby realizing world peace and creating opportunities for those who search for goodness and truth."

The defeatist expressions set forth in the declaration are nothing out of the ordinary. Instead, the declaration's chief poison is its attempt to try to grow closer to and cease hostilities with the West—in all its blasphemy and evil, which it inflicts upon Islam and Muslims. It presents a pattern of injustice—a pattern of intellectual prostrations and deep bows to the West and to the Americans particularly (perhaps so they would go easy on the writers?). And how can it describe the West, which has colonized the lands of Islam, killing and displacing millions—how can it describe it in this manner? And instead of enumerating its atrocities, and its exportation of secularism and atheism to the lands of the Muslims, the intellectuals praise it and describe it as being closer to us than the East, with "bridges of communication," and [suggestions] that the West can benefit from our economy—as if to say: Please do not cut off from us what your right hand gives—for only you yourself will suffer, you wretch.

Why all the lies and false claims that the conflict with the Americans is not over values of justice and the choice of freedoms? For indeed, the conflict with the Crusading Americans *is* over values of justice—both in theory and practice; likewise with freedoms—in theory and practice. Know that lying in order to satisfy the West and disavowing our religion serves only to weaken Muslims, benefiting them neither now nor in the future.

Furthermore, how can they claim that we have no right to force a people to change its particular values, when they transgress the bounds of nature? Such are lies. In fact, Muslims are obligated to raid the lands of the infidels, occupy them, and exchange their systems of governance for an Islamic system, barring any practice that contradicts the *sharia* from being publicly voiced among the people, as was the case at the dawn of Islam.

IF ISLAM IS TRUE THEN WHY DON'T YOU CALL THE WEST TO IT?

They said in their declaration: "We believe that Islam is the truth; however, it is not possible for the entire world to become Muslim: it is neither in our capacity to achieve this, nor is it permissible under our *sharia* to impose our particular beliefs on others. This is our [Islamically] legal choice."

The signatories were daring to use such expressions—saying to the face of the West that Islam is the truth!—but they did not follow up on this boldness by calling the West to submit [to Islam], as the Prophet did with the kings of the infidels and whomever of their numbers he happened upon. Instead they found a way out for themselves by saying that we are incapable of making the whole world Muslim.

Thus they make claims and speak about Allah without understanding. They say that our *sharia* does not impose our particular beliefs upon others; this is a false assertion. For it is, in fact, part of our religion to impose our particular beliefs upon others. Whoever doubts this, let him turn to the deeds of the Companions when they raided the lands of the Christians and Omar imposed upon them the conditions of *dhimmi[tude]*. These conditions involve clothing attire, specific situations, and class distinctions known to *ulema* as the pact of Omar,[25] and they are notoriously famous. Let the signatories review them so they know that we *are* to force people by the power of the sword to [our] particular understandings, customs, and conditions, all in order to induce debasement and humility, just like Allah commanded when he said: "[. . .]until they pay the *jizya* by hand, in complete submission and humility" [9:29]. Now, if you are incapable of *jihad* and placing people into the religion, like the Companions did, your impotence does not mean that it is not a legitimate aspect of the religion. Instead, it [the declaration] is a product of your defeat and your desire to live with the Christians.

We do not desire your intercessions; but we do desire the intercession of the Prophet. They said in their declaration: "Muslims have the right to hold on to their religion, its values and teachings. This is an option too difficult to force [them away from]. However, we present a moderate and balanced understanding, and we strive for its radiance. And the West will discover in it a great difference than the understandings and perceptions they have about Islam. That is if it [the West] is in earnest about acknowledging us, our religion, and our capabilities—or, at the very least willing to study the facts of our religion and our values in a rational and objective manner."

They claim that they will present a "moderate" and "balanced" way of life, contrasting greatly from the understandings and perceptions the West has over Islam. If your moderation greatly contradicts what the West, and in particular their intellectuals, know, then it is not Islam, nor does it possess any relationship to Allah Most High's religion. Consecutive Western exchanges and examinations of Islam have enabled them to understand the principles and foundations of the religion more than many Muslims. The picture of Islam that Western governments and [their] intellectual circles have is very exact and minute. Since the start of colonization, they have devoted whole centers where they research and study Islam—and all this so they can formulate a clear conception of Islam. And the West's notions that Islam is a religion of *jihad* and enmity toward the religions of the infidels and the infidels themselves is an accurate and true depiction. So if the intellectuals wish to present a "moderate" and "balanced" way of life, it is first necessary to abolish Loyalty and Enmity, *jihad*, and especially Offensive *Jihad*, thereby making the Word of Allah apply to them: "Neither the Jews nor the Christians will be pleased with you until you follow their faith" [2:120]. As to the moderation and balance that the West might find satisfactory—that is nothing less than a religion stripped of its reality. Thus the balance and moderation that you claim to present to the West most assuredly is in opposition to the intensity and radicalism that is represented by America's number-one foe, Sheikh Osama bin Laden. Indeed, your moderation will be in opposition to the command of the Prophet who said he had been sent in the final hours with the sword and had willed to battle mankind until they declare that there is no god but Allah. The "middle ground" of the Prophet who said, as recorded in Muslim and Ahmad and others, through Abu Hurreira: "Do not initiate peace with the Jews nor with the Christians; if you find one of them in the way, bully him into a corner." That's his command regarding civilians who made pacts [*dhimmis*], not those who combat. As for those who do combat, such as those you addressed, the Americans, he spoke about them as is recorded in Ahmad through Abd Umru by saying: "Slaughter is come for you." Such, then, is the pattern [of behavior] that we need you to present and that expresses the command of the Prophet. But your new advice, as presented by this declaration, destroys the religion and abolishes the differences between the infidels and us.

SLOW DOWN. DO NOT JOIN THOSE STATES THAT BATTLE ISLAMIC TERRORISM.

They said in their declaration: "The West heavily discusses the problem of terrorism and extremism. From our perspective, this problem is a serious one confronting the entire world, requiring a number of measures to deal with it. . . . However, religious extremism is not tied to any one particular religion. We admit that there are extremist elements among the Muslims, as there are with other [religions]."

And so at last the intellectuals proclaim that they will join the American campaign to battle Islamic "terrorism"—that is, *jihad*. Such is what we finally get out of these balanced moderates: that they perceive "extremism" to be a serious problem in the world needing to be remedied and treated. And they have decided that among the different kinds of extremism is Islamic extremism. And naturally, of course, Islamic extremism is primarily depicted by Sheikh Osama bin Laden, and al-Qaeda, and Abu Sayyaf's organization, and the *mujahidin* in Chechnya, and Hamas, and others.[26] If all or some of these are not meant by "Islamic extremism," as the intellectuals call it, then which group is being described?! And who do they mean?! Clearly they have agreed with the West regarding this perception of extremism.

After the *mujahidin* were expecting aid from ones such as these [the intellectuals], instead they opt to acknowledge the West's interpretation of extremism—though after widening the scope. Moreover, they have also decided on the necessity of finding ways to "solve" it. The ways of remedying extremism are to cancel the doctrine of Loyalty and Enmity along with the rites of *jihad*, O you intellectuals!

Woe to them! They neither aid Islam nor do they crush the infidels. And while the *mujahidin* are painted in colors of shame and torture in defense of the religion and the weak, these [intellectuals] conclude that they [*mujahidin*] are radicals and that they will come up with a plan to treat radicalism. May Allah forgive them!

Cooperation with the West against what they call Islamic extremism [or "fundamentalism," "radicalism"], whether it's performed by one word, or a declaration, or any other manner, either directly or indirectly, is apostasy from the religion of Allah Most High. And there's enough evil in these words [of theirs] in that they even *admit* that there exists extremes in Islam. And the extremism meant by the West is [found in] Allah Most High's Word: "Muster against them what fighting men and steeds of war you can, in order to strike terror in the enemy of Allah and your enemy, and others besides them whom you do not know, but Allah knows well" [8:60]. Thus whoever refuses the principle of terror[ism] against the enemy also refuses the commandment of Allah the Exalted, the Most High, and His *sharia*. The West prepares to defend itself in face of this extremist verse. So, have the intellectuals learned to deny the truth of the religion? But what is truly amazing is that they have promised a moderate and balanced approach—which is its number-one characteristic.

THE WEST IS BATTLING THE VERY ESSENCE OF ISLAM, SO DO NOT DECEIVE THE MUSLIMS, O INTELLECTUALS!

They said in their declaration: "We seriously call upon the West to become more open toward Islam and its textual principles, and to deal temperately with the Islamic reality. [We call upon them to] seriously review their position against Islam. Moreover, [we call upon them to] open channels of dialogue between prominent Islamic thinkers representative of the broad current of Islamic thought, and the thinkers and policy makers of the West."

Although they are intellectuals, they still remain ignorant—or are willfully ignorant—that the West understands their religion and the foundations of their exclusive creed more than the Muslim laity. So they think that the West's position toward us is due to its lack of understanding Islam, its principles, and its laws. In fact, the West did not treat Islam in this atrocious manner until after it [first] understood the truth about Islam—comprehended its essence and soul. And the West is knowledgeable of all religions, but it would never confront any of them, nor persecute their people. But it is bent on pulverizing the Muslims, since first learning of their enterprise [Offensive *Jihad*].

And despite their [the intellectuals'] ignorance that the West knows the details and foundations of their religion, to make things worse, they call the Western thinkers and policy makers to talks with a select group of intellectuals "representative of the broad current of Islamic thought." Enough dissembling, deception, and word plays already! For we do not accept that any utter on behalf of the *umma* except the true *ulema* [of Islam]. We do not accept that the intellectual and defeatist party speaks on our behalf, conversing with the West and calling it to live with us, abolishing enmity for it and *jihad* against it. And those who call the West to dialogue do not call that the dialogue be with the *ulema*, for they know that the *ulema* forbid living with the West. So they solved this critical issue by [appointing] the intellectual party, which does not distinguish between root and branch.

WHICH "MODERATION" DO YOU MEAN?

They said in their declaration: "It is imperative for the West to appreciate that the majority of Islamic movements in the Islamic world, and elsewhere, are essentially moderate. It's important to preserve this and respect the rights of these organizations that behave with temperance. [It is also imperative to] cease creating or approving instigations from any party and under any pretext—all so that [people] can cooperate rationally and securely."

Still do the intellectuals play with words and technical terms—the chief character of their declaration. They describe the majority of Islamic movements as being moderate. But what is meant by "moderation"? Is it based on the understandings of the *sharia* or the understandings of the West? The evolution of the[ir] talk evinces that what is meant is the Western understanding, not the *sharia*'s. For the *sharia*'s notion of moderation is represented by the Word of the Most High: "So We have made you a just ["middle-way"] *umma*, so that you may testify against mankind, and so that the Messenger may testify against you" [2:143]. And His Word: "Who but a foolish man would forsake the religion of Abraham?" [2:130]. "Moderation" is demonstrated by our Prophet who did not remain more than three months in Medina without raiding or sending a raiding party into the lands of the infidels to beat down their strongholds and seize their possessions, their lives, and their women. "Moderation" is clear from one look to the life of the Prophet and the lives of his Companions after him. "Moderation" is apparent from the action of the Prophet when he joined the community of faith of our forefather, Abraham. This is what moderation based on *sharia* law is like, O you assembly of intellectuals. And of course by calling the West to "preserve moderation," you clearly do not mean the *sharia*'s moderation, but rather Western moderation, which it approves of. And the most important feature of the moderation the West favors is elimination of *jihad*—especially Offensive *Jihad*; also elimination of enmity for the infidels and the things they worship, and their religions and idols. Or, at the very least, to disregard and overlook these duties. Truly, this is the sort of moderation that "behaves with temperance." The intellectuals entreat the West to safeguard against instigations, so it [moderation] does not die out.

And so what if instigations occur against the moderates? Will they jump to defend their religion and manhood? Not at all. Instead, they will submit a declaration to the hostile Crusaders, bowing to them, and entreating them, in order that they approve of them, reach an understanding, and disavow those [al-Qaeda] who influenced the West to rise up against them. And they request an investigation into finding a way to coexist outside of *sharia* law. Thus, at a time when the intellectuals and theologians of the West, backed by their governments and the Jews, support a butchery of Muslims everywhere, our intellectuals write a verbose prostration to please the West.

The Camp David Accords[27] have been transferred into the minds of the intellectuals. They said in their declaration: "Now, if the goal is to sever terrorism at its root, the most appropriate course of action is not universal war but equitable peace. This is what the world looks for in Palestine and elsewhere."

Amazing! After a good number of our intellectuals were warning against peace and naturalization [of relations] with the Jews and the West in general—[indeed] even the secularists who acknowledge Islam—we find today that cloning experiments do work indeed, but by transferring the beliefs and expressions from the halls of Camp David into the minds of the intellectuals. So now they've begun to call for universal and equitable peace in Palestine and elsewhere. The notion of "peace" as thrown around today and that the West calls for, and the intellectuals consider a shared aspect, is none other than surrendering and selling land to the foe. So repent to Allah, and leave off from these useless expressions!

BACKSTABBING AND TREACHERY IN REPRESENTING THE *MUJAHIDIN*

They said in their declaration: "Terrorism, according to the universally agreed meaning being used today, is but one of many manifestations of unjust aggression against life and property. However, only one who is morally devoid would focus on but one form of unjust aggression while turning a blind eye to all other manifestations—even if they are more atrocious, producing more deaths and corruption around the land: such would be a clear case of selective vision and the use of double standards." How so many had hope that Islam would receive aid from the signatories through the publications of declarations uplifting the religion and the people of the faith and the *mujahidin*. But behold! Today they are agreed to the meaning and definition of "terrorism" as acknowledged and agreed to by the Americans, that is, "unjust aggression against life and property." And such acknowledgment by necessity must apply to and include the Prophet who assaulted the lives, properties, and women of the infidels, who were living in secure and settled cities. As did his Companions after him. Such aggression, as understood by the West, is not justified; nor does such hostility agree with the Western notion of "freedom of religion." Thus our Prophet and his Companions and the righteous forefathers have all now become "terrorists."[28] The intellectuals are agreed to today's widespread and acknowledged definition [that] terrorism is loathsome—unless, of course, they mean as acknowledged under the conventions of *sharia* law, which is another matter. However, the message is to the West, and they only understand international—that is, American—definitions.

Such prostrations count as a powerful stab in the back of the *mujahidin*—who expect help and support from every Muslim. Instead they [the intellectuals] reject the terrorism of the *mujahidin*, which attacks lives and property. But if the intellectuals grow hostile toward you, O *mujahidin*, [know that] Allah is with you and will never forsake you.

ALLAH SAYS *JIHAD* IS A GOOD THING FOR YOU, AND THE INTELLECTUALS SAY "NOT SO!"

They said in their declaration: "The engagement of struggle does not necessarily result in any positive outcomes—for either of the opposing parties. Nor are those who represent the struggle always the best suited to represent this group or that. And nothing can fend off the specter of clashes [of civilizations] as can justice and the preservation of rights and the commitment to values and morals, even during wars, if we are forced into them."

[More] insistence from them that *jihad*—what they have dubbed "struggle"—cannot produce good results for both parties, thereby disagreeing with the Word of Allah Most High: "You are obligated to fight, though you may hate it. For it may well be that you hate that which is good for you and love that which is evil for you. Allah knows [best]; you do not know" [2:216]. And His Word: "O you who have believed! Respond to Allah and the Messenger when he calls you to that which will give you life" [8:24]. And a faction of the original forefathers asserted: "*Jihad* is what enlivens you." And the saying of the Prophet: "No nation ever forsook *jihad* without becoming degraded." Yet these [intellectuals] claim that "struggle"—*jihad*—cannot produce any good for either party. What matters to us here is the Muslim party; and *jihad*, as demonstrated and agreed upon, produces nothing for them [Muslims] except always the best—whether it be a Defensive *Jihad* or Offensive *Jihad*, and even if they all die [realizing it].

So now *jihad* has become a specter and a clash to the intellectuals. And they reject the clash of civilizations, and mean to ward off its specter through justice, the preservation of rights and values—especially any rights present in the West and any value we might possibly agree upon.

Their reluctance in acknowledging that Offensive *Jihad* is one of the exclusive traits of our religion demonstrates nothing but defeat. As for concluding that clashes and struggles cannot produce anything positive, this is great delusion and an outrageous claim—such that whoever utters it should fear that his work shall perish.

WE WERE EXPECTING THEM TO PREPARE FOR *JIHAD*, BUT INSTEAD THEY SAY . . .

They said in their declaration: "[We need] to find greater room for dialogue and the exchange of ideas whereby theorists, *ulema*, and intellectuals—from our perspective—will find a substitute for the language of force and destruction. And this is our motivation for writing this paper and participating in this debate."

Here in this section they pronounce their excuse and motivations—that is, a dialogue for theorists, intellectuals, and *ulema*, in place of violence and destruction, offering assurances for both parties. But our "party" has nothing else but *jihad* in the way of Allah, by which we raid the infidels on their own ground. So it was the furthest thing from our mind and beyond our wildest imaginations that one day people such as these would come out, at the van of the *mujahidin*, emulating the Prophet and all the Companions and the righteous forefathers—and then all of a sudden like a thunderbolt they dumbfounded every well-meaning person toward them. They call for talks to put an end to the exchange of force and destruction. Verily, there is no ability or power save in Allah alone! We were expecting a *jihad* from them, but they are suddenly resolved to wage war against the *mujahidin* by way of dialogues and condemnation of the *mujahidin*. And this declaration is but the beginning; what's to come is greater. We ask Allah for security and well-being.

Way of life? Or is there some reasonable objection?

CONCLUSION

Truly, this declaration was a flash of lightning striking down many of the pious who read it—especially because it contained some names [the signatories] renowned for [religious] learning. However, we request that these be excused; for they agreed to the substance of the declaration without closely inspecting the details, thereby [hastily] including their names without knowing the final form, as the best of them said. But let them beware that they have no excuse in front of Allah Most High except by disclaiming the great errors found in the declaration—especially those things that have to do with the foundations [of the faith]. And the criticisms contained in what we wrote are not meant to vex those more righteous ones who were deceived; instead, we maintain goodwill toward them and ask for guidance for ourselves and them.

And just as the intellectuals' decision to coexist with the West by agreeing to the West's principles and values—and all in the name of Islam and Muslims—cut to our very being, what has perturbed us even more, much more, is what the person who put this declaration together did, when he asked the common people to endorse his signature by supporting it with theirs. And if the request for the people's opinions was sincere, there would have been a square [to check] in agreement and another square [to check] for disagreement. However, he knew that the people would all [choose to] disagree. And this manner of deciding truth from falsehood, through the ballot box, is one of the methods the writer of the declaration utilized straight from the West. For they [Westerners] vote over everything—even over legalizing homosexual marriage! They raised their voices in all their parliaments and thus legalized it. But he who tried to portray all these doctrinal matters as legitimate to the people [Muslims] knew that such supplementation [of "yes" and "no" boxes] would only have led to rejection. Nonetheless, what is false is false—even if a billion individuals agree to it; and truth is truth—even if only one who has submitted [i.e., a Muslim] holds on to it. Abundance or dearth [by way of votes, opinions, etc.] is not indicative of truth and falsehood. Allah said, "If you were to obey the greater part of those on earth, they would lead you astray from the path of Allah. They follow nothing but idle fancies and [utter] nothing but lies" [6:116]. And He said: "Strive as you may, most men will not believe" [12:103]. And the Messenger, as [recorded] in the two authentic [*hadiths* of Bukhari and Muslim], said that on the Day of Judgment the Prophet will come alone, and [that] the Prophet will come with one man, and with two men. Now, are these prophecies mistaken [simply] because no one confirmed them? Bush loudly proclaims the rightness of his decisions against Islam and Muslims [supported] by 85 percent of Americans—but does that make it right? Just because people agree to your falsehoods does not mean that falsehood has become truth—even if people unanimously reject it [truth] and wage war against it. Truth and falsehood are discerned through the Book [Koran] and the *sunna*—not by the amount of votes from the voters. So are you willing to go back to the *ulema* who are deeply rooted in theology and ask them if your declaration is true or false? Between us stand the Book and the *sunna*—not a million signatures, O you intellectuals! We ask Allah Almighty to show us and them truth as truth and grant us [the will] to adhere to it; and to show us falsehood as falsehood, and grant us [the will] to avoid it, for He [alone] is sovereign and capable of doing so.

2

The following lengthy treatise, written by Ayman al-Zawahiri, portrays a world divided into two warring camps: Muslims and the rest. The Arabic words rendered here as "loyalty" and "enmity," *wala'* and *bara'*, can be variously translated, but always a dichotomy exists ("love and hate" or "friendship and animosity," for instance). *Wala'* essentially means friendship, benevolence, fealty, and devotion, while *bara'* means disavowal, repudiation—essentially being "clean" of something. While all these words are to varying degrees applicable (and are utilized within the translation according to context), as an Islamic doctrine what is being relayed is most appropriately captured by the words "loyalty" and "enmity." "Enmity" toward infidels especially best translates *bara'* since al-Qaeda insists that the basic relationship between the infidel and Muslim is described by this Koranic verse: "You have a good example in Abraham and those who followed him, for they said to their people, 'We disown you and the idols that you worship besides Allah. We renounce you: enmity and hate shall reign between us until you believe in Allah alone' " [60:4]. (In fact, in "Moderate Islam Is a Prostration to the West," bin Laden makes this verse the cornerstone of Islam's relationship to the non-Muslim world.)

The entire doctrine is dedicated to showing that true Muslims must always strive to be in a state of *wala'* by being devoted to Allah and loyal to one another, while maintaining a state of *bara'* by hating or at least being clean from everything—and everyone—outside of Islam. In fact, if every Muslim followed this doctrine, a clash between the Muslim world and the non-Muslim world would inevitably occur—which is precisely what al-Qaeda seeks.

The many Koranic verses alone that form the centerpiece of this doctrine seem straightforward enough. For instance, "O you who believe! do not take the Jews and the Christians for your friends and protectors; they are friends and protectors of each other. Whoever among you takes them for a friend, then surely he is one of them" [5:51]; or "You shall find none who believe in Allah and the Last Day on friendly terms with those who oppose Allah and His Messenger [i.e., non-Muslims]—even if they be their fathers, their sons, their brothers, or their nearest kindred" [58:22]; or "Neither the Jews nor the Christians will ever approve of you until you follow their ways" [2:120]. Aside from these divine verses and more like them, *hadiths* and exegeses by the *ulema* regarding the legitimacy of this doctrine are plentiful.

The comprehensive nature of this doctrine is such that once it is upheld, everything else that radicals such as al-Qaeda yearn to see falls into place. The entire world becomes black and white, good and evil. In such a setting other doctrines that al-Qaeda endorse become more obligatory and urgent. Upholding *sharia* (Islamic) law becomes more pressing, since that is the primary way for Muslims to differentiate themselves and be clean of the ways of the infidels. Waging Offensive *Jihad* against the infidels becomes even more logical and palatable, since Muslims can never love or befriend infidels anyway until the latter submit to Islam. All Muslims would be obliged to help, fund, and shelter the *mujahidin*, since they must at all times be loyal to fellow Muslims. And so forth. In short: the Muslim must "know that he is obligated to befriend a believer—even if he is oppressive and violent toward you, while he must be hostile to the infidel—even if he is liberal and kind to you."

This treatise is further revealing in that it acknowledges another little-known doctrine—that of *taqiyya*. According to this doctrine, Muslims may under certain circumstances openly deceive infidels by feigning friendship or goodwill—even apostasy—provided that their heart remains true to Islam. A favorite verse justifying this sort of dissimulation while also supporting the doctrine of Loyalty and Enmity, which Zawahiri quotes innumerable times, states: "Let believers not take for friends and allies infidels rather than believers: whoever does this shall have no relationship left with Allah—*unless you but guard yourselves against them, taking precautions*" [3:28, italics added for clarity].

Due to the overall importance of this treatise—and despite its length and repetitiveness—it is presented wholly unedited. The redundant quotes from the Koran, the *hadith*, and *ulema*, aside from furnishing the treatise with solid backing, probably serve an indoctrinating purpose.

This treatise is split into two parts. In part 1, Zawahiri meticulously delineates the many Koranic, *hadithic*, and *ulemaic* quotes that support the doctrine of Loyalty and Enmity. In part 2, he tries to demonstrate how almost all of the Muslims' woes are due to their lack of faithfully upholding this all-encompassing doctrine. Underlined sentences were underlined in the original for emphasis.

"LOYALTY AND ENMITY:
An Inherited Doctrine and a Lost Reality"

AYMAN AL-ZAWAHIRI

In the Name of Allah, the Compassionate, the Merciful

INTRODUCTION

This point in Islamic history is witness to a furious struggle between the powers of the infidels, tyrants, and haughtiness, on the one hand, and the Islamic *umma* and its *mujahid* vanguard on the other. This struggle peaked with the blessed raids against New York and Washington [9/11 attacks] and what followed: [U.S. president George W.] Bush's declaration to carry out his new Crusade against Islam, or what he dubbed the "War on Terror."[1]

Due to the events of this war and its realities, there is an urgent need to comprehend the doctrine of Loyalty and Enmity in Islam. Negligence and indolence have spread in regard to upholding this great pillar of Islamic faith. Moreover, deception has spread among the masses of the Islamic *umma*, reinforced by the foes of Islam, along with their followers and minions. They have obliterated this firm pillar, portraying enemies as friends, while casting accusations of depravity against the pious.

These enemies have launched a campaign of intellectual and doctrinal deception in tandem with their militaristic, Crusading campaign. Their goal is to patch up the tattered fabric that represents the reigning regimes in our lands—in all their corruption and power to corrupt, and their submission to the international, tyrannical powers of the Crusaders and the Jews.

This campaign means to wipe out the dividing line between truth and falsehood, till even friend and foe are intermingled. But it also intends—in its frenzied attempt to confront the ascending, Islamic *mujahid* tide—to decorate the realities of effeteness, subjugation, and submission to that which is not Allah, and governance that does not accord with His *sharia*. Side by side with this goes an attempt to distort the call for truth, *jihad*, and honor, [all] that make up the banner that the Islamic *mujahid* vanguard raises aloft, along with its supporters and the masses rallied around them.

Every time the call for *jihad*, truth, and honor has grown in strength, so too has the call for falsehood, idleness, and humiliation—to the point that the advocates of this latter did not hesitate to take up the stance of the Murji'ites of old,[2] despite their incessant crowing and talk that they are the guardians of the faith of the forefathers and the glorious first centuries [of Islam]. And yet they have no qualms in taking up the articles of debauched secularists, despite their boasts that they are the guardians of the *sharia* and its defenders. They see no evil in having government officials—whether from the military, security forces, media outlets, or courts—calling for secularism and promoting recognition of Israel, along with submission to it—all while supposedly remaining pious, Allah-fearing Muslims, fasting, praying, pilgrimaging, giving alms!![3]

We have even seen the oldest and noblest reigning families serving America's interests, all while asserting that they are the guardians of the doctrine of *tawhid*. And we have seen the imams of infidelity imposing secular constitutions and ruling according to secular laws. They race toward a policy of normalization with Israel while sponsoring competitions at memorizing the Koran for students attending universities where wearing the veil [for women] is prohibited! And we have seen the most severe scourgers and tormentors of Muslims performing the greater and lesser pilgrimages. And we have seen brigands in Afghanistan [i.e., "The Northern Alliance"], who earn their wages from American forces, as the latter send them out in front of them to do battle with the *mujahidin*. After this, they [the "brigands"] try to sanctify themselves with the clothes of the martyred *mujahidin* and the soil about their graves!! As the Sheikh of Islam, Ibn Taymiyya, said regarding the Tatars: "The people have even seen them [Tatars] praise an area and then seize all the possessions therein. They have seen them heap praise upon a man and seek his blessings—only to snatch the clothes off his back, violate his women, and then subject him to a form of torment the likes of which are only exercised by the most unjust and depraved of peoples. The interpreter of religion punishes only those whom he considers disobedient to the faith. And yet they [Tatars] glory in the religion of the one they punish, saying that he is more obedient [to Allah] than they: so what justification is left them?"

Nor is there anything strange in this; the foaming, fuming mechanism of falsehood confuses and blends all things, as it seeks to perpetuate the corruption that oppressively lies atop our chests and the occupation that stains the pure soil of our *umma*—especially in our most sacred of lands: the Two Holy Sites [cities of Mecca and Medina, i.e., Saudi Arabia] and blessed Jerusalem.

So this is their intention—evident to any contemplative person: to perpetuate corrupt, corrupting rule that contradicts *sharia* law and to make the [Islamic] lands vulnerable to conquest by the new Crusading forces. This is their agenda, observed in every word they utter, broadcast, or print.

The Koran exposed the forebears of this faction, revealing the truth about them—that they seek to sow sedition among the Muslim ranks; that they are the quickest people to accept it; that they scurry to the infidels to secure what is in their personal interests and material gains. The Most High said: "If they had intended to come out, they would certainly have made some preparation theretofore: but Allah was averse to their being sent forth; so he made them lag behind, and they were told, 'Sit among those who sit.' If they had come out with you, they would not have added to your [strength] but only [made for] disorder, hurrying to and fro in your midst and sowing dissension among you, and there would have been some among you who would have listened to them. But Allah knows well those who do wrong!" [9:46–47]. And the Most High said: "And behold! the hypocrites and those in whose hearts is a disease said, 'Allah and his Messenger promised us nothing but delusions!' And another faction among them said, 'O you men of Yathrib [original name of Medina]! You cannot withstand [the attack]! Go back!' And a band of them asked for leave from the Prophet, saying 'Truly, our houses are bare and exposed,' though they were not exposed: they intended nothing but to run away" [33:12–13].

So we see that deviating from the doctrine of befriending the believers [Muslims] and maintaining hostilities against the infidels [all non-Muslims] is, in this age, the greatest threat to *tawhid* and the Islamic faith. Thus we wrote these pages as a caution and warning to our Muslim *umma* in its sacred awakening and victorious *jihad*—Allah willing—to vanquish the American-Jewish Crusading campaign against the Islamic *umma*.

We have divided the essay into two parts and a conclusion:

Part One: The basis of Loyalty and Enmity in Islam
Part Two: Various deviations from the doctrine of Loyalty
    and Enmity
Conclusion: Main points we wish to emphasize

Whatever is found to be worthy here was approved by the Most High and Exalted One; whatever is not is from ourselves and Satan. And our final call is, Thanks be to Allah, Lord of the Worlds. Allah's prayers on our leader Muhammad and his family and his Companions—and peace.

Ayman al-Zawahiri
December 2002

PART ONE: THE FOUNDATIONS OF LOYALTY
AND ENMITY IN ISLAM

1. THE PROHIBITION AGAINST BEFRIENDING INFIDELS

Allah Most High said: "Let believers [Muslims] not take for friends and allies infidels [non-Muslims] rather than believers: whoever does this shall have no relationship left with Allah—unless you but guard yourselves against them, taking precautions. But Allah cautions you [to fear] Himself. For the final goal is to Allah" [3:28]. Al-Tabari said: "The meaning of this, O believers, is that you are not to take infidels as helpers and sponsors; nor show consideration for their faith; nor enable them to overcome Muslims in preference to believers; nor reveal your weaknesses [to them]. For whoever does this shall receive nothing from Allah. And thus he abandons Allah and Allah abandons him, for he has left his faith and entered into [a state of] infidelity."

Allah Most High said: "Offer glad tidings to the hypocrites, that they have painful torments [in store]—they who take infidels as friends instead of believers. What?! do they seek praise from them? All praise is to Allah" [4:138–39].

Allah Most High said: "O you who have believed! do not take infidels as allies and friends instead of believers. What! do you desire to offer Allah a clear proof against yourselves?" [4:144]. Al-Tabari said: "He says to them, O you who have believed in Allah and his Messenger: do not befriend the infidels, supporting them instead of the people of your *umma* and faith—the Muslims. [If you do] you will be like unto the hypocrites who have been consigned to the flames."

Allah Most High said: "O you who have believed! do not take the Jews and the Christians for friends; they are but friends of each other; and whoever among you takes them for a friend, then surely he is one of them. Verily Allah does not guide the unjust people. But you will see those in whose hearts is a disease hastening toward them, saying: We fear lest a calamity should befall us; but it may be that Allah will bring the victory or a punishment from Himself, so that they shall be regretting on account of what they hid in their souls. And those who believe will say: Are these they who swore by Allah with the most forceful of their oaths that they were most surely with you? Their deeds shall go for nothing, so they shall become losers. O you who believe! whoever from among you turns back from his religion, then Allah will bring a[nother] people; He shall love them and they shall love Him. Lowly before the believers, mighty against the infidels, they shall strive hard in Allah's way and shall not fear the accusation of any accuser. This is Allah's Face: He gives it to whom He pleases, and Allah is generous, knowing. Only Allah, His Messenger, and those who believe are your friends and helpers, those who uphold prayers and pay the alms tax while they bow. And whoever takes Allah and His Messenger and those who believe as a guardian, then surely the party of Allah are they that shall be triumphant. O you who have believed! do not take for friends and allies those who take your religion for a mockery and a joke, from among those who were given scriptures [Jews and Christians] before you, and the infidels; and be careful of [your duty to] Allah, if you are believers. Whenever you call to prayer they make it a mockery and a joke; this is because they are a people who do not understand" [5:51–58].

Al-Tabari said: "When the Most High said, '[A]nd whoever among you takes them for a friend, then surely he is one of them,' He means that whoever turns to the Jews and Christians in friendship, in place of the believers, becomes one of them." He adds: "For whoever allies with them and enables them against the believers, that same one is a member of their faith and community. One seeks not the friendship of another unless he is of the same faith and confession. If someone finds another person and his religion agreeable, [like him] he becomes hostile to whatever opposes and angers him. Their principles become one and the same."

Ibn Hajar al-Asqalani said in explanation of the *hadith* relayed by Ibn Omar: "If Allah brings down torment upon a tribe, the torment afflicts those of the group. Then they go back to tending their affairs."

Ibn Hajar said: "One learns from this that fleeing the infidels and the oppressors is legitimate: to reside with them jeopardizes one's soul. This is so even if one does not aid them or approve of their deeds. But if he aids or approves, then he is definitely one of them."

It is because of this that Allah Exalted consigned them to fire everlasting. The Most High said: "You will see many of them befriending those who disbelieve. Evil is that to which their souls prompt them: in torment shall they abide. And had they believed in Allah and the Prophet and what was revealed to him, they would not have taken them for friends. Yet most of them are evil doers" [5:80–81].

Allah Most High said: "O you who have believed! if your fathers and your brothers love unbelief more than belief, then do not befriend them; and whoever of you befriends them sins. Say: 'If your fathers and your sons and your brethren and your mates and your kinsfolk and the property that you have acquired, and the slackness of trade that you fear and dwellings that you like, are dearer to you than Allah and His Messenger, and *jihad* in His way, then wait till Allah fulfills His decree: Allah does not guide a sinful people'" [9:23–24]. Ibn Kathir said: "The learned al-Bayhaqi narrated a *hadith* that was conveyed by Abdallah bin Shawdhab. He said: 'The father of Abu Ubayda bin al-Jarrah was praising idols to him on the day of [the battle of] Badr.[4] So Abu Ubayda began avoiding him. But when al-Jarrah's persistence grew, his son, Abu Ubayda, attacked and slew him. Thus Allah revealed this verse in reference to him.' And it has been firmly established in the authentic account [*hadith* of Bukhari] that he [Muhammad] said: 'By him who holds my soul in his hand, none of you believes unless I am dearer to him than his father, his son, and all of mankind.'"

A. The Difference Between Befriending and Dissembling
The *sharia* differentiates between befriending infidels, which is forbidden, and fearing their evil. Allah Most High said: "Let believers not take for friends and allies infidels rather than believers: whoever does this shall have no relationship left with Allah—unless you but guard yourselves against them, taking precautions. But Allah cautions you

[to fear] Himself. For the final goal is to Allah" [3:28]. Ibn Kathir said: "The Most High said, '[U]nless you but guard yourselves against them, taking precautions'—that is, whoever at any time or place fears their evil may protect himself <u>through outward show—not sincere conviction.</u> As al-Bukhari records through Abu al-Darda the words, 'Truly, we grin to the faces of some peoples, while our hearts curse them.' And Thawri records through Ibn Abbas this statement: 'Protection is not secured by deeds but with the tongue.' " "Kashr" [word rendered "grin" in al-Darda's *hadith*] means to display one's teeth while smiling.

He [Ibn Kathir] also says in his commentary regarding the Word of the Most High: "To the faithful, Allah has set an example in pharaoh's wife, who said: 'Lord! Build me a house with You in Paradise and deliver me from pharaoh and his misdeeds. Deliver me from a wicked nation' [66:11]": "Allah provided this instance to show the believers that no harm will come to them should they intermingle with the infidels whenever they have need of them. As the Most High said: 'Let believers not take for friends and allies infidels rather than believers: whoever does this shall have no relationship left with Allah—unless you but guard yourselves against them, taking precautions' [3:28]."

Al-Qurtubi said: "Mu'adh bin Jabal and Mujahid say, '*Taqiyya* [self-preservation through dissembling] was a novelty of Islam before the Muslims grew strong. But today Allah has ennobled Islam to overcome its enemies.' Ibn Abbas said: 'He but speaks with his tongue, but his heart is secure in faith; <u>he murders not nor does he commit any sin.</u>' Al-Hassan says: '*Taqiyya* is acceptable till the Day of Judgment— but not if it causes deaths [of fellow Muslims].'

"Thus it is said that if a believer resides with infidels, and if he fears for himself, he should cajole with his tongue, while his heart remains secure in its faith. However, *taqiyya* is permitted only should one fear being <u>killed, scarred, or severely harmed.</u> But whoever is forced into apostasy, it is his right to resist and refuse to respond to any utterance of infidelity, if he can."

Al-Tabari said [regarding the verse]: "[U]nless you but guard yourselves against them, taking precautions" [3:28]. "Only when you are in their power, fearing for your selves, are you to demonstrate friendship for them with your tongues, whilst harboring hostility toward them. But do not join them in the particulars of their infidelity, and do not aid them through any action against a Muslim."

The Sheikh of Islam, Ibn Taymiyya, confirms this when he tells of those whom the Tatars forced to ride out with their army. He says: "If *jihad* is required, and if Muslims, according to the will of Allah, should be killed, let as many Muslims perish from the ranks [of *jihad*] for the sake of *jihad*—for there is nothing more glorious than this.

"However, the Prophet commanded anyone compelled to partake in seditious warfare to break his sword. He is not to fight, even if he is killed. Just as Sahih al-Muslim relays Abu Bakr saying: 'So spoke the Messenger of Allah: "There will be sedition, followed by sedition, followed by sedition. Behold! The one who will be sitting will be more blessed than the one standing; the one standing more blessed than the one running. And behold! when it [sedition] descends or plummets, let the one who has a camel stay close to his camel; the one who has sheep, stay close to his sheep; the one who has land, stay close to his land." A man said: "O Messenger of Allah, what is your opinion regarding the one who possess neither camel, nor sheep, nor land?" [Muhammad replied:] "He should lay hold of his sword, beating its edge with a stone; then he should attempt to escape. O Allah I have delivered [Your Message], O Allah I have delivered, O Allah I have delivered." A man said: "O Messenger of Allah, what is your opinion if I am coercively enlisted among the ranks or made to march, and a man strikes me dead with his sword or arrow?" He said: "He shall bear the punishment of his sin and yours, and become a denizen of hell." '

"Thus in this *hadith*, he forbids fighting in seditious warfare. And in order to prevent fighting, he commands that one stand aloof, or damage his weapons of war. Should anyone be forced to enter battle or anything else, and should he be killed unjustly, the murderer bears the punishment of his own sin and the sin of the man slain, as the Most High related in the story of Adam's sons.[5]

"The point [here] is that if one is compelled to fight in seditious warfare, he should not fight. Instead, <u>he is to damage his weapon and remain steadfast till he is unjustly slain.</u> So then, what about the one who is coerced to fight against other Muslims with a sect that opposes the *sharia*—for instance, those who deny the alms tax, apostates, and such? <u>He earns no punishment if, while forced to be present, he refuses to fight, even if Muslims slay him—just like if the infidels force him to join their ranks fighting the Muslims.</u> It is just as if someone forced another to kill an innocent Muslim: He cannot kill him with the consent of Muslims; and yet if he is forced to kill, he will not save his soul by killing this innocent person."[6]

To conclude: Should a Muslim encounter circumstances that expose him to murder, scarring, or severe injury, he may utter some words [i.e., lie] to stay the infidels' torments. But he must not undertake any initiative to support them, commit sin, or enable them through any deed or killing or fighting against Muslims. Nobler for him that he should endure the torments, even if they are the cause of his death.

2. HATING THE INFIDELS AND RENOUNCING THEIR LOVE

A. Allah Most High Forbade Us from Showing Affection to Those Who Oppose Allah and His Messenger

Allah Most High said: "You shall find none who believe in Allah and the Last Day on friendly terms with those who oppose Allah and His Messenger—even if they be their fathers, their sons, their brothers, or their nearest kindred. Allah has inscribed the faith in their very hearts, and strengthened them with a spirit from Himself. He will admit them to gardens watered by running streams, where they shall dwell forever. Allah is well pleased with them and they are well pleased with Him. They are the party of Allah, and surely it is the party of Allah that shall triumph!" [58:22]. Ibn Kathir said: "It was said that the phrase from the Most High—'even if they be their fathers'—that it was revealed about Abu Ubayda when he slew his father at [the battle of] Badr; 'their sons' was about Abu Bakr [Muhammad's successor and first caliph] when he intended to slay his son, Abd al-Rahman; 'their brothers' was about Mus'ab bin Umayr, who slew his brother, Ubayd bin Umayr; 'or their kin' was about Omar, who slew one of his relatives. Also Hamza, Ali, and Ubayda bin al-Harith: They slew Utba, Sheeba, and al-Walid bin Uitba [their kin] at that battle. Allah knows [best].

"Moreover, when the Messenger of Allah consulted with the Muslims regarding the captives of Badr, Abu Bakr advised that they should pay ransom, thereby enabling the Muslims to grow stronger. Also, since they [captives] were cousins and relatives, perhaps Allah Most High would have eventually guided them. But Omar said: 'This goes against my thinking, O Messenger of Allah. Let me slay so-and-so (a relative of Omar), and let Ali [slay] Aquil [Ali's brother], and so-and-so [slay] so-and-so—so that Allah may know that there is no love in our hearts for the idolaters. . . .' This is the whole story.

"Ibn Abbas said: 'He strengthened them with a spirit from Himself' [from 58:28]—that is, He empowered them.

"Within the saying of the Most High—'Allah is well pleased with them and they are well pleased with Him' [from 58:28]—is a marvelous, hidden meaning: When they [Muslims] became enraged at their relatives and kin in the Most High's [cause], He rewarded them, by being pleased with them and making them pleased with Him."

Allah Most High said: "O you who have believed! Do not make friends with those who are My enemies and yours. Would you show them kindness, when they have denied the truth that has been revealed to you and driven out the Messenger and yourselves—all because you believe in Allah your Lord? If it was indeed to fight for My cause, and out of a desire to please Me, that you left your city, how can you be friendly to them in secret? I well know all that you hide and all that you reveal. Whoever of you does this strays from the straight path. If they gain ascendancy over you, they will plainly show themselves your enemies, stretching out their hands and tongues against you with evil. They long to see you become infidels. On the Day of Judgment neither your kinsfolk nor your children will avail you. Allah will separate you: He is cognizant of all your actions. You have a good example in Abraham and those who followed him. They said to their people: 'We disown you and the idols you worship besides Allah. We renounce you: enmity and hate shall reign between us until you believe in Allah alone.' (But do not emulate the words of Abraham to his father: 'I shall implore forgiveness for you, although I can in no way protect you from Allah.') [Abraham said:] 'Lord! in you have we put our trust; to You we turn and to You we shall come at last. Lord! Do not expose us to the designs of the infidels. Lord! Forgive us. You are the Mighty, the Wise.' Truly, in those there is a good example for everyone who puts his hopes in Allah and in the Last Day. He that gives no heed shall know that Allah alone is sufficient and worthy of praise. It may well be that Allah will put goodwill between you and those with whom you have hitherto been at odds. Allah is mighty; Allah is forgiving and merciful. Allah does not forbid you from being kind and equitable to those who have neither made war on your religion nor driven you from your homes. Allah loves the equitable. But He forbids you from befriending those who have fought against you on account of your religion and driven you from your homes, or abetted others to drive you out. Those that befriend them are wrongdoers" [60:1–9].

Ibn Kathir said: "This noble chapter was revealed due to the story of Hatib bin Abi Balta.

"The Imam Ahmad 179 said: Ubaydalla bin Abi Rafi informed him that he heard Ali say: The Messenger of Allah sent me, al-Zubayr, and al-Miqdad out, saying, Go from here till you come to Rawda Khakh, for yonder there is a woman with a parchment. Take it from her. So we set out, horses agallop, till we arrived at al-Rawda. And behold! We happened upon the woman and said, Relinquish the parchment. She said, I have no parchment with me. So we said, Either give up the parchment, or we shall strip you naked [i.e., rape you]. So she took the parchment out of her braid and we took it to the Messenger of Allah. And behold, its contents were from Hatib ibn Abi Balta to the idolaters of Mecca informing them of some of the designs of the Messenger of Allah. So the Messenger of Allah said, O Hatib, what is this? He [Hatib] said, Do not hasten [to judge] against me, for I was a man closely associated with the [tribe of] Quraish, though I was not related to the tribe. The others who emigrated with you [from Mecca to Medina] have relatives to protect their families in Mecca. So I desired to compensate for my lack of blood relation by doing them a favor, in order that they might protect my relations. I did not do this as an infidel or an apostate from my faith, nor as one who favors infidelity over Islam. So the Messenger of Allah said: Hatib has told you the truth. Omar said, Command me to chop this hypocrite's head off. The Messenger of Allah said, He was a participant of [the battle of] Badr, and who knows, maybe Allah has looked at the people of Badr and said, Do what you like, for I have forgiven you. With the exception of Ibn Majal, the majority, X [Bukhari] 3007, M [Muslim] 2494, D [Dawud] 2650, T [Tirmidhi] 3305, S [Sunan al-Sughra] 11585, included this saying with chains of transmission through Sufyan bin Uyayna. Al-Bukhari adds in his narration in the Book of Raids 4274 that Allah revealed the [aforementioned] verses [regarding this event]. 'O you who have believed! Do not make friends with those who are my enemies and yours' [60:1].

"Allah said to his faithful servants regarding the infidels whom he commanded to disavow, to be hostile toward, and to keep clean from by keeping [them] at a distance, 'You have a good example in Abraham and those who followed him,' for 'they said to their people, We disown you'—that is, we disavow you—'and the idols you worship besides Allah. We renounce you'—that is, your religion and way [of life]—'Enmity and hate shall reign between us until you believe in Allah alone'—that is, enmity and hate between us has been decreed from now until you renounce your infidelities, so we [must] start to disavow and hate you—'until you believe in Allah alone' [60:1]—that is, until you exercise *tawhid* and worship Allah alone, partnerless, and break from whatever other idols and rivals you worship besides him."

Allah Most High said: "O you who have believed! Do not befriend those who have incurred the wrath of Allah: such men despair of the Hereafter, just as the infidels are in despair over the inhabitants of the graves" [60:13]. Al-Qurtubi said: "The Word of the Most High—'O you who have believed! Do not befriend those who have incurred the wrath of Allah'—refers to the Jews. This is because some poor Muslims provided the Jews with news of the believers, maintaining close relations with them, and thus suffered the same fate [as the Jews]. They are forbidden from doing this.

"It is said that Allah concluded the verse the way he started it—forsaking the friendship of infidels. It was an address to Hatib bin Abi Balta and others.

"Ibn Abbas said: 'O you who believe! Do not befriend—that is, do not befriend and advise them; the Most High is referring to Hatib bin Abi Balta.' "

B. The Almighty Has Informed Us That the Infidels Despise the Muslims

Allah Most High said: "The infidels among the People of the Book [Christians and Jews] and the idolaters resent that any blessings should be sent down to you from your Lord" [2:105].

Allah Most High said: "Many among the People of the Book wish, through personal envy, to lead you back into infidelity, now that you have embraced the faith" [2:109].

Allah Most High said: "See how you love them and they do not love you! You believe in the entire Book [Koran]. When they meet you they say, 'We believe!' But when alone, they bite at their fingertips in rage. Say 'May you perish in your rage!' Allah knows your innermost thoughts. When you are blessed with good fortune, they are grieved. Yet when evil befalls you, they rejoice. But if you persevere and guard yourselves against evil, their machinations shall never harm you" [3:119–120]. Al-Qurtubi said: "The meaning of this verse is that one should not keep close relations with those who are hostile and spiteful, and who rejoice when misfortunes befall the believers. This applies particularly to the great command of [waging] *jihad*, which is the foundation of this world and the next."

C. Likewise, the Most High Has Informed Us That They [Infidels] Shall Never Be Content with the Believers as Long as They Persist in Their Faith

Allah Most High said: "Neither the Jews nor the Christians will ever approve of you until you follow their lifestyle. Say 'Allah's guidance [i.e., the *sharia*] is the only guidance.' And if after all the knowledge you were given you yield to their desires, there shall be none to help or protect you from the wrath of Allah" [2:120–121].

D. Instead, They Wish to Turn the Believers Back into a State of Infidelity
Allah Most High said: "O you who have believed! If you obey [any] faction from among those who were given the Book, they [Jews and Christians] will revert you, after you had believed, into infidels" [3:100]. Allah Most High said: "O you who have believed! If you obey the infidels, they will drive you back on your heels, and you will turn back [from faith] to your own detriment" [3:149]. Ibn Jarir al-Tabari said: "He means by this, O you who have believed Allah and his Messenger, Allah's promise and His threat, His commandment and prohibition: 'If you obey the infidels'—that is, those who rejected the prophesy of your Prophet Muhammad, the Jews and Christians. [Should you obey] what they command and forbid you to do, you accept their views and accept their counsel. They claim that they can give you sound counsel on this, but 'they will drive you back on your heels.' Thus He says <u>they will lead you to apostasy after you had believed, and rejection of Allah, His Revelation, and His Prophet after your submission to Islam.</u> 'You will turn back [from faith]'—that is, you will turn away from your faith and the religion to which Allah had led you, 'to your own detriment'—that is, you will perish. For you have lost yourselves and <u>strayed from your religion;</u> and all things in this life and the next are lost to you. And for this reason are the people who believe in Allah forbidden to obey the infidels, adopt their views, or accept their counsel regarding their religions."

E. The Relationship Between Loving the Lord Almighty,
Befriending the Believers, and Jihad *in the Path of Allah*
And now that we have demonstrated the precepts of the *sharia* regarding befriending the believers and maintaining hostility toward infidels, we wish to evoke some profound words by the Sheikh of Is-

lam, Ibn Taymiyya, in reference to the strong tie between loving the Lord Almighty and [waging] *jihad*. Ibn Taymiyya said: "Love is an unrestricted and general word. The believer loves Allah, His messengers and prophets, and His faithful servants. Thus is the love of Allah, and no one else deserves the love that belongs to Allah. This is why the love of Allah is mentioned in the context of worship, repentant appeal, devotion, and so forth. All of these words contain the love of Allah Almighty, the Most High.

"It is also shown that love for Him is the basis of religion. Faith is made complete through the completeness of love, lacking through a lack of love. The Prophet said: 'Islam is the head of the order; prayer, its back; *jihad* in the way of Allah, its summit'. So he declares that *jihad* is the summit—the highest and noblest aspect. The Most High said: 'What! do you make [one who undertakes] the giving of drink to the pilgrims and the guarding of the sacred mosque like him who believes in Allah and the Last Day and strives hard in Allah's way?! To Allah, they are not equal; and Allah does not guide the unjust people. Those who believe, and suffer exile and strive with might [i.e., wage *jihad*] in Allah's way, with their goods and their persons, have the highest rank in the sight of Allah: they are the people who will achieve [salvation]' [9:19]. There are many texts regarding the virtues of *jihad* and its practitioners. Therefore, it is established that *jihad* is the most excellent work a servant [Muslim] can render. *Jihad* is proof of absolute love. The Most High said: 'Say: If your fathers and your sons and your brethren and your mates and your kinsfolk and property that you have acquired, and the slackness of trade that you fear, and dwellings that you like, are dearer to you than Allah and His Messenger and *jihad* in His way, then wait till Allah brings about His command: and Allah does not guide the transgressing people' [9:24]. And the Most High said, describing the characteristics of those that love and are loved: 'O you who have believed! whoever from among you turns back from his religion, then Allah will bring a[nother] people. He shall love them and they shall love Him. Lowly before the believers, mighty against the infidels, they shall wage *jihad* in Allah's way and shall not fear the accusation of any accuser' [5:54].

"Thus love is a prerequisite of *jihad*. The lover loves and hates whatever the Beloved loves and hates: He develops friendship and adversity to whatever the Beloved is friendly and adverse to; he is content or angry with whatever makes [the Beloved] content or angry; he governs and prohibits in accordance with [the Beloved's] rules and prohibitions [i.e., the *sharia*]. He is agreed to this.

"These are the ones whose approval and anger are one with the Lord's: pleased by what is pleasing [to the Lord], angered by what angers Him. As the Prophet said to Abu Bakr at Ta'if regarding Suhayb and Bilal: 'Perhaps you have angered them; for if you have, so have you angered your Lord.' So he said to them: 'My brothers, have I made you angry?' They said, 'No, may Allah forgive you, O Abu Bakr.'

"When Abu Sufyan bin Harb passed by them, they said: 'The swords have not received their due.' So Abu Bakr said to them: 'Do you speak thus to a lord of the Quraish?' Abu Bakr then relayed [this incident] to the Prophet so he replied to him as aforementioned. They spoke so out of anger on behalf of Allah, in complete perfection of affection for Allah and his Prophet and adversity to their enemies. This is why, in an authentic *hadith*, the Prophet speaking on behalf of his Lord, said: 'My Servant ceaselessly toils to do above and beyond what is required in order to be near Me, that I may love him. Thus when I love him, I become the Ears through which he hears, the Eyes through which he sees, the Hand with which he strikes, the Leg with which he walks. Through Me he hears; through Me he sees; through Me he strikes; through Me he walks. If he asks [for something], I give it. If he asks for protection, I protect him. And though I hesitate in none of the things I do, I hesitate in taking the breath of my faithful servant. He hates death, and I hate causing him pain—yet it is inevitable.' "

Ibn Taymiyya said in regard to befriending the Jews and Christians: "If similarities in worldly matters produces love and friendship, how then when there are similarities in religious affairs? This results in a more serious and intense form of friendship.

"Love and friendship for them contradicts faith. Allah Most High said: 'O you who believe! do not take the Jews and the Christians for your friends and protectors; they are but friends and protectors to each other. Whoever among you takes them for a friend, then surely he is one of them. Truly, Allah does not guide the unjust people. Those in whose hearts is a disease—see how eagerly they run about among them [Jews and Christians], saying: We fear lest a change of fortune bring us disaster. Ah! But when Allah grants you victory or makes known His will, then shall they regret the thoughts that they secretly harbored in their hearts. Then shall the faithful say: Are these the men who solemnly swore oaths by Allah that they would stand with you? Surely their works shall come to naught and they will be losers' [5:51–53]. Censuring the People of the Book, the Most High said: 'Curses were pronounced on those among the Children of Israel who rejected the Faith, by the tongue of David and of Jesus the son of Mary: because they disobeyed and persisted in innovations. Nor did they forbid one another [from] the iniquities that they committed: evil indeed were the deeds that they did. You will see many of them turning in friendship to the infidels. Evil indeed are [the works] that their souls have prompted them to, so that Allah's wrath is on them, and in torment will they abide. If only they had believed in Allah, in the Prophet, and in what has been revealed to him, never would they have taken them for friends and protectors, but most of them are re-bellious wrongdoers' [5:78–81].

"So the Exalted and Most High One shows that faith in Allah, the Prophet, and the revelation he received requires one to cease associating with them [infidels]. Close relations with them demonstrates a lack of faith: failure to fulfill an obligation means not accepting the obligation.

"The Exalted, Most High said: 'You shall not find a people who believe in Allah and the Last Day befriending those who act in opposition to Allah and His Messenger, even though they were their [own] fathers, or their sons, or their brothers, or their kinsfolk. These are they into whose hearts He has impressed faith, and whom He has strengthened with a Spirit from Himself' [58:22]. Thus the Almighty, the Most High informs [us] that <u>no believer will love an infidel; and whoever does love an infidel is not a believer.</u> It might be expected that outward similarity breeds affection, which is forbidden, as indicated in the previous resolution."

He [Ibn Taymiyya] also goes on to say: "The believer is to love and hate *only* in Allah. It is his duty to befriend a fellow-believer— even if the latter is unjust to him; for injustice does not break the bond of loyalty imposed by [similar] faith. The Most High said: 'If two parties of believers fall to fighting, then make peace between them. And if one of them transgresses against the other, then fight the one who does wrong till they return to the command of Allah; but, if they return, make peace between them with justice and be fair. Lo! Allah loves the equitable' [49:9]. Thus He makes them brothers in the midst of quarreling and oppressing [each other], by commanding that they make peace among themselves.[7]

"The believer needs to reflect on the difference between these two ways, for often they are confused with one another. He needs know that <u>he is obligated to befriend a believer—even if he is oppressive and violent toward you, while he must be hostile to the infidel—even if he is liberal and kind to you.</u> Allah Almighty sent prophets and revealed scripture so that all religion would be Allah's alone; that there would be love for His allies, hatred for His enemies; honor for His allies, contempt for His enemies; rewards for His allies, punishments for His enemies.

"If within a single man are found good, evil, depravity, obedience, disobedience, tradition, and heresy—insofar as the good qualities go, he is deserving of friendship and rewards; insofar as the evil qualities, he is deserving of hostility and punishment. And so since a single individual invites both respect and revulsion, he reaps some of the former, some of the latter—like an impoverished thief who gets his hand chopped off for stealing while receiving money from the state treasury to meet his needs. This is the principle on which the people of the *sunna* and consensus have agreed."

F. Refuting a Disingenuous Argument

Some have asked, Well, what about this verse of the Most High: "Allah does not forbid you from those who have not made war against you on account of [your] religion, and have not driven you forth from your homes, from showing them kindness and dealing with them justly. Surely Allah loves the doers of justice" [60:8].

Does this not demonstrate that love for infidels is permissible?

The answer is that kindness, which is the source of all goodness, and fair-mindedness, which is justice, are not considered forbidden forms of friendship. [What is forbidden, however] is love, friendship, aid—by word or deed—shared outlooks and actions, and the taking of infidels as confidants, familiarizing them with the secrets of the Muslims.

Al-Shafi'i said: "Allah the All-Powerful, the Exalted, said, 'Allah does not forbid you respecting those who have not made war against you on account of [your] religion . . .' [60:8]. It has been said—and Allah only knows—that some Muslims ceased having relations with the idolaters; this likely occurred when it was revealed that they were obligated to wage *jihad* against them and sever relations with them. Allah also revealed that: 'You shall not find a people who believe in Allah and the Last Day befriending those who act in opposition to Allah and His Messenger . . .' [58:22]. But when they began fearing having amicable financial ties [with them], it was then revealed: 'Allah does not forbid you from those who have not made war against you on account of [your] religion, and have not driven you forth from your homes, from showing them kindness and dealing with them justly. Surely Allah loves the doers of justice. Allah only forbids you those who made war upon you on account of [your] religion, and drove you forth from your homes and supported [others] in your expulsion—these do not befriend. And whoever befriends them is unjust' " [60:8–9].

Al-Shafi'i said: "Financial ties, kindness, fair dealing, fair speech, and appeal to the judgment of Allah do not constitute the sort of friendship that was forbidden. Allah permitted kindness and just treatment toward those infidels who do not help [the enemies of Muslims]. The reference, then, is to those who help [the foes of Islam]: friendship with these is forbidden. Therefore, friendship is not the same thing as kindness and fair dealing. The Prophet ransomed [showed mercy to] some of the hostages at [the battle of] Badr; and Abu Izzah al-Jumahi was one of those to whom he showed mercy—though he was notorious for being quarrelsome and an instigator. After Badr, he also showed mercy to Thumama bin Uthal, also notorious for his hostilities. He [Prophet] had originally commanded that he be killed, but showed mercy after he was captured. Thereafter, Thumama submitted [i.e., embraced Islam]. He proceeded to cut off supplies from the people of Mecca. So they asked the Messenger of Allah if he would allow him [Thumama] to supply them; he gave him leave and he supplied them. Allah the Exalted the Supreme said: 'And they give food out of love for Him to the poor and the orphan and the captive' [76:8]. The 'captive' are those who opposed Allah and his Messenger."

Ibn al-Qayyim expounded on the permissibility of distributing alms taxes and public endowment money to dispossessed persons of the *dhimmi*: "Regarding the Most High's Word: 'Allah does not forbid you respecting those who have not made war against you on account of [your] religion, and have not driven you forth from your homes, from showing them kindness and dealing with them justly; surely Allah loves the doers of justice. Allah only forbids you respecting those who made war upon you on account of [your] religion, and drove you forth from your homes and backed up [others] in your expulsion, that you make friends with them, and whoever makes friends with them, these are the unjust' [60:8–9]. When, in the beginning of the chapter Allah Almighty prohibits Muslims from taking infidels as friends and cutting all love between them, some supposed that kindness and charity is the same as friendship and affection. But Allah Almighty has shown that this is not the sort of friendship that is prohibited, and that it is therefore not forbidden. Instead, this is charity, which He loves, approves, and has assigned in all things. What is forbidden is befriending the infidels, and turning to them with love."

Ibn Kathir said: "The Word of the Most High—'Allah only forbids you respecting those who made war upon you on account of

[your] religion, and drove you forth from your homes and backed up [others] in your expulsion, that you make friends with them, and whoever makes friends with them, these are the unjust' [60:9]— means that you are not prohibited from being charitable to those infidels who do not fight you regarding religion, such as women and the weak, nor from being kind and fair-dealing with them.

"The Imam Ahmad 6345 relays from Hisham bin Urwa, who relays from Fatima daughter of al-Mundhir, who heard Asma' daughter of Abu Bakr say: "My mother, an idolatress during the time of the treaty with the Quraish, came to me. So I went to the Prophet and said: 'O Messenger of Allah, my mother approached [me], desiring something [of me]. Shall I maintain relations with her?' He said: 'Yes, maintain relations with your mother.' "

3. THE PROHIBITION AGAINST TAKING THEM [NON-MUSLIMS] AS INTIMATES AND SHARING THE SECRETS OF MUSLIMS WITH THEM

Allah Most High said: "O you who have believed! Take not into your intimacy those outside your ranks: They will not fail to corrupt you. They only desire your ruin. Rank hatred has already appeared from their mouths. What their hearts conceal is far worse. We have made plain to you the revelations, if you but have wisdom" (3:118). Al-Qurtubi said: " 'Intimacy' applies to both singular and plural. A man's exclusive intimates are those who know his innermost thoughts.

"With this verse, Allah Almighty prohibited the believers from taking infidels, Jews, people of delusion, foreigners, and interlopers into their confidence, and entrusting money to them. Therefore, it is maintained that you need not converse with anyone who is of a different sect or religion. So says the poet: 'Ask not about a man but about his companion; for each companion emulates his own [friend].'

"Sunan Abu Dawud contain a *hadith* of the Prophet relayed by Abu Hurreira: 'A man embraces the faith of his bosom friend: let each of you, then, consider well whom he befriends.' And Ibn Mas'ud relayed that he [Muhammad] said: 'Judge people based on their brethren [i.e., the people they consort with].'

"The Most High then showed why it is He forbids close relations [with non-Muslims], saying: 'They will not fail to corrupt you'—that is, they shall never cease striving to corrupt you—that is, though they do not fight you openly, still they shall not cease from trying to corrupt you with cunning and deceit.

"The verse 'They only desire your ruin' is the source of the meaning that they only desire to cause you pain and affliction, for *anat* [word rendered as "ruin" in the verse] means pain."

4. THE PROHIBITION AGAINST APPOINTING INFIDELS TO DIGNIFIED AND IMPORTANT POSTS

Ibn Taymiyya said: "Imam Ahmad, through a sound chain of support, narrates from Abu Musa al-Ash'ari—Allah be pleased with him: 'I told Omar that I have the Christian book [Gospels]. He replied: What's wrong with you?! Allah curse you! Have you not heard Allah's words?—"O you who have believed! Take not for friends and helpers the Jews and Christians, for they are but friends and helpers of each other" [5:51]. And do you now take them to be righteous?! I said, emir of the faithful, I have [only] his book [while] he has his religion. He said: I honor them not, for Allah has debased them; I ennoble them not, for Allah has laid them low; I do not draw close to them, for Allah has set them at a distance.' "

Al-Qurtubi said: "It is told that Omar said: 'Do not employ the People of the Book [Jews and Christians], for they regard bribes as lawful. Instead, for your affairs and [those of your] subjects, ask the aid of those who fear Allah Most High.' It was said to Omar: 'Behold, here is a man from among the Christians of [the tribe of] al-Hirra. None write better than he, nor do any supersede his calligraphy. Shall he not be your scribe? He said: I take none in place of the believers as my intimates.' Thus it is not permitted to employ the *dhimmis* as scribes, or to make use of them otherwise, in buying or selling, or as emissaries.

"The situation is reversed in these times, as the People of the Book are taken as scribes and intimates; how they have darkened the ignorant and foolish, [among the] governors and emirs."[8]

Ibn Taymiyya said: "One is not to use the *dhimmis* for employment or scribe-duties, for this entails or leads to corruption.

"Abu Talib relays that Ahmad was asked, What about the land tax? He said: 'Do not seek their aid [the *dhimmis*] for anything.' [He was asked again]: 'What if one of them runs an office for Muslims—shall his contract be annulled?' [He said]: 'If one of them injures or tries to corrupt Muslims, it is not permitted to employ him. Others are more preferable to him.' Abu Bakr the righteous made an oath that he would never employ any of the apostates—even if they returned to Islam; for he feared the corruption of their beliefs."

5. THE PROHIBITION AGAINST GLORIFYING THE INFIDELS'
RELIGIOUS CEREMONIES AND CUSTOMS, ENCOURAGING
THE INFIDELS AND APOSTATES IN THEIR FALSEHOOD,
AND EMBELLISHING OR PRAISING IT

The Sheikh of Islam [Ibn Taymiyya] said [in his] section on Friendship and Animosity: "The believers are loyal to Allah, and so they are [naturally] one another's allies. The infidels are the enemies of Allah and thus the enemies of the believers. He [Allah] has decreed that believers are to be unified together, and he showed that this is one of the necessities of faith. He prohibited befriending the infidels, making it clear that this is impermissible for the believers, and showing that such an act is a show of hypocrisy.

" 'Those who return to infidelity after Allah's guidance has been revealed to them are seduced by Satan and inspired by him. That is because they say to those [infidels] who abhor the Word of Allah, We shall obey you in some matters. Allah knows their secrets' [47:25–26]. Clearly, then, befriending the infidels was the cause for their relapse into apostasy. This is why He mentioned the leaders of the apostates right after issuing a ban against befriending infidels. 'And whoever among you turns to them [Jews and Christians] in friendship is of them' [5:51]. He said: 'O you Messenger! Grieve not over those who plunge headlong into infidelity, those who say with their tongues, We believe, but they have no faith in their hearts—and those Jews, men who will listen to any lie, will listen even to others who have never so much as come to you! They twist words out of their context and say, If this be given you, accept it; if not, then beware!' [5:41]. He mentioned the hypocrites and infidels who concluded a truce, telling [us] that they listen to other peoples, who have never so much as come to you. This means that the [Muslim] hypocrites and [dhimmi] infidels, at times of peace, give ear to the committed infidels who have not even concluded a truce.

"Thus there are among the believers those who will give ear to the hypocrites, as He said: '[T]here would have been some among you who would have listened to them' [9:47]. And some people have surmised that 'listened' here means listening in the manner of a spy—that is, listening to what is said, and then revealing it to them.

"But 'listening to them' means to respond to them and follow them. Just as it is said that Allah listens to whoever praises him, that is, he responds to whoever praises him by doing what he asks. Saying that so-and-so listens to so-and-so means that the former responds to and obeys the latter.

"Thus, whoever from the [Muslim] umma befriends infidels—whether they be pagans or People of the Book—in any of the various forms of friendship, such as visiting these people of falsehood and joining them in their false words or deeds—to that extent, he will earn the same measure of censure, punishment, and hypocrisy.

"Allah Most High desires to separate the good from the evil, the true from the false, that He may know if these [people] are hypocrites, or if there is any hypocrisy in them—even if they stand among the Muslims. For, just because a man is to all outward appearances a Muslim, does not mean he is not a hypocrite within.

"All hypocrites are outwardly Muslims. But the Koran has revealed their characteristics and principles. If they were around during the time of the Messenger of Allah and in the prime of Islam, when the banners of prophecy and the light of the Message shone forth, then surely afterward they are an even stronger presence. The cause of hypocrisy is the same as the cause of infidelity: resistance to that which the apostles have delivered."

6. THE PROHIBITION AGAINST AIDING THEM [INFIDELS] AGAINST MUSLIMS

Allah Most High said: "O you who have believed! take not the Jews and the Christians for your friends and protectors: They are but friends and protectors to each other. And he among you that turns to them [for friendship or protection] is of them. Truly, Allah guides not a transgressing people. Those in whose hearts is a disease—see how eagerly they run about among them [Jews and Christians], saying: We fear lest a change of fortune bring us disaster. Ah! But when Allah grants you victory or makes known His will, then shall they regret the thoughts that they secretly harbored in their hearts. Then shall the faithful say: Are these the men who solemnly swore oaths by Allah that they would stand with you? Surely their works shall come to naught and they will be losers" [5:51–53]. Al-Tabari explained the circumstances of this revelation: "The correct reading of this verse is that Allah Most High forbade all believers from taking Jews and Christians as supporters and allies instead of the people who believe in Allah and his Messenger. He declares that whoever takes them as supporters, allies, or friends, in the place of Allah, his Messenger, and the believers, this same one sides with them against Allah, His Messenger, and the believers. Allah and His Messenger are clean [have washed their hands] of that one."

Regarding the Tatars, Ibn Taymiyya said: "Every military commander who crosses over to them accepts their rule: They are both equally apostates from the *sharia* of Islam.

"And if the righteous forefathers called those who opposed the alms tax apostates, even though they fasted and prayed and did not fight the Muslim majority, what then when they side with the enemies of Allah and His Messenger, killing believers?!"

Ibn Hazam said: "We know that anyone who exits the Abode of Islam and goes to the Abode of War[9] flees Allah the Most High, abandoning the leader of the Muslims and the *umma*. His [Muhammad's] *hadith* confirms this: 'Sever [relations] with every Muslim who resides with obvious idolaters.' And he broke only with those who were infidels. Allah Most High said: 'The true believers, men and women, are friends to one another' [9:71].

"Abu Muhammad said: 'It follows from this that whoever hastens to join the Abode of Infidelity and War, choosing to battle any Muslim he encounters, by this action demonstrates his apostasy. All condemnations pertaining to apostasy apply to him: the duty to fight him whenever fate decrees; forfeiture of his property; annulment of his marriage; and so forth. For the Messenger of Allah does not break off from a [true] Muslim.'

"As follows, any Muslim living in India, Sind [west Pakistan], China, Turkey, Sudan, Rome [all part of the Abode of War], who cannot quit them due to an abundance of children, lack of funds, physical debilitation, or blocked roads, is forgiven. However, if he is there as a combatant against Muslims—aiding the infidels either through physical or scribal service—then he is surely an infidel.

"If an infidel holy warrior [*mujahid*] conquers a Muslim realm, leaving the Muslims there free [to practice their faith], with the exception that he is the sole sovereign and king, and yet he professes a faith other than Islam, those who aid him and remain with him are infidels, even if they claim to be Muslim." (The phrase "infidel holy warrior" [*kafir mujahid*] is perhaps a misprint, which should have read "outspoken infidel" [*kafir mujahir*]. Allah knows.)

So, what would al-Tabari, Ibn Hazam, and Ibn Taymiyya say if they were made witness to the American planes, troops, and their allies launching off from the [Arabian] Gulf to strike Muslims in Iraq?

And what would they say if they were witness to American planes taking off from Pakistan in order to kill Muslims in Afghanistan? And what would they say if they witnessed American and Western ships and planes, stocking up on fuel, provisions, and ammunitions from the Gulf States, Yemen, and Egypt, on their way to lay siege to Iraq, occupy the Arabian Peninsula, and safeguard Israel's security?

And what would they say if they witnessed homes collapsed atop the heads of their Muslim, Palestinian inhabitants, by the weapons of the Americans (the "friends" of our rulers)? What would they say if they witnessed American planes bombarding the *mujahidin* with missiles in Yemen, in compliance with its government?

7. THE COMMANDMENT TO WAGE *JIHAD* AGAINST THEM, EXPOSE THEIR FALSEHOOD, HAVE NO LOVE FOR THEM, AND KEEP AWAY FROM THEM

Not only did the Almighty and Exalted One forbid us from befriending the infidels, but he also ordered us to wage *jihad* against the original infidels [those who never submitted to Islam], the apostates [Muslims who have strayed from the faith], and the hypocrites.

A. Jihad *Against the Original Infidels Is Obligatory If They Occupy the Lands of Islam*

Ibn Taymiyya said: "If the enemy enters the lands of Islam, he must surely be repelled as soon as possible <u>for all Islamic lands are one umma. There must be a general call to arms, without requiring permission from the father nor</u> [any other] <u>opposition.</u> The writings of Ahmad evince this." He also said: "Defensive warfare is the most critical form of warfare, [since we are] warding off an invader from [our] sanctities and religion. It is a unanimously accepted duty. After faith, there is no greater duty than to repulse the invading enemy who perverts faith and the world. There are no rules or conditions for this; he must be expelled by all possible means. Our learned *ulema* and others have all agreed to this. It is imperative to distinguish between repulsing the invading, oppressive infidel [Defensive *Jihad*] and pursuing him in his own lands [Offensive *Jihad*]."

Ponder well this extremely powerful statement by the honorable *mujahid*, the Sheikh of Islam, Ibn Taymiyya, demonstrating the consensus to wage *jihad* against the infidels who raid the Abode of Islam. Note his emphasis that there is nothing after faith more obligatory than expelling them [infidels]. This is something agreed upon by the *ulema* of the *umma*. Then compare these assertions with the assertions of the *ulema* who serve the sultan, the propagandists of idleness, who employ every ruse in order to keep Muslims from waging *jihad*, to the point that the infidels are secured in their raids against our lands, accomplishing what they will, in ease, comfort, and security.

B. Jihad *Against the Apostate Rulers of the Lands of Islam*

One of the greatest and most individually binding *jihads* in this day and age is *jihad* waged against those apostate rulers who reign over Islamic lands and govern without the *sharia*—the friends of Jews and Christians. The *ulema* are agreed upon this and have made numerous declarations about it. We cite only a few of them here.

Allah Most High said: "But they will not—I swear by your Lord—they will not be true believers, until they make you [Muhammad] judge in all disputes [that arise] between them, and find in their souls no resistance against your verdicts, but accept them with full conviction and submission" [4:65]. Al-Shafi'i said, regarding the chapter on obedience to the Messenger: "Allah Most High said: 'Obey Allah and obey the Messenger' [4:59]. The Almighty also said: 'And We sent forth messengers so that men should do their bidding by Allah's leave' [4:64]. The Most High said: 'He who obeys the Messenger also obeys Allah' [4:80]. Again, the Most High said: 'But they will not—I swear by your Lord—they will not be true believers, until they make you [Muhammad] judge in all disputes [that arise] between them, and find in their souls no resistance against your verdicts, but accept them with full conviction and submission' [4:65].

"Thus He—the Almighty, the Exalted—confirms through these

verses that it is obligatory [for believers] to obey the Messenger. It is proven that obeying the Messenger *is* obeying Allah; defying him *is* defying Allah. Allah Most High said: 'Let those beware who withstand the Messenger's command, lest some trial befall them, or a grievous penalty be inflicted on them' [24:63]. Thus He warns against contradicting the Messenger's command, likening the one who opposes the command of the Messenger, rejecting his Message and doubting him, to one who abandons the faith. Allah Most High said: 'But they will not—I swear by your Lord—they will not be true believers, until they make you [Muhammad] judge in all disputes [that arise] between them, and find in their souls no resistance against your verdicts, but accept them with full conviction and submission' [4:65].[10]

"It is said that resistance is doubt, as was conveyed by *mujahid*; and the root cause of resistance is apprehension. An acceptable reading [of the aforementioned verse] is that it means one must submit [to the Messenger's *sunna*] without doubt or apprehension. Instead, it should be accepted calmly, deliberately, and confidently.

"This verse confirms that whoever rejects any of Allah the Most High's commandments or the commandments of His Messenger this same one has departed from Islam, whether the rejection stems from doubt or refusal to submit.

"This confirms that the Companions [of Muhammad] were right to brand as apostates those who refused to pay the alms tax, slaying them and imprisoning their children. For Allah Most High has decreed that whoever refuses to submit to the Prophet and comply with his orders is not of the people of faith."

Allah Most High said: "Is it pagan laws that they wish to be governed by?! Who is a better judge than Allah, for men whose faith is firm?" [5:50]. Ibn Kathir said [in his commentary on the aforementioned verse]: "The Most High denies those who turn away from Allah's decrees, which permit all good and forbid all evil, and stray toward the opinions, whims, and agreements established by men without support from the *sharia* of Allah—just as was the case with the people of pagan times [*jahiliyya*], who ruled in darkness and ignorance, through their vain imaginings and caprices. And just like the Tatars, who ruled through the royal policies of their king, Genghis Khan, who established for them the *yasiq*.[11] This [the *yasiq*] was essentially a book consisting of decrees derived from the diverse legislations of the Jews, Christians, Muslims, and others; and many were based merely on his own opinions and desires. This went on to become supreme law among his descendants, superseding the commandments of the Book of Allah and the *sunna* of his Messenger. . . . Thus, whosoever does this, the same is an infidel who needs to be fought till he returns to the commandments of Allah and his Messenger, so that he reigns in evil for the shortest amount of time."

C. Jihad *Against the Hypocrites Who Propagate Specious Arguments*

Allah Exalted commanded his Prophet to wage *jihad* against the hypocrites with great ruthlessness, force, clear arguments, and the imposition of limits [as set forth by the *sharia*].

Allah Most High said: "O Prophet! Wage war against the infidels and the hypocrites, and be ruthless against them. Their abode is Hell—an evil fate!" [66:9]. Al-Qurtubi said: "There is but one theme—and that is zeal for the religion of Allah. He commands the waging of *jihad* against the infidel by use of the sword, sound sermons, and the summons to Allah [proselytization]; as for hypocrites, wage *jihad* with ruthlessness against them, restrict them, and notify them of their fate in the Hereafter, for they shall have no light to walk the [straight] road with the believers. Al-Hassan said: 'Wage *jihad* against them by restricting them.' "

8. LEGALLY UNACCEPTABLE EXCUSES FROM THOSE WHO BEFRIEND INFIDELS

The Most High does not accept the excuses of the hypocrites, [who claim that] they befriend the infidels and enable them to victory simply because they fear the vicissitudes of time and chance, especially since if the infidels overcome the Muslims, the hypocrites will stand to gain from the infidels. Allah Most High said: "O you who believe!

do not take the Jews and the Christians for your friends and protectors; they are friends and protectors of each other. Whoever among you takes them for a friend, then surely he is one of them. Truely, Allah does not guide the unjust people. But you will see those in whose hearts is a disease hastening toward them, saying: We fear lest a calamity should befall us; but it may be that Allah will bring the victory or a punishment from Himself, so that they shall be regretting on account of what they hid in their souls. And those who believe will say: Are these they who swore by Allah with the most forcible of their oaths that they were most surely with you? Their deeds shall go for nothing, so they shall become losers" [5:51–53]. Ibn Kathir said: " 'You will see those in whose hearts is a disease'—this means doubt, hesitation, and hypocrisy. 'Hastening toward them,' that is, they rush to offer them their friendship and allegiance, both secretly and publicly. 'Saying: We fear lest a calamity should befall us'—that is, they offer up excuses as to why they befriend and ally with infidels, saying that they fear it may come to pass that the infidels overcome the Muslims: should this happen, they want to be assured of favor with the Jews and Christians."

9. THE COMMAND TO BEFRIEND AND AID BELIEVERS

Having delineated how Allah Almighty forbade us from befriending infidels, we shall now clearly demonstrate how Allah has commanded that we befriend the believers. Allah Most High said: "Those who have embraced the faith and fled their homes, and fought for the cause of Allah with their wealth and their lives, and those that sheltered them and helped them shall be as friends to one another. As for those who have embraced the faith but have not fled their homes, these you are not obligated to protect until they come into exile. But if they seek your help in religion, it is your duty to assist them, except against a people whom you already have a treaty [i.e., "temporary truces" according to *sharia* law]. Allah knows all that you do. Infidels give aid and comfort to one another; if you fail to do likewise, there will be disorder in the land and great corruption. Those that have embraced the faith and fled their homes and fought for the cause of Allah, and those that have sheltered them and helped them—they are the true believers! For them is forgiveness of sin and a provision most generous. Those who have since embraced the faith and fled their homes and fought alongside you—they too are your brothers; yet according to the Book of Allah [Koran], those who are bound by ties of blood are nearest to one another. Allah knows all things" [8:72–75]. Al-Qurtubi said: "Regarding the Word of the Most High '[I]f they seek your help in religion' [Allah] desires that, if those believers who did not emigrate from the Abode of War call for your aid, whether through a call to arms or for money to save them, then help them. However, if they ask for your aid against a group of infidels lying in between you with which there is a treaty, then do not aid them against them. Do not annul the treaty until its time is up.

"Ibn Arabi: 'Even if they [believers] are enfeebled captives, still, loyalty to them stands. Helping them is a duty imposed on us as long as we have eyes to see. If our numbers can bear it, we must ride forth and save them. We must spend all our money—till no one has a single *dirham* [silver coin] left—to bring them out. So say Malik and the consensus of *ulema*. For we are Allah's and to Him we return. This applies to those who abandon their brethren to the prisons of the enemy, though they hold in their hands money, reserves, strength, numbers, and perseverance.'"

Ibn Kathir said: "The Most High mentioned the different kinds of believers and he distinguished them thus: those who, abandoning their homes and possessions, emigrated coming to the aid of Allah and His Messenger and the establishment of His religion—giving up their money, possessions, and lives for this cause; and al-Ansar [i.e., "the helpers"], the Muslims living in Medina[12] who provided asylum for their fugitive brethren in their homes, comforting them with their wealth, and aiding Allah and His Messenger by fighting alongside them. These [two] are surely allies to one another, that is, they have greater obligation to one another than anyone else. To this end, the Messenger forged ties of brotherhood between the emigrants and al-Ansar—they are brethren.

"And the saying of the Most High: 'As for those who have embraced the Faith but have not fled their homes, these you are not obligated to protect until they go into exile.'

" '[N]ot obligated to protect until they go into exile.' This is the third category of believers—they who believed and yet did not emigrate, choosing instead to remain in place. These have no share in the plunder—not even a fifth—unless they take part in battle.

"The Most High said: 'But if they seek your help' those Arabs who did not emigrate—in battle for My religion—against their enemy, help them. You are duty-bound to assist them, for they are your brothers in faith [Islam]—unless they ask you to aid them against infidels whom you already have made a truce with. In that case, betray not your treaties, nor break faith with those whom you made contract with. This was relayed by Ibn Abbas."

Allah Most High said: "The believers—both men and women—are protectors of each other: they enjoin what is just, and forbid what is evil: they observe regular prayers, practice regular charity, and obey Allah and His Messenger. On them will Allah pour His mercy: for Allah is Exalted in power, Wise" [9:71]. Ibn Kathir said: "When the Most High evoked the hideous traits of the hypocrites, he also evoked the praiseworthy traits of the believers: 'The believers—both men and women—are protectors of one another,' meaning they help and aid one another, as is found in the authentic accounts [of Muhammad] Bukhari, Muslim: 'A believer to a believer is like unto a building that makes firm all its parts together.' At this, he [Muhammad] interlocked his fingers. Another trustworthy saying Bukhari, Muslim: 'In the compassion and mercy the believers possess for one another, they are like one body: Should one of its members be struck ill, the rest of the body suffers from fevers and insomnia.' "

10. SUMMARY

A. Allah Exalted has forbidden us from taking infidels as friends and allies, and aiding them against the believers, by either word or deed. Whoever does this is an infidel like them.

Sharia law allows [through the doctrine of *taqiyya*] whoever fears being killed, scarred, or severely harmed to say whatever will prevent the infidels from harming him—without making them intimates, and without helping them against Muslims, either by way of action, murder, or fighting. But the better way is to be steadfast and endure.

B.   The Lord Almighty has commanded us to hate the infidels and reject their love. For they hate us and begrudge us our religion [i.e., way of life], wishing that we abandon it. Omar al-Khitab deemed Hatib bin Abi Balta a hypocrite, simply because he sent word to the infidels that the Prophet was headed toward them with a force that could not be withstood. [Due to this] he [Omar] wanted to kill Hatib. Yet the Prophet did not renounce him [Hatib]; instead, he forgave him his great sin, for his righteous and mighty deed of participating at [the battle of] Badr.[13]

There is a firm bond between loving the Lord, befriending the believers, and [waging] *jihad* in the path of Allah. Kindness and fair-dealing with those infidels who are not hostile toward us are not the same thing as friendship, which is forbidden.

C.   The *sharia* has forbidden us from taking infidels as confidants, inducting them into our secrets.

D.   The *sharia* forbids us from appointing infidels to important posts.

E.   The *sharia* forbids us from adopting or praising the beliefs and views of the infidels.

F.   The *sharia* forbids us from assisting infidels against Muslims; even the one who is coerced has no excuse to fight under the banner of the infidels.

G.   The *sharia* commands us to battle infidels—both original infidels and apostates, as well as hypocrites. As for waging *jihad* against those infidels who have usurped the lands of Islam, this is a duty considered second only to faith, by *ulemaic* consensus.

H.   The *sharia* does not accept the excuses made by hypocrites—that they befriend the infidels because they fear the vicissitudes of time.

1. We are duty-bound by the *sharia* to help Muslims overcome infidels.

PART TWO: ILLUSTRATIONS OF DEVIATION FROM THE DOCTRINE OF LOYALTY AND ENMITY

1. RULERS [WHO] HAVE FUSED GOVERNANCE WITHOUT THE *SHARIA* WITH FRIENDSHIP FOR CHRISTIANS AND JEWS

The most exceptional group deviating from the doctrine of Loyalty and Enmity at this [point in] time—despite their claim that they adhere to Islam—is that clique of [secular] rulers who, while domineering over the lands of Islam, oppose *sharia*.

The danger this clique poses to the Muslim *umma* has become perilous, diverting the *umma* from the creed and preventing by force the practice of its faith. This is a clique that has utterly deviated from the path of Islam, [while possessing] absolute authority over the affairs, souls, and livelihoods of the Muslims; simultaneously, its [authority] is exceedingly widespread, so that not a single Muslim country has been able to escape the grasp of its evil.

The deviations of this clique are interrelated: for, while this clique governs without the *sharia*, it also befriends and submits to the external enemies of Islam—in particular, the Jews and Christians.

If we look to their friendship with the Jews and Christians, we will see that they have transformed the lands of Islam—particularly [in] the Arab world—into bases that feed and house Jewish and Christian forces. Any observer of the Arabian Peninsula, Gulf Emirates, Egypt, and Jordan will see that they have been changed into bases and camps providing administrative and technical support to the Crusader's forces in the heart of the Islamic world. And on top of that, these governments have placed their armies into the service of the new Crusading campaign against the Islamic *umma*.

Any observer will discover that these rulers who oppose *sharia* and dictate over the lands of Islam have a legacy stretching over decades of our modern history. Through a chain of conspiracies, secret relationships, direct support, bribes, salaries, secret accounts, corruption, and recruitment, the enemies of Islam—especially Americans, Jews, French, and English—have succeeded in giving this clique power over the fates of Muslims. There is no space here to explain this history; nonetheless, we can point out that the forces hostile to Islam were, after World War II, able to take control of these governments, pouring them into the mold of the victorious Allies' world order—that is, the United Nations.

In brief, the United Nations, through the eyes of Islam, is essentially a hegemonic organization of universal infidelity: [a true Muslim] is not permitted to join or have recourse to it. It exists in order to prevent rule by *sharia* and to guarantee submission to the rule of five of the greatest criminals on earth. They dominate the leadership of the United Nations, known as the Security Council [the United States, Britain, France, Russia, and China]. We also point out that the foes of Islam have made these governments accept as lawful the existence of the Jewish entity [Israel] in Palestine through a number of official treaties and practical arrangements, starting with the 1949 Armistice Agreement to the 1993 Oslo Accords. Then there was the Beirut Summit of 2002,[14] where the Arab states confirmed that they completely and unanimously accept the existence of Israel.

It should be borne in mind that peace with Israel and acceptance of its usurpation of Palestine repudiate binding and necessary tenets of the *sharia*. It is a rejection of *jihad*—an individual duty imposed on Muslims to drive out all raiding infidels from the Abode of Islam, as we have enumerated above. It also denies the obligation of aiding Muslims in Palestine—another binding individual duty affirmed by the faith. Allah Most High said: "Why would you not fight in the cause of Allah and of those who, being weak, are ill-treated?—men, women, and children whose cry is: Our Lord! Rescue us from this town, whose people are oppressors; raise for us from Your [presence] one who will

protect! raise for us from Your [presence] one who will help!" [4:75].
Al-Qurtubi said: "The Word of the Most High—'Why would you not
fight in the cause of Allah'—is an incitement for *jihad*, which ensures
the salvation of the weak from the hands of the idolatrous infidels
who torment them and prevent them from practicing their religion.
Thus the Most High obligated *jihad* in order to lift up His Word, make
known His religion, and rescue the weak believers among his slaves—
even if, to this end, some should perish."

This is not only about a failure to [actively] perform individual
obligations: most Arab states participated in the 1996 Sharm al-
Sheikh Conference with Israel, America, Russia, and most Western
states, where all parties agreed and promised to defend Israel from the
attacks of the *mujahidin*.

Against this backdrop of acquiescence to the will of the greatest criminals, those powers hostile to Islam—headed by the Neo-
Crusaders—have succeeded in subjugating the governments of our
lands to do their militaristic and economic bidding.

Finally, we arrive at what we see today: a state of absolute submission to the Neo-Crusaders. Palestine is torn asunder and demolished,
its children slaughtered every day—yet its Arab neighbors respond
with either silence or connivance. Iraq is victim to one campaign after
another, in order to slay its Muslim populace, divide the land, and pillage its oil—yet its Arab neighbors perform every sort of assistance
and support to the new Crusading forces. Afghanistan is victimized
by the Crusading forces—yet its neighbors connive to give the Americans dominion over Afghanistan and its people.

Such, then, is this clique—a clique of rulers that violate *sharia*.
Their corruption and power to corrupt, crimes against the general
Muslim populace, not to mention the elite, and their friendship to
Jews and Christians, are evident for all to see. Because of this, they fear
an uprising against them from the Muslim *umma*, and its *mujahid*
youth—particularly in light of the rising tide of Zionist-American aggression against Palestine, Iraq, Chechnya, and Kashmir. They have
utilized a number of groups in order to numb the *umma*, ensuring its

continued incapacity, depression, and submission. And the most dangerous of these groups are those that cloak themselves in the garb of Islam and its summons, worming their way into the *umma*'s beliefs, mind, and heart. They are like lethal bacteria trying to overcome the human immune system, trying to destroy it to sow corruption in the cells of the human body.[15] We will summarize this phenomenon in the following paragraphs.

2. THE RULER'S HENCHMEN

Official Ulema, Journalists, Media Personnel, Writers, Thinkers, and Other Officials Who Receive Their Pay for Aiding and Embellishing Falsehood, and Combating [These] People of Falsehood and Their Distortions

Now this is the loudest class proclaiming its loyalty to the puppet rulers and the Crusading forces that invade the Abode of Islam—or the "*dhimmis*," as they call [the Crusaders]. However—and for shame!—they evade an embarrassing question of utmost importance: Who pays the *jizya* to whom?[16]

This class, in all its myriad confusion, engages in ideological fakery, by embracing deviant beliefs that have been rejected by the imams of Islam, past and present, along with the Sunnis and the[ir] consensus. This class combines:

1. The doctrine of *irja'* [i.e., postponement],[17] in its most despicable forms, shamelessly conferring legitimacy on the worst forms of dissolution, subjugation, corruption, and plunder, by the reigning, apostate, *sharia*-opposing regimes.
2. The path of the Kharijities,[18] branding as infidels the *mujahidin* who serve Islam, vilifying them, accusing them of heresy, and legitimizing their slaughter and degradation.

The Grand *Mufti* of Egypt is an official employee of the Egyptian government who receives his salary from it in order to render his service, that is, conferring legitimacy onto the secular regime, which op-

presses Muslims and befriends Jews—and in a manner that far sur-
passes the fervor of the Murji'ites [Postponers] of old! He [the *mufti*]
himself issued a *fatwa* allowing a secular, military court to condemn
[to death] the six *mujahidin* heroes of Islam in Egypt—Muhammad
Abd al-Salam Faraj, Abd al-Hamid, Abd al-Salam, Khalid al-Islambuli,
Hussein Abbas, and Atta Tayil—they who slew Anwar al-Sadat [for-
mer president of Egypt]. He signed four treaties with Israel, thereby
recognizing the state of Israel and its seizure of Palestine, while
promising never to attack it or support any state that does, and removing weapons from Sinai to insure Israel's security, along with
other covert agreements.

The most popular of these treaties is the 1979 peace treaty with Israel,[19] which permanently ended the state of war between Egypt and
Israel and prevented Egypt from aiding any country that might fall
under Israeli aggression. Moreover, it called for naturalization with
Israel in every field—political, economic, and intellectual. Soon
thereafter, al-Azhar[20] issued a *fatwa* blessing this treaty, claiming that
it agrees with the *sharia*!!

Another sort of *muftis* call us to obey the powers-that-be. At the
same time, they consider the *mujahidin* as spreaders of sedition.
These are the ones who approved the call to aid the Americans, reasoning that this massive army that blots out the horizon, this gigantic
fleet that chokes the oceans, these hundreds of thousands of raiding
soldiers are a guarantee of security [for them]!! But we do not
know—who is securing whom?? They issued joint *fatwas* making it
legitimate to aid the American forces confront the [then-reigning]
Baathist regime in Iraq—calling it a necessity. And then they conferred legitimacy on the presence of the infidel host that raids the
Muslims' holiest places. These forces have been present for nearly
twelve years since Iraq withdrew [from Kuwait] and capitulated
[since the 1991 Gulf War]. During that time—and due to sanctions—
nearly two and a half million Iraqi children have been killed, without
these wage-workers uttering so much as a single word about it.

The issue is not about helping infidel forces against the forces of the Baathist Saddam [Hussein]; instead, it is about the usurpation of the oil wells in the Arabian Peninsula. There was no need for an American presence; the armies of Arab and Islamic states were sufficient and able to protect and liberate Kuwait.[21]

However, these rulers possess no will. Rather, they are the products of the British plans that drew their borders and established them on their thrones. Afterward, the Americans inherited the status of the British: they came to possess absolute authority over all the rulers of the Arabian Peninsula along with the rest of the Arab world.

And so the masters came to defend their possessions. And all these sheikhs and kings had no say insofar as securing or defending the Arabian Peninsula.

And so now, after Iraq surrendered, accepting an aerial blockade over half its land, and after the Kurdish north gained independence from the government of Baghdad, and after the imposition of inspection commissions and coercion to pay reparations—after all this, the presence of the Crusader military remains in the Arabian Peninsula, in ever-growing numbers. Indeed, they are preparing for a new campaign against Iraq wherein hundreds of thousands of Muslims are expected to die until the oil wells of Iraq are well secured.[22]

Thereafter, they will attempt—as they plainly disclosed in Congress—to divide Saudi [Arabia]; then to Egypt—the "grand prize," as they call it.

Seems the issue is not about aiding. No, the issue is about occupation, thievery, plunder, domination, and the Crusaders' suppression of Muslims in their holiest of lands: the Arabian Peninsula. These rulers are nothing more than a drab coat of paint covering the American presence. Then come the sultan's *ulema* to sign *fatwas* delivered from the palace, to legitimize this seizure, this pillaging, this Crusader overlordship—nay more, this pouring of Muslim blood in [neighboring] Iraq!

On top of all that, the Grand *Mufti* of the Saudis issues a ruling that [making] peace with Israel is legitimate, since the one who concluded it with them was a legitimate Muslim ruler (Yasir Arafat).

A number of persons connected with the call in Kuwait screamed ["murder!"] after *mujahidin* slew Americans in Failaka.[23] They grew angry at the hostilities toward the Crusaders whom they described as "*dhimmis*." They seem to have forgotten that the *dhimmis* live under Muslim domination, pay them the *jizya*, and are governed under the *sharia*. These sheikhs and their rulers live under the yoke of the Crusaders and are in their power; they run to them for defense and, in obedience or through coercion, pay them exorbitant sums to curry favor with them. Nor can they lift a finger in defiance to their will. So, then, who is a *dhimmi* to whom? Who pays the *jizya* to whom? Who is in whose power?

They have also forgotten that Kuwait is a part of the Arabian Peninsula: The Jews and Christians, from the start, are not permitted to be there.[24]

And all these people—who block the path to Allah—command the people to obey the opponents of *sharia* by abandoning the obligatory *jihad*. They have, thereby, caused a number of misfortunes:

A.   They have helped enable the infidels to continue dominating the lands of Islam.
B.   They have prevented the people from carrying out *jihad*, that personal duty decreed them.
C.   They have conferred legitimacy on the false governments that oppose *sharia*.
D.   They have cursed and slandered the *mujahidin*.

One of the tricks they use is to claim that, Yes, *jihad* is true and obligatory, and the path to salvation—and yet now is not the time for it: now is the time for preparations; now is the time to exhaust all appeals—until the right time.

And they make strenuous arguments in defense of this specious claim; yet they flee the embarrassing, critical question: Why, after all these decades of humiliation, are you [still] completely unprepared? And when will these "preparations" be completed? They have no response, because, for them, "preparations" are endless. Allah Most High said: "If they had intended to come out, they would certainly have made some preparation therefore" [9:46].

If only they had reformed the beliefs of the people, clarifying for them the pure creed of *tawhid*, as it was revealed to the Prophet and as it was transmitted by the pious forefathers. But to great regret, instead they reveal some of it, and hide much.

They talk a great deal about *tawhid* to the general populace and the enfeebled; yet they do not touch upon the idolatrous rulers' betrayal of Islam and their friendship to Jews and Christians.

It is truly amazing that the lands of Islam have been under foreign influence for decades! Nor is the presence of this current Crusader military occupation the result of a surprise [attack] or a sudden coup. No, it is the fruit of a continuing policy of submission to the West that has gone on for over a century. And as for all that, we hear not a word from them regarding this disaster, save the rare, ambiguous hint.

At times they make a commotion saying the *mujahidin* do not know the difference between right and wrong and that they have caused more harm than good. And yet they do not respond to the embarrassing question: Very well, what then is the approach to *jihad* that you propose that will do good and avoid harm? Their response? Abandon *jihad* altogether.

But ask them: If we made the *mujahidin* forsake their duty [*jihad*], joining your ranks, the ranks of those who sit and abandon *jihad* under various pretexts, would then the enemies of the *umma* halt their aggression? Would corruption and its influence be stayed? And would the Jews leave Palestine? Would Israel abandon its plan to "judaize" Palestine, and raze the Aqsa Mosque [in Jerusalem], and the goal of establishing a Greater Israel?[25] Would the secularists then cease from their deviations and deceptions? Would there be hope that the wicked would repent and be pardoned? Would the idolatrous tyrants forsake their thrones, opening the doors of the prison houses? Would their hangmen tire of tormenting their people? Would, would, would . . . ?

Then they proceed to add much murk and mire to these specious arguments, preaching to the youth, saying: Why not preoccupy yourselves with your studies? Why not busy yourselves with trying to dialogue and debate with the infidels? Why not spend time founding religious schools, taking care of orphans, and helping the sick? Why not preoccupy yourselves with the call to the "true creed"? Would that they were honest in their call to correct the creed! But instead, the reality of their call is: Why not distract yourselves from *jihad*??

This disease robs its victims [the Muslim masses] of their intellectual and doctrinal immunity. We issue the strongest warning against it, for its consequences are great losses, humiliation, and submission.

The purpose of their call is to prevent the *mujahidin* from waging *jihad* and disabling the fighting youth so that the aggressors will be assured of their raid against any reprisals or resistance. This is why the enemies of Islam look on them with contentment and point to their governments with broad satisfaction.

3. SUPPORTERS OF AN ILLUSORY RECONCILIATION

The third group that deviates from the doctrine of Loyalty and Enmity is that class that calls for a reconciliation with those [secular, dictatorial] governments that oppose *sharia*, [all supposedly] in order to resist the *umma*'s enemies [the West, etc.].

In short, their logic is that we should cooperate with the thief in order to regain what he stole from us; that we should reconcile with the debauchee in order to guard the honor he has desecrated. And if they were evicted from their bases, they would say: Let us make peace with the Jews and Christians in order to convince them to give up our lands and depart in peace. They ask us to discredit the reality we witness and believe these dreams.

They call [on us] to cease resisting the *umma*'s primary foe. They would have us surrender the leaders of the *mujahidin* to the traitors whose history teems with crimes against Islam—they who did not for one day defend Palestine, who hurried to recognize Israel and expose our lands to the Crusaders' forces.

4. AMERICA'S *MUJAHIDIN*

The fourth group that deviates from the doctrine of Loyalty and Enmity, at this point in time, are those groups and leaders associated with the *jihad* in Afghanistan, and who have befriended the Americans [e.g., the Northern Alliance, which helped oust the Taliban]. Some among them are well known. International peacekeeping forces protect them under the banner of the United Nations. American forces surround them; [U.S.] bombers provide them with air cover. They are overjoyed with the crumbs of power they received over the corpses of their people and the blood of the *mujahidin*!!

Allah Most High said: "But if you renounced the faith, you would surely have made mischief in the land and violated the ties of kinship! Such are those whom Allah has cursed; He has made them deaf and blinded their eyes. Do they not then reflect on the Koran? Are there locks upon their hearts? Surely those who return on their backs [apostatize] after guidance was revealed to them are seduced by Satan, who has made it a light matter for them, and inspired them. That is because they say to those [the infidels] who hate what Allah has revealed: We will obey you in some matters—but Allah knows their secrets. But how will it be when the angels cause them to die, smiting their faces and backs. That is because they follow what is displeasing to Allah and are averse to His pleasure; therefore He will surely nullify their deeds. Or do those in whose hearts is a disease think that Allah will not expose their malice? And if We willed it, We could have made you know them so that you would certainly have recognized them by their marks and most certainly you can recognize them by the intent of [their] speech; and Allah knows your deeds. And so most assuredly We will try you until We know who among you are the righteous *mujahidin*, for We shall try your mettle" [47:22–31].

In the name of Allah, the Compassionate, the Merciful

CONCLUSION

In conclusion, we wish to emphasize a number of key points in these pages:

1. Befriending believers and battling infidels are critical pillars in a Muslim's faith. His faith is incomplete without it. Allah Most High said: "O you who believe! do not take the Jews and the Christians for your friends and protectors; they are but friends and protectors of each other. Whoever among you takes them for a friend, then surely he is one of them. Truly, Allah does not guide the unjust people" [5:51].

   This hostility toward infidels, which is a pillar of faith according to Allah, cannot be achieved except by [first] renouncing the idolatrous [tyrants].[26] Allah Most High said: "[W]hoever rejects idolatry and believes in Allah grasps the most trustworthy handle, [one] that never breaks. And Allah hears and knows all things" [2:256]. And the Most High said: "Have you not seen those who assert that they believe in what has been revealed to you along with what was revealed before you? They desire to summon one another to the judgment of Satan, though they were commanded to rebuke him. Satan desires to lead them astray" [4:60]. Thus it is imperative that we separate from the evil tyrants and their helpers—keeping clear of them: "You have a good example in Abraham and those who followed him, for they said to their people, We disown you and the idols that you worship besides Allah. We renounce you: enmity and hate shall reign between us until you believe in Allah alone" [60:4].

2. Failure to uphold this fundamental pillar has opened a fissure whence the enemies of Islam penetrate in order to annihilate the Muslim *umma*—betraying it, dulling its senses, sucking it into

catastrophe and misfortune. Allah Most High said: "If they had come out with you, they would not have added to your [strength] but only [made for] disorder, hurrying to and fro in your midst and sowing sedition among you. And there would have been some among you who would have listened to them. But Allah knows well those who do wrong" [9:47].

3. Failure to uphold this fundamental pillar leads to the dissolution of a Muslim's creed; he sloughs it off. Allah Most High said: "O you who have believed! if you obey those who disbelieve they will turn you back upon your heels, and you will become losers" [3:149].

4. We have an urgent need to distinguish between those loyal to Islam, who defend it, and the enemies who attack it, and the oscillators who seek only to pursue their own interests by weakening the resistance of the *umma* and diverting it from the truth. Allah Most High said: "When you see them, their good looks please you; and when they speak, you listen to what they [have to] say. Yet they are like propped-up beams of wood. Every shout they hear, they take to be against them. Truly, they are the enemy: guard yourselves against them. Allah confound them! How perverse they are!" [63:4]. He has also said, glory be to the Speaker: "Wavering between this [and that], [belonging] neither to these nor to those. Whoever Allah causes to go astray, you will find no way for him" [4:143].

5. How can we accept appeals that aim to clear a way for the enemies of the Muslim *umma*? How can we keep silent as they strive to deny Muslims of their right to resist their enemies? This is a right all peoples enjoy. How can we keep silent as they are held back, while the *umma* possesses such enormous resources and such reliable *mujahidin*? How can we permit these appeals to circulate among us after the criminals have attacked us from every corner? They have shown us no mercy, granted us no quarter.

Any Muslim zealous over the triumph of Islam cannot accept

any call to halt or postpone *jihad*, or turn the *umma* away from it. Despite the presence of all these resources we just mentioned, our enemies daily sink their teeth into our holy places, sacred [things], and wealth. Allah Most High said: "They break faith with the believers and set at naught all ties of kinship. Such are the transgressors" [9:10]. Ibn Omar said: "I heard the Messenger of Allah say: 'If you enter business transactions, grabbing hold of cows' tails, are content with farming, and you abandon *jihad*, Allah will allow humiliation to overtake you and will not restrain it until you return to your religion' " narrated by Ahmad and Abu Dawud.

6. Nor is it enough that we reject any and all calls to halt *jihad*. Instead, we call the *umma*—in all its factions, classes, and groups—to join the caravan of *jihad*, proceed in its journey, vying with one another in its performance and in defiance of its enemies. Allah Most High said: "O you who have believed! Shall I point out to you a profitable course that will save you from a woeful scourge? Have faith in Allah and His Messenger, and fight in the path of Allah with your resources and lives. That would be best for you—if you but only knew it! He will forgive you your sins and usher you into gardens watered by running streams. He will lodge you in pleasant mansions in the gardens of Eden. That is the supreme triumph! And He will bestow other blessings that you desire: help from Allah and a speedy victory. Proclaim the good tidings to the faithful!" [61:10–13].

7. We also extend our hands to every Muslim zealous over making Islam triumph till they join us in a course of action to save the *umma* from its painful reality. [This course of action] consists of staying clear of idolatrous tyrants, warfare against infidels, loyalty to the believers, and *jihad* in the path of Allah. Such is a course of action that all who are vigilant for the triumph of Islam should vie in, giving and sacrificing in the cause of liberating the lands of the Muslims, making Islam supreme in its [own] land, and then spreading it around the world.

8. We warn our *umma* against falling to defeatism and ignoring the dangers that oppressively lie atop our chests. Behold! the Crusader-Jewish military machine occupies exalted Jerusalem! It crouches a mere ninety kilometers from the shrine in Mecca. It surrounds the Islamic world with a series of bases, armies, and fleets. It gears its aggression against us through a network of submissive rulers.

    We do not wish to live as if in another world, behaving as if the danger is yet another thousand years hence. We could open our eyes—any given morning—to discover the Jewish tanks that have destroyed homes in Gaza and Janin [in Palestine] surrounding our homes.

    This is but the beginning of the campaign against Iraq. And when Abu Ali al-Harith was killed by American missiles in Yemen, it was a warning that the Israeli way for killing *mujahidin* in Palestine had been exported to the Arab world. Tomorrow, each one of us shall be the target of an American missile. And no sincere preacher or honest writer will be able to escape the all-accusing finger of America.

    We must act and act quickly. Enough time has been lost. Let the Muslim youth not await anyone's permission, for *jihad* against the Americans, Jews, and their alliance of hypocrites and apostates is an individual obligation, as we have demonstrated. Young people of every class must assume responsibility for the *umma* and make plans to defend it from its foes. We must set our lands aflame beneath the feet of the raiders; they shall never depart otherwise.

9. In closing, we call to our Muslim *umma*—and particularly its *mujahid* youth—to be patient and sure. To be patient in bearing the burdens of religion, and particularly its glorious peak— *jihad* in the way of Allah. Allah Most High said: "O you who have believed! Be patient and forbear. Stand firm in your faith and fear Allah, so that you may triumph" [3:200]. And to be sure

in the promise of Allah the Exalted One. Allah Most High said: "Allah has decreed: I shall surely triumph—Myself and my messengers! For Allah is Powerful and Mighty" [58:21]. Muslim conveyed Uqba bin Omar saying: "I heard the Messenger of Allah say: 'A band of people from my *umma* shall continue to fight in obedience to the command of Allah, vanquishing their foes. They who oppose them shall not bring them any harm. Thus shall they remain till the hour [of death] overtakes them.' "

Our final call is, Praise be to Allah, Lord of the Worlds, and Allah's prayers be upon our leader Muhammad, his family, and his Companions—and peace.

Ayman al-Zawahiri
December 2002

3

The following treatise, made up of two short parts, is extracted from Ayman al-Zawahiri's widely circulated book *The Bitter Harvest: The [Muslim] Brotherhood in Sixty Years*, which first surfaced around 1991. The book is mostly a history dedicated to demonstrating how and why Egypt's notorious Muslim Brotherhood—one of the oldest and most far-reaching Islamic organizations—has lost its way by choosing to participate in elections instead of waging the obligatory *jihad* against the current "apostate" government of Egypt. Zawahiri, who joined the Brotherhood when only fourteen years old but later abandoned it for more radical groups, wrote the book

> not to criticize the many errors of the Brothers—for if that was the case, it would be much longer. Rather, our book will limit itself to researching how and why the Brothers have abandoned pursuing [the creation of] a legitimate Muslim government in place of the current governments that rule Muslim lands. This deviation has made the Brothers idle from fulfilling their true calling, as Allah wills it. And not only have the Brothers been idle from fulfilling their duty of [waging] *jihad*, but they have gone as far as to describe the infidel governments as legitimate, and have joined ranks with them in the[ir] *jahiliyya* [-style of] governing, that is, democracies, elections, and parliaments. Moreover, they take advantage of the Muslim youths' fervor by bringing them into their fold only to store them in a refrigerator. Then, they steer their onetime passionate Islamic zeal for *jihad* against tyranny toward conferences and elections.

In order to justify his scathing condemnation of the Brotherhood's interactions with the Egyptian government, Zawahiri first delineates two theological concepts that validate his accusations: (1) the Islamic obligation to fight and overthrow any leader who does not govern according to the *sharia* of Allah, and (2) the belief that democracy and Islam are antithetical and thus can never coexist. Both these, plus an abridged version of the introduction of the book (which unabridged deals primarily with the temporal affairs of the Brotherhood), make up the following translation.

Based on these two principles, Zawahiri depicts the Brotherhood as having betrayed the true cause of Islam—that is, enforcing Allah's rule here on earth by any direct means, preferably *jihad*, not passive roundabout ways, such as elections. (It is ironic to note, however, that participating in democratic elections has in fact paid off for the Brotherhood: to international consternation, the partially banned Brotherhood won 88 seats [20 percent of the total] to form the largest opposition bloc in the 2005 Egyptian parliamentary elections.)

The issue of *sharia* law is confusing to many Westerners. Coming from a Christian heritage, Western peoples see no reason why democracy and religion cannot happily coexist. This, however, is mostly due to the fact that the word "religion" in the West connotes Christianity. And Christianity is such that it can be literally practiced under any set of secular laws. Christian theology, often metaphysical, preaches passivity to this world. Jesus declared, "Render unto Caesar [the government] that which is Caesar's [the corporeal] and unto God that which is God's [the spiritual]" (Matt. 22:21). Thus the separation of church and state inherent in Western democracies in no way contradicts Christian principles. Indeed, the reverse argument can be made—that Christianity did away with the concept of law altogether:

> Knowing that a man is not justified by the works of the Law,
> but by the faith of Jesus Christ, even we [Christians] have be-
> lieved in Jesus Christ, that we might be justified by the faith
> of Christ, and not by the works of the Law: for by the works
> of the Law shall no flesh be justified [Galatians 2:16].

As will be demonstrated in the following treatise, however, not only is Islamic law supreme, but there is no such distinction between "mosque" and state in Islam. Beyond the Five Pillars—profession, prayer, fasting, tithing, and pilgrimaging—Islam is extremely involved with this life and how it is to be lived. To that end, Allah, through his Prophet, has pronounced meticulous laws governing every facet of Muslims' lives.

This is the *sharia*, which is etymologically related to the word "road" or "pathway." Derived from the divine words of the Koran and the *sunna* of the Muslim prophet, the *sharia* has something to say about almost everything, sometimes by analogy in modern times. The divine words of Allah declare: "And now We have set you [Muhammad] on a straight road [*sharia*]. So follow it, and do not follow the whims of those who are ignorant" [45:18].

The fundamental issue that Zawahiri dwells upon can best be captured by the following question: How can Muslims—rulers or otherwise—establish or abolish that which has already been fixed from on high? In fact, based on Islamic jurisprudence, every conceivable action performed in this life is categorized as being either forbidden, disliked, permissible, recommended, or obligatory.

The Islamic ideologue Sayyid Qutb, whom Zawahiri quotes at length regarding the evils of democracy, while defining the word religion (*deen*), concludes that "the word 'religion' includes more than belief; 'religion' actually means a way of life." The very words "Islam" and "Muslim" ("submission" and "one who has submitted," respectively) denote the centrality of upholding the *sharia*, since the one who is willing to submit (i.e., a Muslim) submits to Allah. Yet exactly how does one go about submitting to Allah? The most standard and traditional answer has been, By striving to perform Allah's will as revealed in the Koran and Muhammad's *sunna*—which is precisely what the *sharia* consists of. In this context, not only democracy but every other form of man-made governance—from monarchy to communism—is *shirk*, or "partnership," with Allah, the greatest blasphemy.

The last two sentences of the following treatise perhaps best summarize the matter: "Thus whoever claims to be a 'democratic-Muslim,' or a Muslim who calls for democracy, is like one who says about himself 'I am a Jewish Muslim,' or 'I am a Christian Muslim'—the one worse than the other. He is an apostate infidel."

"SHARIA AND DEMOCRACY"

✥

INTRODUCTION

Allah Most High said: "O you who have believed! Do not behave presumptuously in the presence of Allah and His Messenger, but fear Allah: for Allah hears all and knows all" [49:1]. Allah Most High commands his servants to hold off from doing anything until they first learn the verdict of Allah and his Messenger. The words of the exegetes have revolved around this [command], for it forbids the servant from initiating any work until he first learns its legitimacy: Is this work obligatory or recommended or permissible or disliked or forbidden?[1]

Just as Allah Most High decrees that his servants are to know before doing, so too has He commanded that they submit whatever they disagree over to the judgment of Allah and his Messenger: "Whatever the subject of your disputes, the final decision rests in Allah alone" [42:10]. However, even if the servant learns the judgment of Allah regarding any [particular] act, he truly does not hear unless he also obeys the Words of the Most High: "It is not fitting for true believers—men or women—to take their choice in affairs if Allah and His Messenger have decreed otherwise. He that disobeys Allah and His Messenger strays far indeed!" [33:36].

Thus every statement or opinion or command that contradicts the commandments of Allah and his Messenger is false and unacceptable, forbidden [for believers] to perform or participate in—even if decreed by one of the imams [e.g., as a *fatwa*]. As the saying [*hadith*] of the Messenger goes: "He who performs a deed not sanctioned by us is an apostate."

Today, the stark reality that needs to be confronted by Islamic organizations is none other than the regimes ruling Muslim lands. It first behooves these groups to inquire whether these governments are Islamic or infidel, and whether the ruler is a Muslim or an infidel—this before they begin mustering Muslims and raising the banner of change. For we have shown that it is obligatory to first research before acting.

Now, if this ruler is a Muslim but transgresses by becoming cruel and despotic, the Sunni *madhhabs* say that it is forbidden to overthrow him. Ibn Hajar said: "Ibn Batal said: 'In the *hadith* there is evidence for not deposing a sultan even if he transgresses. The jurists have agreed unanimously on the necessity of obeying the victorious sultan and waging *jihad* with him. Obeying him is better than fighting him, so as to not cause bloodshed. However, should the sultan become an infidel, then he is not to be obeyed, and it is obligatory for you to wage *jihad* against him, if you can.'

"The first part of the *hadith*, where Ibn Batal indicated that there is evidence regarding deposing a sultan if he transgresses, is based on one of the sayings of the Messenger of Allah: 'Should someone hate his commandments for any reason, let him be patient, for he who distances himself from the sultan even a handbreadth dies the death of the ignorant' (in Bukhari and relayed by Ibn Abbas).

"As for the second part, where Ibn Batal indicates that it is obligatory to depose a sultan [or any 'authority figure'] if he becomes an infidel, this is based on Abada bin al-Samat's account: 'The Prophet called us to pledge our allegiance to him and to take an oath that we will hear and obey, earnestly or reluctantly, in good times as well as bad times, and never to revolt against the will of his successors unless you see clear proofs that they have become infidels, then you have evidence from Allah [to overthrow them].' " It is agreed.

Again, Ibn Hajar says: "Ibn al-Teen and al-Dawudi said: 'If you are able to break away [from an apostate ruler] without civil strife or oppression, you should do so; otherwise, your duty is to be patient. But if he is become an infidel, then you must overthrow him.' "

To summarize: It is forbidden to overthrow a tyrant, but it is a duty to overthrow an infidel. If the ruler is despotic, it is unlawful for a Muslim to rally other Muslims in order to condemn him, for if they do so then they become the aggressors and it becomes incumbent for the sultan to fight them, just as the Most High said: "Even the one who committed great evils found salvation in Allah's commandments."

The current rulers of Muslim countries who govern without the *sharia* of Allah are apostate infidels. It is obligatory to overthrow them, to wage *jihad* against them, and to depose them, installing a Muslim ruler in their stead.

Though they have concluded that it is dangerous to openly confront Islam as enemies, these current organizations lording over our Islamic *umma* continue betraying Islam and cheating its people by, above all, scattering and dividing them—all which lead to two situations:

1. They have Muslims abandon the *sharia* and guidance of Allah in [exchange for the opportunity to] participate in *jahiliyya* democracies[2]—thus ultimately yielding Allah's absolute truths for human truths, meaning submission to the right of humanity to choose what it wants from laws and ideologies.
2. They attack and belittle those who call for that [*jihad*], slander them, and call on the [apostate] governments to destroy them. They disavow themselves from [those who call for *jihad*] in front of those idolaters, contrary to Allah's Word: "Fight against them [infidels] until idolatry is no more and Allah's religion reigns supreme" [2:191].

The Word of the Most High: "O you who have believed! Do not behave presumptuously in the presence of Allah and His Messenger, but fear Allah: for Allah hears all and knows all" [49:1].

And the Word of the Most High: "It is not fitting for true believers—men or women—to take their choice in affairs if Allah and His Messenger have decreed otherwise. He that disobeys Allah and His Messenger strays far indeed!" [33:36].

And the saying of the Messenger of Allah, preserved in Muslim's *hadith*: "He who performs a deed not sanctioned by us is an apostate."

PART ONE: IN CONDEMNATION OF THOSE WHO GOVERN WITHOUT ALLAH'S *SHARIA*

The Book [Koran], the *sunna*, and the sayings of the *ulema*, both past and present, all clearly demonstrate that exchanging the Islamic *sharia* with something else is infidelity—especially in the despicable manner that we see today in the lands of Islam. These regimes that exchange the *sharia* of Allah are outcasts from the Muslim *umma* for the following reasons:

1. [Because they] abandon the *sharia* of Allah in exchange for a motley set of contrived rules. Sheikh Ahmad Shakir called it "the modern-day *yasiq*," as we shall show, Allah willing.
2. [Because they] ridicule the *sharia*.
   And is there any greater mockery than withholding the *sharia*, or superimposing another [law] over it, or putting together a piece of paper and presenting it to the idle chatter of the so-called "people's council"—whoever agrees agrees, whoever disagrees disagrees—deeming this the only way to govern?
3. [Because they] institute democratic rule, which is, as Abu al-Ali al-Mawdudi described in his book *Islam and Modern Civilization*, "rule of the masses" and "the deification of man."
   "Democracy is partnership with Allah. The difference between democracy and monotheocracy [*tawhid*][3] is that monotheocracy makes Allah the sole Legislator while democracy is rule of the people for the good of the people. The legislator in democracies is the people, and the Legislator in monotheocracies is Allah, the Glorious and Most High. Thus,

democracy is partnership with Allah, for it divests the Almighty of the right to legislate and gives it to the people."

4. [Because they] legitimize what is forbidden and forbid what is legitimate.

The basis of this notion of theirs [Egyptian secular government] exists in the Egyptian Constitution in the sixty-sixth article[4] where it says: "No crime and no punishment except through the law"—in other words, anything that the Constitution and its subsequent laws do not stipulate as being criminal is not criminal. Even if tens of [Koranic] verses and hundreds of *hadiths* agree that a certain act is criminal, and yet the Constitution and laws do not deem it criminal, then said act becomes legitimate, thanks to the Constitution and law. Any citizen, then, under the Constitution and law, has the right to perform said act with impunity. Indeed, whoever tries to prevent him becomes the criminal in the sight of the Constitution and law, even if the *sharia* praises and recommends [his actions]. Instead, he becomes the one deserving of punishment.

Dr. Muhammad Naeem Yasin says in his *Book of Faith*, "He commits great blasphemy, whoever proclaims that he has the right to legislate that which Allah has not permitted due to its [effects on] authority and governance. He [in effect] proclaims that he has the right to permit that which is forbidden, and to forbid that which is permitted. From this, laws and regulations are established that permit adultery, usury, and the exploitation of vices, or that alter the established punishments which Allah has decreed in the Book of Allah and the *sunna* of his Messenger."

Here we quote excerpts from the writings of the *ulema* regarding this question:

1. Allah Most High said: "Is it *jahiliyya* [-style] laws that they wish to be governed by? Who is a better judge than Allah for men whose faith is firm?" [5:50]. In his exegesis over this verse, Ibn

Kathir said: "The Most High rejects those who, turning away from Allah's decrees, which encompass all good and forbid all evil, stray toward the opinions, whims, and traditions of men without support from the *sharia* of Allah—just as was the case with the people of *jahiliyya*, who ruled in darkness and ignorance through their vain imaginings and caprices. And just like the Tatars, who governed in accordance to the royal policies of their king, Genghis Khan, the codifier of their *yasiq*.[5] This [the *yasiq*] was essentially a book consisting of decrees derived from the diverse legislations of the Jews, Christians, Muslims, and others; and many were based merely on his own opinions and desires. This [the *yasiq*] went on to become supreme law among his descendants, superseding the Commandments of the Book of Allah and the *sunna* of his Messenger. . . . Thus, whosoever does this, the same is an infidel who needs to be fought till he submits to the Commandments of Allah and his Messenger, so that he reigns in evil for the shortest amount of time."

The most learned Muhammad Hamid al-Fiqi states: "In this manner, evil comes whenever someone implements laws borrowed from the Franks [i.e., Europeans] and governs according to them in [matters related to] blood, sex, and money, giving them precedence over what he has learned and has been made clear to him from the Book of Allah and the *sunna* of his Messenger. If such a one persists in this, and does not return to governing in accordance to what Allah has revealed, he is without any doubt an apostate infidel. No other name is suitable for him, regardless of all outward shows of prayer, fasting, pilgrimaging, and so forth."

2. The *fatwas* of Sheikh Ahmad Shakir in his book *Amdat al-Tafsir* (a commentary of Ibn Kathir) remark on the aforementioned words of Ibn Kathir: "Now, have you seen the powerful words of the learned Ibn Kathir—in the fourteenth century—regarding the conventional laws established by that enemy of Islam,

Genghis Khan? Do you see how he portrays the plight of
Muslims during that age, in the fourteenth century—but for
one difference [between now and then], which we pointed
out previously: This occurred only among one specific group
of rulers, which quickly and through the passage of time
assimilated into the Islamic *umma*, ceasing to have any
influence.[6] Today, however, Muslims are in a worse plight,
suffering even greater injustices. For the majority of Islamic
nations today are on the verge of adopting these laws that are at
variance with the *sharia* and that resemble the *yasiq*, which itself
was formulated by an infidel [Genghis Khan]—a man who
publicly reveled in his infidelity. Such also are the laws being
promulgated by people associated with Islam today. The sons of
the Muslims go on to learn them, and both fathers and sons take
pride in them, letting their rebellious wills embrace it—the
modern-day *yasiq*. . . .

   "The issue regarding these made-up laws is as clear as the
sun is bright: it is flagrant infidelity. There is nothing hidden or
ambiguous about it. There is no excuse for anyone adhering to
Islam—be he whom he may—to exercise [such laws], or to
relate to them or their decisions. So let each person be wary
of himself; for every man is responsible for his own self."

3.   The *fatwas* of the Sheikh of Islam, Ibn Taymiyya, where he says:
"It is well known and compulsory, based on Islam and the
consensus of Muslims, that whoever justifies adherence to
something other than Islam, or adherence to a law other than
the *sharia* of Muhammad, such a one is an infidel—like the
infidels who believe in some parts of the Book while
disbelieving others. As the Most High has said: 'Those who
reject Allah and His messengers, who seek to distinguish
between Allah and His messengers by saying we believe in some
[verses] and reject others, hoping thereby to find a middle
road—surely these are the infidels. We have prepared a shameful
doom for the infidels!' [4:150–151]."

4. Al-Shanqiti, according to his exegetical study regarding the verse "He [Allah] allows none to share in His governance" [18:26], writes: "What is to be understood from verses such as 'He allows none to share in His governance' is that rulers who legislate something other than what Allah has decreed make themselves the partners of Allah [one of the greatest sins]."

    And regarding the verse "Verily this Koran guides men to that which is most upright" [17:9], he says: "The verse, 'Verily this Koran guides men to that which is most upright,' is in regard to all who associate with legislations that contradict what was revealed by [our] leader, son of Adam, Muhammad bin Abdullah. Thus taking part in such contradictory [to Allah's *sharia*] legislation is clear blasphemy and a departure from the Muslim *umma*."

5. In former Saudi *mufti* Sheikh Muhammad bin Ibrahim's *fatwa* regarding the fixation of laws, which starts with the assertion: "One of the most obvious and severest of blasphemies is when the accursed [secular] law is established—though it was never revealed to the heart of Muhammad by the faithful spirit."

    He goes on to say, on page 10: "The fifth (that is, the fifth of the severest sorts of blasphemies that exclude one from the *umma*) is the greatest, most universal, and most apparent: resistance to the *sharia* and condescension to its commandments, a vexation to Allah and his Messenger. [Such resistance manifests itself in] a similar manner to the *sharia* courts: [resulting in] arrangements, jurisdictions, centers, subdivisions, formulations, decisions, requirements, and a constitution of codes [i.e., secular courts go on to take the exact role of *sharia* courts]. So just like the *sharia* court has references stretching in authority all the way back to the Book of Allah and the *sunna* of his Messenger, these courts have as a source of authority a concocted code made up of various legislations and many laws, stretching back to the French laws, the American laws, British laws, as well as various innovations, and so forth, from among the ideologies of both the heretics [i.e., innovators] and the followers of *sharia*, as well as others.

"Today these courts are all ready and prepared in the major capitals of Islam, with doors wide open. The people flock to them in droves. Its judges govern them with these laws that contradict the *sunna* and the Book. It makes them uphold, ratify, and impose [these laws] upon others. . . . Is there any greater infidelity than this?" So end the words of Muhammad bin Ibrahim; and it behooves every Muslim brother to read it in its entirety, for it is truly a gem.

6. Sayyid Qutb wrote in [his book] *In the Shade of the Koran*: "Sovereignty is the most exclusive prerogative of godhood. Therefore, whoever legislates to a people assumes a divine role among them and exercises its privileges. Men become his slaves, not the slaves of Allah; they accept his religion, not the religion of Allah. . . . This issue is extremely critical for the faith, for it is an issue concerning godhood and worship [i.e., the relationship between man and Allah], an issue concerning freedom and equality, an issue regarding the very liberation of man—nay, the very coming into being of man! And thus, due to all this, it is an issue of infidelity or faith, an issue of *jahiliyya* or Islam.

"Nor is *jahiliyya* merely a historical period, but rather it is a condition that comes into existence every time its prerequisites are established or organized. Its ultimate goal is to return justice and legislation back to the whims of the nations."

Thus, judgment upon this question is settled: he is an infidel, whoever does not rule in accordance to what Allah has revealed [i.e., the *sharia*].

So what are Muslims required to do in face of a ruler who has abandoned the Islamic faith? The learned Ibn Hajar, in his commentary on a *hadith* of the Prophet where he said: ". . . unless you see clear proofs that they have become infidels, then you have evidence from Allah (agreed upon [by the *hadith* compilers])," says: "The jurisprudents are agreed regarding the duty of obeying the triumphant sultan and waging *jihad* with him; for obeying him is better than evicting him. There is no exception to this unless the sultan clearly falls into [a state of] infidelity. In that case, it is forbidden to obey him—nay more! he is to have *jihad* waged *against* him by those who have the ability to do so. In the *hadith* narrated by al-Bukhari on the authority of Janada, the latter said: 'We came in to Abada bin al-Samat while he was ill and said, May Allah recover you, and may Allah serve you well by this discussion I heard from the Prophet. The Prophet called us to pledge our allegiance to him and to take an oath, that we will hear and obey, eagerly or reluctantly, in good times as well as bad times, and never to revolt against the will of his successors unless you see clear proofs that they have become infidels, then you have evidence from Allah [to overthrow them].' "

Ibn Hajar also said in his *Fath*: "And let the emir be exiled in all [his] infidelity. . . . It is incumbent upon every Muslim to revolt in this situation: whoever overcomes will be rewarded; whoever flatters or deceives, sins; whoever is incapable [of fighting] is obligated to emigrate that land."

Regarding the aforementioned *hadith* of Abada, al-Nawwawi comments in his *Kitab al-Imara*: "The judge Ayad said: 'All the *ulema* have agreed that the role of leader should never be filled by an infidel; and if all of a sudden he becomes an infidel he should be exiled. Likewise if he ceases to uphold prayer and the call to it [i.e., stops upholding the Pillars of Islam].'

"The judge Ayad also said: 'Now, if he suddenly becomes an infidel—by way of altering the *sharia* or [introducing] innovations—he forfeits all authority and obedience. Instead, it becomes the duty of the Muslims to rise up against him, overthrow him, and place in his stead a just leader, if they are so able. . . . Even if this only occurs among a small group, still they are obligated to rise up and overthrow the infidel.' "

And we have already mentioned the words of Ibn Kathir when he described the condition of the Tatars in his exegesis over verse 5:50, that all who do this are infidels who need to be deposed.

[The final paragraph deals with historic events regarding the Muslim Brotherhood and how they have completely abandoned their above-delineated obligation to overthrow through *jihad* "apostate" regimes.]

PART TWO: THAT DEMOCRACY CONTRADICTS ISLAM

Know that democracy, that is, "rule of the people," is a new religion that deifies the masses by giving them the right to legislate without being shackled down to any other authority. For sovereignty, as has been shown earlier, is [the equivalent of] absolute authority; nothing supersedes it. Regarding this, Abu al-Ali al-Mawdudi said: "Democracy is the deification of man . . . and rule of the masses." In other words, democracy is a man-made infidel religion, devised to give the right to legislate to the masses—as opposed to Islam, where all legislative rights belong to Allah Most High: He has no partners. In democracies, however, those legislators [elected] from the masses become partners worshipped in place of Allah. Whoever obeys their laws [ultimately] worships them. The Most High said: "What! have they partners [of Allah], who have established for them some religion without the permission of Allah?" [42:21]. "Religion" as used here means the regularization and ordering of people's lives—whether these accord with truth or falsehood, as shown by the Word of the Most High: "You have your religion and I have mine" [109:6]. Thus the infidelities that the infidels practice, the Most High has called "religion"[7]; and so it is that those people who legislate for the masses in democracies are partners worshipped instead of Allah. These are the "lords" mentioned in the verse: "Do not take each other for lords in place of Allah" [3:64]. So what greater blasphemy and infidelity is there? Udi bin Hatim, a former Christian who submitted [i.e., converted to Islam], said: "I came to the Messenger of Allah while he was reciting Surat Bira [the ninth chapter of the Koran] till he arrived at the verse: 'They [Christians and Jews] take their priests and monks for lords beside Allah' [9:31]. So I said, O Messenger of Allah, we do not take them for lords. 'Indeed!' said he. 'Do they not allow for you that which is forbidden you, and you permit it, and forbid that which is allowed you, and you forbid it?' I said yes. He said, 'Such, then, is their worship' " (narrated by Ahmad and al-Tirmidhi and considered a strong *hadith*). In his commentary on this passage, al-Alusi said: "The majority of exegetes have interpreted this as meaning that the main issue at hand regarding these 'lords' is not that they [the people] believed them to be universal gods, but rather that they obeyed their commands and prohibitions [thereby treating them as gods]."

Here we relay, in abridged form, the words of Sayyid Qutb regarding the Word of the Most High: "Let not some take others for lords in place of Allah" [3:64]. He said: "This universe, in its entirety, shall never maintain order nor possess a sound countenance, unless it has but one god to order it: 'If there were, in the heavens and the earth, other gods besides Allah, there would have been chaos in both!' [21:22]. The prerogatives of godhood in respect to mankind are: to be obeyed by the slaves [mankind]; to give them laws to govern their lives; and to balance their lives. Whoever, then, claims any one of these for himself [also] claims the most exclusive rights of godhood for himself. He sets himself up as a god among the people, in place of Allah. No worse corruption befalls the earth as when gods multiply in this manner—when slaves become enslaved to other slaves; when one of the slaves claims he personally has the right to be obeyed by the slaves; that he personally possesses the right to legislate for them; that likewise he personally has the right to establish values and standards. This is a call for godhood, no less than was spoken by Pharaoh: 'I am your lord most high' [79:24].

"The bottom line is that this is either partnership with Allah or infidelity against Him. . . . This makes for the most obscene form of corruption on earth. Allah Most High said: 'Say, O People of the Book [Jews and Christians]! let us come to an agreement: that we shall worship none but Allah—associating nothing with Him. Let not some take others for lords beside Allah.' But if they resist, then say: 'Bear witness that we are Muslims' [3:64]. This is a call to worship Allah alone; to associate absolutely nothing with Him—neither man nor stone [idols]. It is a call to not take each other as lords in Allah's place—neither prophets [e.g., Jesus] nor apostles. They are all slaves of Allah. He chose them to spread His Message—not to join him in divinity and lordship: 'But if they resist, then say: Bear witness that we are Muslims' [3:64]. This encounter is between Muslims and those who take each other as masters instead of Allah alone [i.e., infidels]. This is what distinguishes them [Muslims] from the rest of the religious communities and denominations; this is what differentiates their way of life from that of the rest of mankind. Now, if this particularity [being governed by Allah alone] is realized, then they are Muslims; if not, then they are not Muslims—no matter how much they claim to be. Indeed, throughout the world and in most governments, people take each other for lords and masters in place of Allah. . . . This occurs in both the most progressive democracies and the basest of dictatorships. But the very first prerogative of godhood is the right to be obeyed by the people: the right to establish order, guidelines, laws, regulations—the right to establish values and standards, to say what is good and what is evil. . . . Yet, in various ways, this right is usurped by a group of people in every government around the world; and power is delivered them through one of many systems [e.g., democracies, dictatorships, etc.]. This group of people then subjects the rest to its laws, its distinctions between right and wrong, [in short] its vain imaginings. These, then, are the masters of the world, which the people take for lords in place of Allah, allowing them to the claim of godhood and lordship. And so in this manner they ultimately worship them instead of Allah—even if they do not prostrate and kneel [before them]. For obedience is a form of worship that should be rendered only to Allah. In this manner, then, Islam [i.e., submission to Allah and His *sharia*] is *the* religion before Allah. It is what every messenger sent from Allah delivered. Indeed, Allah sent these messengers with this religion in order that people would cease being enslaved to slaves and become enslaved to Allah alone—from oppressive servitude to the justice of Allah. . . . Whoever does not embrace this is no Muslim, by Allah's witness, no matter what they say or whom they mislead."

So, as you can see, my brother, the foundation of democracy is built atop the premise "rule by the people for the people" and rejection of the Commandments of Allah, which are all-comprehensive for mankind. Its [democracy's] essence revolves around the whims and fancies of man, which are articulated in a number of ways, and which become the ruling godhead. It rebels against and prevents the *sharia* of Allah from becoming established law. The Most High said: "And now We have set you [Muhammad] on a straight road [*sharia*]. So follow it, and do not follow the whims of those who are ignorant" [45:18].

In what follows, we summarize the many faces of blasphemy inherent to democracies:

1. Democracies grant the rights of legislation to the masses, as found in the eighty-sixth article of the Egyptian Constitution: "The People's Council holds the authority to legislate"[8]—and this, when legislation is an exclusive right of Allah Most High! "Judgment belongs only to Allah" [12:40]. Thus, democracies raise up gods, establish masters, and assign partners to Allah Most High: "What! have they partners [to Allah], who have established for them some [other] religion without the permission of Allah?" [42:21].

    And the Most High said: "They [Christians and Jews] take their priests and monks for lords beside Allah" [9:31].

2. The bottom line regarding democracies is that the right to make laws is given to someone other than Allah Most High. Such, then, is democracy. So whoever is agreed to this is an infidel—for he has taken gods in place of Allah. Legislation is an exclusive right of the Most High. Whoever legislates anything

for mankind erects himself up as a god among them. Whoever permits him to do this takes him for a god. "They take their priests and monks for lords beside Allah" [9:31].

Whoever agrees [to give] the rights of legislation to anyone else, instead of Allah, makes him Allah's equal in regard to the sovereignty of law-giving. And whoever makes another equal to Allah by giving him the sovereign rights of legislation—by making him *equal* to Allah—this one is surely an infidel, as shown by the Word of the Most High: "Infidels are they who set up equals with their Lord" [6:1].

3. If a democracy is built upon the premise that the nation holds authority, and if authority is the highest form of power, then it becomes the deciding factor for all matters. All controversies and differences must be settled at its feet. Now, then, everyone agreeing to this is an infidel—for the settling of disputes and differences is an exclusive right of Allah Most High, as found in the judgments revealed in the Book and *sunna*. And whoever contradicts this and decides to grant this right to someone or -thing other than Allah Most High—that is, agrees to the authority of the "nation"—this one is an infidel for he rejects the Word of Allah Most High: "Whatever the subject of your disputes, the final decision rests in Allah" [42:10]. For authority—that is, the highest form of command—in Islam belongs to the *sharia*, not to the nation and not to the people. Whoever disagrees with this—he is an infidel, one who makes the verses of Allah lie. Allah Most High said: "None, save for the infidels, deny Our Revelations" [29:47].

4. If democracy is built upon the premise of the nation's authority, and if authority is the highest form of power, it then follows that the power of the nation supersedes the power of Allah Most High. The power of the nation is built atop that which Allah Most High has not decreed, and thus upon contradiction. In the same way, the *sharia* of Allah Most High cannot be ratified unless the nation agrees to it: in other words, the word of the

Nation is above the Word of Allah Most High. Allah Most High said: "It is not fitting for true believers—men or women—to take their choice in affairs if Allah and His Messenger have decreed otherwise. He that disobeys Allah and His Messenger strays far indeed!" [33:36].

5. As for the principle of equality regarding rights and duties among the citizens of democracies, this makes for a number of situations—all of them blasphemous.[9] We have indicated these before, and among them are:

A. No limit to apostasy [which, under *sharia* law, earns the death penalty], since the Constitution declares freedom of religion; likewise abolition of *jihad* against the apostates.

B. Abolition of *jihad* in the way of Allah—that is, [Offensive] *Jihad* against infidelity and blasphemy—since the Constitution has established freedom of religion.

C. Abolition of the *jizya* and the *dhimmi* conditions[10] applied to those who are not Muslim—since there is no difference between citizens, due to the fissure created by the premise of equality, rights, and obligations.

D. Abolition of man's dominion over woman. The Most High said: "Men have authority over women, for Allah has made the one superior to the other" [4:34]. But in a democracy, women have the right to emulate the dignity and legal status of men. Such are the fruits of "equality"—the essence of democracy: for man's domination over woman contradicts the concept of equality. Like we said, the principles of democracy confront the commands of the *sharia* in direct opposition.

But, to the point—

Islam is so much richer than all these blasphemous principles. The Most High said: "This day I have perfected your religion [i.e., way of life] for you" [5:3]. So whoever once doubts the perfection of Islam, renouncing it in favor of one of the [governmental] systems of the infidels, such a one is an infidel, rendering false all the previous [Koranic] verses mentioned. Allah Most High said: "None, save for the infidels, deny Our Revelations" [29:47]. Islam ennobles and is not ennobled; it does not accept mixing with other [ideologies]. The Most High said: "Say, 'O you infidels! you have your religion and I have mine' " [109:6]—in other words, a complete separation and total disavowal [of their systems]. The Most High said: "Verily, it is We Who have revealed the Book to you in Truth: so serve Allah, offering Him sincere devotion. Is it not to Allah that sincere devotion is due? But those who choose friends and allies besides Allah [say], 'We worship them only that they may bring us nearer to Allah.' Truly Allah will judge between them in that which they differ. But Allah guides not such as are false and ungrateful" [39:2–3].

Such, then, is democracy, and the infidelities and blasphemies born of it. And the members of the people's council, my brother, are the lords [taken] in place of Allah. This is enough to prohibit voting [someone into] a representative, democratic council, as well as prohibit [one] from participating in elections in this council. And whoever participates while fully aware of the truth of democracy is an apostate infidel, an outcast from the Islamic *umma*.

And if their constitutions stipulate that the state is a democracy while the official religion is Islam,[11] this does not change one thing from their infidelity. This is like one who says "I witness that Allah is no god, and Muhammad is the Messenger of Allah, and Musailima is the Messenger of Allah."[12] Can anyone once doubt the blasphemy of this?! So anyone who calls for Islam while presenting [a system of] infidelity, such as democracy or socialism, is an apostate infidel. Allah Most High said: "And most of them believe not in Allah except by associating [others as partners] with Him!" [12:106]. Thus whoever claims to be a "democratic-Muslim" or a Muslim who calls for democracy, is like one who says about himself "I am a Jewish Muslim" or "I am a Christian Muslim"—the one worse than the other. He is an apostate infidel.

4

It is unclear when the following treatise was written, though the atypical lack of reference to the attacks of 9/11 would indicate that it was produced prior to that date. It is also unclear who physically wrote it, though it clearly states that it was overseen by Ayman al-Zawahiri and thus can be treated as his own.

After demonstrating the importance of *jihad*, as per Muhammad's assertion—"If you take up a domestic life, hold on to the tails of cattle, are content with farming, and thus abandon *jihad*, Allah will let humiliation lord over you until you return to your religion"—this treatise revolves around two highly controversial questions, both of which are related to *jihad*: (1) Is it legitimate for a Muslim to kill himself for the sake of Islam? and (2) Is it legitimate to bombard the infidels if Muslims, women and children, or *dhimmis* are intermingled with them? Al-Qaeda's answer to both questions is yes (as was evinced on 9/11). But unlike *jihad*, which is easily demonstrated in the Koran as well as Islamic history, "martyrdom operations"—commonly known in the West as "suicide bombings"—are not, and need to be somewhat rationalized and analogized from the Muslim texts.

At the outset, Zawahiri initiates this by quoting the Muslim Prophet's famous statement, "War is deceit." Based on this assertion, martyrdom operations, which due to their surreptitious nature are deceitful, become legitimate in the context of warfare.

Zawahiri goes on to ground his argument that martyrdom operations are legal in the lengthy "boy and king" *hadith* (reproduced here in full).[1] It is significant, however, that a *hadith*—as opposed to a Koranic injunction—is used as the primary justification for martyrdom

operations (ideally, Koranic verses form the foundation of an argument while *hadiths* serve to exemplify). Even the grand point of the
hadith—that the youth revealed to the tyrant king how to kill him in
order to magnify the religion—is still not the same as killing oneself:
it was still the king's will and action, not the youth's, that took the life
of the latter. In other words, Zawahiri is somewhat stretching it in his
quest to find theological backing for suicide bombings.

Thereafter the bulk of the argument consists of other anecdotes
from the *hadith* and Islamic history supporting the thesis that martyrdom operations are not only legitimate but laudable acts of worship warranting the highest paradisical rewards.

But again, the same problem inherent to the "boy and king" *hadith* is encountered: all the *hadiths* depict *mujahidin* who place themselves in "suicidal" situations (the usual scenario is an overzealous or
Paradise-seeking *mujahid* recklessly hurling himself into the center of
the enemy's ranks); they are not depicted, however, as *willing* themselves to die, nor are they the very instruments of their own deaths. In
other words, despite all odds, there is always a slim chance that the
warrior will survive in the *hadiths*—whereas one who hijacks and
drives a plane into a building is sure to die, thus willfully killing
himself.

Zawahiri attempts to get by this troublesome technicality by re-
sorting to analogy (*qiyas*), which is a legitimate tool of Islamic jurisprudence. (See p. 8 for a discussion of *qiyas*.) By admitting that suicide is a
great sin while simultaneously maintaining that fighting to death in the
path of Allah is the most worthy endeavor, Zawahiri suggests that the
dividing line is *intention*: whether one literally kills himself (such as in
a suicide bombing) or is killed by another (such as in the *hadiths*) is ir-
relevant. *Why* he wills his own death is all-important. Here the end
clearly justifies the means: "Thus the deciding factor in all these situations is one and the same: the intention—is it to service Islam [martyr-
dom] or is it out of depression and despair [suicide]?"

There is also an anachronistic element at work here that sides
with Zawahiri's view. Considering that there was no technology in the
guise of explosives in the early years of Islam, there were few ways—if

any—for *mujahidin* to inflict damage to the enemy by causing their own deaths. Thus even if suicide bombings are legitimate, there is no way to find a precedent for them in the traditional texts of Islam.

Although there are countless *hadiths* demonstrating the legitimacy of fighting to certain death, Zawahiri shrewdly selects those that most strike a chord in Muslim readers due to current circumstances. For instance, the first *hadith* he notes after the "boy and king" has to do with a "poverty-stricken and haggard-looking" man who gladly fights to the death in order to gain Paradise. It would seem that this particular *hadith* was included with the express purpose of motivating the many poor and dispossessed Muslims around the world to martyrdom. Also, there are certain *hadiths* (found also in Loyalty and Enmity) that depict Muslims who, in order to make up for their less-than-ideal Muslim lifestyles, atone by fighting to the death. These *hadiths* are probably directed to those many Muslims who, from being indifferent in regard to their faith, have developed a renewed piety.

Before going on to the second question, Zawahiri adds a few more circumstances in which it is permissible for a believer to kill himself, despite the Koranic ban—"Do not destroy yourselves"[4:26]—including killing oneself in order to escape being made captive to the infidels, expose crucial secrets of the Muslims under pain of torture, or accept death rather than renouncing the faith. Again, in all these circumstances, the deciding factor is the potential martyr's intentions: Are they destroying themselves in order to aid the faith (martyrdom), or is it for some personal reason, such as fear or despair (suicide)?

As to the legality of bombarding infidels when those whose blood is forbidden from being shed—Muslims, women, children, and *dhimmis*—are among them, Zawahiri delineates the three different legal views (i.e., *madhhabs*). Two of these views legitimize bombarding, while the third prohibits if the Muslim is there against his will, used as a human shield.

Furthermore, Zawahiri stresses an authentic *hadith* from Bukhari that contradicts the ban on bombarding infidels if they have women and children among them and that was carried out at the hands of the Muslim Prophet himself: when Muhammad was laying siege to the

town of Ta'if, he used catapults, which clearly did not differentiate between women and children on the one hand and fighting male infidels on the other. When Muhammad was asked about this
discrepancy, he replied: "They [women and children] are from among
them [infidels]."

Zawahiri, in agreement with the middle view of the three different perspectives, concludes that it is permissible to bombard infidels
even if those whose blood is guarded are among them, as long as there
is a need or an obligation for Muslims to do so, or if holding off
causes the *jihad* to be delayed. (The other two views offer extremes:
one maintains that it is impermissible to bombard, while the other asserts that it is permissible—even if there is no pressing need or obligation to attack.)

Zawahiri goes on to state that the blood of those Muslims who
are intermingled with the infidels of their own free will is surely not
as sacred as the blood of Muslims who are held captive (which was the
usual scenario in the early days of Islam, when the various schools
were being formed).

Finally, Zawahiri points out that all of the *hadithic* references and
the history of the early Companions have to do with Offensive
Jihad—that is, when the Muslims, unprovoked, launched campaigns
into infidel territory with the express purpose of enforcing Islamic
rule. Zawahiri insists that it is in this context that women, children,
Muslims, and *dhimmis* are nominally exempt. However, in a Defensive *Jihad*, which al-Qaeda time and time again claim to be waging
and where Islam itself is perceived to be under attack, all these stipu-
lations fade away in the background of Muslims fighting any way they
can for their very existence.

The following is an abridged version of the original, which in the
Arabic is nearly thirty thousand words and includes a part 3 (not re-
produced here) dedicated to demonstrating the need to battle those
Muslim regimes that do not rule in accordance with the *sharia*, a
common theme of Zawahiri's, well delineated in both "Loyalty and
Enmity" and "*Sharia* and Democracy."

"*JIHAD*, MARTYRDOM, AND THE KILLING OF INNOCENTS"[2]

PREPARED FOR THE COUNCIL OF THE *JIHAD* ORGANIZATION
UNDER THE SUPERVISION OF DR. AYMAN AL-ZAWAHIRI

In the name of Allah, the Compassionate, the Merciful

Allah Most High said: "O you who have believed! Fear Allah as He should be feared, and die not except as Muslims" [3:102].

And the Most High said: "O you who have believed! Fear Allah and speak accurately, so that He may fix your affairs and forgive your sins; and whoever obeys Allah and His Messenger indeed achieves a mighty victory" [33:70–71].

Allah Most High has imposed *jihad* on His behalf upon His believing slaves. The Most High said: "Fight in the path of Allah those who fight you, but do not transgress, for Allah loves not the transgressors" [2:190].

And the Most High said: "Then, when the sacred months have passed, slay the idolaters wherever you find them—seize them, besiege them, and make ready to ambush them!" [9:5].

And the Most High said: "[A]nd fight the Pagans all together as they fight you all together" [9:36]. And the Most

High said: "[M]ake war on the leaders of infidelity—for no oaths are binding with them—until they give in" [9:12].

The Prophet has shown that war is deceit between the believers and their foes. He said: "War [is] deceit." Structurally, the subject of the clause is "war," the predicate, "deceit"—in other words, the essence of warfare, and its most important cornerstone, is deceit. Just like his saying: "Pilgrimage [is at] Arafat"—that is, the most important thing in pilgrimaging is attaining Arafat, despite the fact that there are other pillars in the pilgrimage. Moreover, these are like his saying: "The religion [is] advice."

Deception in warfare requires that the *mujahid* bide his time and wait for an opportunity against his enemy, while avoiding confrontation at all possible costs. For triumph, in almost every case, is [achieved] through deception: triumph achieved through confrontation possesses many dangers. Nonetheless, this deception needs to be gauged by the *sharia*'s prescriptions—for all advantages not regulated through *sharia* law are unworthy. Therefore, engaging in that which is forbidden as a pretext for deception is inexcusable. To that end, al-Nawwawi said in his commentary regarding this *hadith*: "The *ulema* are agreed that deception against the infidels in war is legal, unless it reneges an existing pact or treaty in which case it is unacceptable." And Ibn Hajar al-Asqalani said: "Revealing one thing while secretly planning another is the essence of deception; moreover, the *hadith* incites [Muslims] to take great caution in war, while [publicly] lamenting and mourning in order to dupe the infidels. Whoever does not do so has no guarantee that he himself is not being deceived [by the enemy]."

Ibn al-Arabi said: "Deception in warfare has to do with [issuing] obvious hints while working in stealth, and things of this nature. And in the *hadith*, practicing deceit in war is well demonstrated. Indeed, its need is more stressed than [the need for] courage. Likewise, the summary of this *hadith* comes to a point—in the same manner as when he said: 'Pilgrimage [is at] Arafat.' " Ibn al-Munir said: "War means deceit: in other words, the most complete and perfect war waged by a combatant is a war of deception, not confrontation, due to the latter's inherent danger, and the fact that one can attain victory through treachery without harm [to oneself]."

In this message we demonstrate, Allah Most High willing, the legality of one of the methods of deception against the enemy—that is, martyrdom operations. Many disputes have revolved around its legitimacy, both from the people of Islam themselves and from their foes. We will discuss the legality of martyrdom operations in the following sections:

Introduction: Regarding the duty of *jihad* and the superiority
of martyrdom
Part one: The *sharia*'s perspective on martyrdom operations
Part two: The permissibility of bombarding infidels when
Muslims and others who are not permitted to be killed are
dispersed among them

INTRODUCTION: REGARDING THE DUTY OF *JIHAD*
AND THE SUPERIORITY OF MARTYRDOM

Allah, the Blessed and Most High, said: "Allah has bought from the believers their lives and worldly goods, and in return has promised them Paradise: they shall fight in the way of Allah and shall slay and be slain. It is a promise binding on Him in the Torah and the Gospel and the Koran. And who is more true to his pledge than Allah? Rejoice then in the bargain you have struck, for that is the supreme triumph" [9:111].

Al-Muqadam bin Ma'ad Yakrub relays that the Prophet of Allah said: "The martyr is special to Allah. He is forgiven from the first drop of blood [that he sheds]. He sees his throne in Paradise, where he will be adorned in ornaments of faith. He will wed the Aynhour [wide-eyed virgins] and will not know the torments of the grave and safeguards against the greater terror [hell]. Fixed atop his head will be a crown of honor, a ruby that is greater than the world and all it contains. And he will couple with seventy-two Aynhour and be able to offer intercessions for seventy of his relatives."

Now, if martyrdom and martyrs are revealed in such a glorious manner, demanding martyrdom and desiring death in the path of Allah becomes legitimate, as was spoken by Abdallah bin Jahsh: "O Allah! Find me among the idolaters a mighty and furious man, full of blasphemy and unbelief, that I may fight him for your sake. Then he will overcome me, plunder me, and chop off my ears and nose. And when I meet You [Allah], You will say: 'O Abdallah bin Jahsh, why were you mutilated?' And I shall respond: 'For you, my Lord!' "

Likewise, in Bukhari's authenticated book regarding the call to *jihad* and martyrdom for men and women, Omar declared: "O Allah! Grant me martyrdom in the land of Your Prophet."

Moreover, Allah Most High has obligated believers to battle all those who reject Him, the Exalted, until all chaos ceases and all religion belongs to Allah. The Most High said: "Fight them until there is no more chaos and [all] religion belongs to Allah" [8:39].

And among those needing to be fought at this day and age are those rulers who govern the people without the *sharia*—they who fight against the people of Islam, who befriend the infidels from among the Jews, Christians, and others. And Ibn Kathir has transmitted the consensus that it is an obligation to battle such rulers.[3]

These rulers and their helpers are the leaders of infidelity, whom Allah Most High spoke of: "[T]hen fight the leaders of infidelity—surely their oaths are nothing—so that they may desist" [9:12].

All *ulema* are agreed that leadership should never fall into the hands of an infidel, or if infidelity should suddenly descend upon him, and he becomes an outcast not ruling in accordance to the *sharia* of Allah, his authority diminishes and it becomes a duty for Muslims to revolt against him and eject him.

When Muslims used to undertake *jihad* in the path of Allah, they were the mightiest of people. But when they abandoned it, Allah humiliated them through division and conquest, just like the Prophet told: "If you take up a domestic life, hold on to the tails of cattle, are content with farming, and thus abandon *jihad*, Allah will let humiliation lord over you until you return to your religion."

Thus the Prophet made abandonment of *jihad* in the way of Allah as the cause for humiliation and disgrace, while making glory—all glory!—incumbent upon a return to *jihad* in the way of Allah Most High, which he regarded as a "return to religion."

Al-Qurtubi said in his commentary regarding the Word of the Most High: "Warfare is ordained for you, though it is hateful unto you" [2:216]. He said: "Abu Abida said: 'You may hate what hardships you encounter in *jihad*, though it benefits you by way of total victory with an acquisition of booty as recompense. But he who dies, dies as a martyr. But perhaps you love being slothful and abandoning warfare? [Know that] this is an evil for you, as you will then be defeated and humiliated, and your authority will pass away.' This is an indisputable truth, as witnessed in Andalusia [modern-day Spain]: they [Muslims] forsook the *jihad* and shrunk away from battle, and a good number of them took to their heels. The result was that the enemy [Christian Spaniards] took over the lands—and what lands!"[4]

All the above demonstrates the greatness of martyrdom and the obligation to fight the imams of infidelity and their aides. Thus, abandoning *jihad* and becoming caught up with [the desires of] this world lead to humiliation and the loss of property, honor, and land, whereas loving martyrdom and engaging in battle lead to glory and strength.

The Prophet showed that the greatest of the believers are those who went out [to battle] with their selves and their possessions only to return empty-handed. As was relayed by Ahmad and others from their chains of authority, Abu Hurreira said that the Prophet said: "Shall I tell you who is the best among the people? A man who takes hold of his horse's reins and plunges headlong in the path of Allah." Another *hadith*, transmitted by Ibn Abbas, says: "The Messenger of Allah when he was haranguing the people of Tabuk, said: 'No one among all the people is like the horseman who plunges headlong in battle on behalf of Allah.'"

The best of people, then, are those who are prepared for *jihad* in the path of Allah Most High, requesting martyrdom at any time or place. Whenever he hears the call to *jihad* he flies to it until Allah's authority is established. By way of Abu Hurreira, the Prophet said: "In order that the people have a livelihood, it is best that they have a man who holds on to the reins of his horse, battling in the way of Allah. He flies upon [his horse's] back every time he hears the call or alarm, wishing for death or expecting to be slain."

Thus, whoever sacrifices himself on behalf of Allah Most High, submitting himself to the path of Allah, is the best of persons, by witness of the truest of all creation [Muhammad].

PART ONE: THE *SHARIA*'S PERSPECTIVE ON MARTYRDOM OPERATIONS

1. PERMISSION TO DESTROY ONESELF IN ORDER TO ENNOBLE AND EMPOWER THE RELIGION

Allah Most High said: "Woe to the makers of the pit [of fire]—fire supplied abundantly with fuel: Behold! they sat over against the fire and witnessed [all] that they were doing against the believers. And they ill-treated them for no other reason than that they believed in Allah, exalted in power, worthy of all praise!" [85:4–8]. Moreover, Muslim narrated in his authentic [account] that Suhaib reported that Allah's Messenger said: "There lived a king before your time who had a sorcerer. As he [the sorcerer] grew older, he said to the king: I have grown old, send me some young boy so that I may teach him magic. He [the king] sent to him a young man to be trained by him [in magic]. And on his way he [the young boy] happened upon a monk sitting there. So he sat there and listened to his talk and was impressed by it. Now, it came to pass that whenever he was going to the sorcerer, he would pass by the monk and sit there [listening], and [later] when he would reach the sorcerer, he would be beaten because of the delay. He made a complaint of this to the monk [so the latter] said: When you feel afraid of the sorcerer, say: Members of my family have detained me. And when you feel afraid of your family, say: The sorcerer has detained me. This continued until [one day] he came upon a huge beast that trapped the people. So he said: Today I will know who is greater—the sorcerer or the monk. He picked up a stone and said: O Allah, if the work of the monk is dearer to You than the work of the sorcerer, cause death to befall this animal so that the people may move about freely. He hurled it and killed it, and the people moved [about freely]. He then went to the monk and informed him, and the monk said: My son, today you are my superior. Your work has come to a stage where I find that you will soon be put to trial. If you are, do not expose me. The youth began to treat the blind and those suffering from leprosy and he in fact began to cure people from [all kinds of] diseases. Now a companion of the king who had lost his sight heard about him and came to him with numerous gifts saying: If you heal me all this amassed [treasure] will be yours. He said: I myself cure no one; it is Allah who heals. If you have faith in Allah, I shall call to Allah to heal you.

"So he believed in Allah and Allah cured him, and he [the companion] went to the king and sat by his side, as was his custom. The king said to him: Who restored your eyesight? He said: My Lord. The king said: Have you a[nother] lord beside me? He said: My Lord and your Lord is Allah. So he seized him and tormented him until he revealed the boy. The young man was summoned and the king said to him: Boy! it has been relayed to me that you have become much proficient in your magic, that you cure the blind and those suffering from leprosy and this and that. He responded: I do not cure anyone; it is Allah who cures. So he [the king] took hold of him and began torturing him until he exposed the monk. The monk was thus summoned and it was said to him: Renounce your religion. He refused. The king ordered for a saw to be brought and he [the king] placed it on the center of the monk's head and sawed it until it split in two. Then the king's companion [whose sight was restored] was brought and it was said to him: Renounce your religion. He refused. Then the saw was placed on the center of his head and it was sawed in two. Then the youth was brought and it was said to him: Renounce your religion. He refused. So he was handed over to a group of [the king's] friends and he [the king] said to them: Take him to so-and-so mountain and ascend it. By the time you get to the summit, if he still refuses to renounce his religion, hurl him down. So they took him and made him climb up the mountain and he said: O Allah, save me from them, as You will! The mountain shook with them and they all fell down. He went [back] walking to the king. The king said to him: What has happened to your companions? He said: Allah has saved me from them. So he [the king] delivered him to a[nother] group of friends and said: Take him and carry him in a small boat, and by the time you reach the middle of the sea, if he still refuses to renounce his religion, cast him in [to the water].

"So they took him and he said: O Allah, save me from them and their intentions. The boat capsized and they were all drowned. He came back on foot to the king, and the king said to him: What has become of your companions? He said: Allah has saved me from them. He said to the king: You will never kill me until you do what I tell you to do. The king said: And what's that? He said: Gather the people into an open field and crucify me on a tree. Then take hold of an arrow from my quiver, string it to the bow, and say: In the name of Allah, Lord of the youth; then fire the arrow. If you do this, you will be able to slay me. So he [the king] called the people in an open field and crucified him to a tree. Then he took hold of an arrow from his quiver, placed the arrow in the bow, and said: In the name of Allah, the Lord of the youth. Then he shot the arrow and it struck his temple. He [the boy] placed his hands upon the temple where the arrow had hit him and died. The people said: We believe in the Lord of the youth, we believe in the Lord of the youth, we believe in the Lord of the youth! Then the king's companions came to him and it was said to him: Do you see that Allah has actually done what you aimed at averting: For

now the people have affirmed their faith in the Lord. So he commanded ditches to be dug at important points in the path. When
these ditches were dug, and the fire was lit in them, it was declared:
Whoever does not renounce his religion will either be thrown into the
fire or commanded to jump. So they did so until a woman came [to
the edge of the pit] with her child, and she hesitated jumping into the
fire. So the youth said to her: O mother, endure [this ordeal] for you
are in the right." *I bet that's what he said.*

There Are a Number of Things to Be Learned from This Hadith:

1. The youth killed himself through his [own] will and choice,
   after the king failed to kill him twice. The youth showed the
   king the way to kill him.

2. This death came by way of empowering the call [to Islam] and
   placing people in the religion of Allah Supreme. Thus this death
   was a victory for the call [to Islam]. It is a legal objective, praised
   for the sake of uplifting the faith. Moreover, it allows for an
   array of disasters to afflict the ranks of the enemy in war.

3. This event [relayed in the *hadith*] is mentioned in the Koran as a
   laudable and stable road for the believers. Also mentioned is
   how the believers chose death over infidelity [i.e., 85:4–8]. And
   several commentators, such as al-Qurtubi, have pointed out that
   this *hadith* was relayed by the Prophet in order to remind people
   of the difficulties they will encounter, and [that they should]
   strive to be like the youth in his patience and firmness, debasing
   himself for the sake of the religion and the placement of people
   in it. Likewise with the monk and the people who, though
   threatened with death and torture, held fast to their faith and
   died—the former sawn, the latter hurling themselves into the
   fire. Thus the youth's command to the king can never be
   [deemed] evil or suicidal.

4. The believers who had faith in the Lord of the youth chose
   death over infidelity, thereby magnifying the faith. Jumping into
   the fire of their own accord can never be [deemed] evil or

suicidal. On the contrary, such a deed Allah loves and extols, associating it with many blessings.

5. Due to this *hadith*'s powerful commentary regarding the question of whether it is permissible for a believer to destroy himself for the good of the religion, many *ulema* have relied upon it, such as the Sheikh of Islam, Ibn Taymiyya, and Muhammad bin Ibrahim.

6. The way to spread Islam and emulate the messengers [of Allah] is through patience against adversity, firmness in the truth, and boldness with the truth in the face of kings, tyrants, and oppressors—even if this leads to death. This is the way of the believers, when they are in a weakened position.

Whenever they are able, however, believers are to enjoin good and forbid evil—which, by nature, is [waging Offensive] *Jihad* in the path of Allah and spreading the call to [conversion to the religion of] the Most High: "Those whom we have given mastery over the earth uphold prayers, render alms, enjoin good, and forbid evil; Allah controls the destiny of all things" [22:41].

Today, however, the world is given over to the tyrants, thanks to the *fatwas* that command people to abandon *jihad*. And if the followers of the prophets [Muslims] oppose the false gods and disavow them publicly and work to depose them, the fake imams rise up against them and urge the tyrants to kill them. But never once do they themselves make mention of *jihad*. Through this it should become clear to you that the true followers of the messengers [seek to] make the religion triumphant through the [use of the] Book and iron, as was spoken by the Most High: "We have sent our messengers with clear signs and sent down with them the Book and the scales of justice, that men might conduct themselves with equity; and We sent down iron, in which is [material for] mighty war, as well as many benefits for mankind, that Allah may test who it is that will help, unseen, Him and His messengers: For Allah is full of strength, exalted in might" [57:25].

Therefore, if believers are weak, they are to wage *jihad* with their hearts and tongues; if they are able, they are to enjoin what is good and forbid what is evil, fight the infidels, and spread the call of *tawhid*. This is how to differentiate between the followers of the messengers of *tawhid* and the hypocrite imams, who sell the verses of Allah for a paltry sum in service to the apostates and enemies of Islam. Allah Most High said: "When Allah made a covenant with those to whom the Scriptures were given [Jews and Christians], He said, 'Proclaim these to mankind and suppress them not.' But they flung the Scriptures behind their backs and purchased with it some miserable gain. Evil was their bargain" [3:187].

The learned Ibn Kathir's following narrative about the battle for Akka strengthens and demonstrates well the meaning of destroying one's self in order to empower the religion:

"[In 1191] the Franks [Crusaders]—may Allah curse them!—led by the English king [Richard the Lionhearted], who had amassed and led a huge and mighty army, the likes of which was never seen before, besieged the city of Akka from all sides. They set up seven catapults and ceaselessly bombarded the city day and night. The city was devastated and many were slain. One day the English king encountered a massive ship coming from Beirut laden with weapons and provisions for the Muslims. So he sent out forty warships to seize the Muslim ship and its provisions. Aboard the latter were six hundred brave and heroic [Muslim] warriors, who upon realizing that their lot was either death or drowning, went about puncturing every side of the ship, so that the Franks were unable to seize anything from it—neither provisions nor weapons. The Muslims grieved greatly over this sacrifice, but, then, we are [all] Allah's and to Him we return."

O you *mujahid* of *tawhid*!—may Allah have mercy on you[5]—look you to these valorous heroes, how they punched a hole in their ship, thereby killing themselves, in order to gain two legitimate and great advantages: (1) preventing their deaths at the hands of their enemies, or falling hostage to them; (2) preventing booty from falling to their enemies. Men such as these are truly the horsemen of *tawhid*, who defend the *sunna* of the Prophet, the enemies of America and Israel, who are described by the hypocrite imams as "terrorists" and described by the [Muslim] Brotherhood as "radicals" and "criminals."

2. PERMISSION FOR A SOLITARY FIGHTER TO ATTACK A GREAT NUMBER OF ENEMIES IN THE *JIHAD*

We have already mentioned two examples found in the Koran and the *sunna* wherein believers killed themselves of their own volition in order to glorify the faith—they are the stories of the youth and the king [as recorded in the aforementioned *hadith*] and the believers who plunged to a fiery death in the trenches [as recorded in the aforementioned Koranic verses, 85:4–8]. We have also mentioned an example from Islamic history—the battle of Akka, where the *mujahidin* drowned themselves instead of allowing their enemy to triumph over them or take their goods.

Here we mention, with the help of Allah, a number of examples from the unadulterated *sunna* and the biographies of the Companions about *mujahidin* who placed themselves in peril and were slain by the[ir] foes. We will then consider the verdicts of the learned regarding this. Finally we will demonstrate—Allah willing—that there is no difference between these examples and those we mentioned earlier.

A. *Examples from the Unadulterated* Sunna *and the Biographies of the Companions Regarding* Mujahidin *Placing Themselves in Peril and Thus Being Killed by Their Enemies*

1. Muslim narrates in his authentic account that Abu Bakr said: "The Messenger of Allah said: 'The gates of Paradise [lay] under the shadows of swords.' So a poverty-stricken and haggard-looking man arose and said: Did you [really] hear the Messenger of Allah say that? He said: Yes. So he [haggard man] went back to his friends and bid them farewell. Then he broke the scabbard off his sword and flung it away. He then proceeded to walk with his sword to the enemy['s camp]. He slashed away till he was slain."

2. Recorded in Muslim, Anas bin Malik said: "The Messenger of Allah and his Companions left and beat the idolaters to Badr.

When the idolaters arrived, the Messenger of Allah said: Let not a one of you do anything until I do it first. Then the idolaters began to advance, so the Messenger of Allah said: Rise up to Paradise, whose width is equal to the heavens and the earth! Umair bin al-Humam al-Ansari said: O Messenger of Allah, is Paradise [really] equal in extent to the heavens and the earth? He said: Yes. Umair exclaimed: Ooh! Ooh! The Messenger of Allah said: What has prompted you to say Ooh! Ooh! He said: Nothing, O Messenger of Allah, only that I desire to be among its residents. He said: You are among its residents. So he took out [some] dates from his bag and began to eat them. Then he said: If I were to live until I have eaten all these dates of mine, it would be a long life indeed. So he threw away all the dates he had with him. Then he attacked and fought them [idolaters] until he was killed."

3. In the two authentic accounts [Bukhari and Muslim], Jabar said: "A man said: Where [do I stand], O Messenger of Allah, if I am killed? He said: In Paradise. So he hurled the dates that were in his hand and fought till he was killed." And Anas said: "A man said: O Messenger of Allah, if I plunge myself into the ranks of the idolaters and fight till I am killed—what then, to heaven? He said: Yes. So the man plunged himself into the ranks of the idolaters, fighting till he was slain." Ibn Ishaq relays from Issam bin Omar: "When the men rejoined on the day of Badr, Awaf bin al-Harith said: O Messenger of Allah, what about His slave does the Lord laugh? He replied: To see him plunge his hand in battle and fight to fatigue. So he threw his shield and advanced, fighting until he died a martyr." *Credulity is key*

4. Aslam bin Umran said: "We were at Constantinople, when a mighty phalanx of Romans [Byzantines] came forth. A Muslim man launched into the Roman phalanx until he penetrated their center. The people screamed, Allah Almighty! 'With his own hand he has cast himself into destruction!' [4:29]. So Abu Ayub responded: O you people, you apply this verse wrongfully. This

verse was revealed because of us, the Ansar [the "helpers" of Medina]. When Islam was dignified by Allah and had received many other supporters, we said secretly among ourselves that our money was lost and that we should attempt to replenish it. At that time, Allah revealed this verse—thus 'destruction' is in response to what we purposed [i.e., forfeiting *jihad* in order to prosper materially]." There is also an authentic *hadith* from Mudrik bin Awaf, who said to Omar: "I have a neighbor who hurled himself into battle and was thus killed. In response, the people said: 'With his own hand he has cast himself into destruction!' Omar replied: They lie! Instead, he has purchased the Hereafter with this life." And at [the battle of] Yarmuk,[6] Akruma bin Abu Jahil was behaving manly. So Khalid [bin al-Walid] said to him: "Don't do it; for your death would hit the Muslims hard. He said: Leave me be, O Khalid; for you were with [i.e., supported] the Messenger of Allah in the past, while I and my father were among the most critical toward him." So he quit him and he was killed.

B. *Verdicts of the Learned* Ulema *Regarding the Legitimacy for a Single Man to Attack a Large Number [of Enemies] Even If It Is Certain That He Will Die*

Muhammad bin al-Hassan al-Shebani said: "There is no wrong for a man to carry out a campaign single-handedly against the enemy— even if he thinks he will be killed—as long as he perceives that he will accomplish something by way of killing, scarring, or defeating [them]. However, if he believes that he will not be able to harm them, then it is not permissible for him to launch [himself] against them. The condition, then, is that his endeavor against them must cause them clear damage.

"There is no harm if a single man attacks a thousand men alone, as long as he hopes to escape or cause harm [to his enemies]; otherwise, it is disliked, for he exposes himself to destruction without any benefit to the Muslims. However, if he does not expect to escape or harm [his enemies] but instead seeks to embolden the Muslims so they may emulate his [courageous] deed, then there is no objection to his doing so. Likewise, if he does not expect escape or damage [to the enemies], and yet he does this to terrify the foe, then it is permissible—for this is even more preferable to destruction and benefits the Muslims."

Al-Jassas said, regarding the above: "What Muhammad [al-Shebani] said is true and legitimate. If his own destruction produces a benefit for the religion, then this undertaking [of his] is noble. Allah praised the Companions of the Prophet for this in His Word: 'For Allah has purchased from the believers their lives and worldly goods in exchange for Paradise. They fight on behalf of Allah, killing and being killed' [9:111]. And He said: 'Do not think that those who were slain fighting in the path of Allah are dead—nay! They live in the presence of their Lord and are well provided for' [3:169]. And He said: 'Among men is he who sells himself to seek the pleasure of Allah' [2:207]."

The Sheikh of Islam, Ibn Taymiyya, said: "Muslim narrated in his authentic account the story of the people of the ditch [see *hadith* on p. 146]. The youth ordered his own death in order to help empower the faith. Therefore, all four schools of jurisprudence[7] have made it permissible for a Muslim to immerse himself in the ranks of the infidels, even if his better judgment tells him that they will kill him—if by so doing the Muslims gain an advantage."

Ibn Hajar said: "Regarding the question of one man taking on many foes, it is collectively agreed that if he undertakes such an initiative in order to magnify his courage, thinking that by so doing he will terrify his enemies, or that he will embolden the Muslims against them, or something to that effect—then it is good. But if it is done merely out of rashness, then it is forbidden."

Al-Qurtubi said: "There is no wrong for a man to single-handedly attack a mighty army—if he seeks martyrdom—provided he has the fortitude. If, however, he is not strong enough, this is [self-] destruction. When the Muslim soldiers encountered the Persians, the Muslims' horses fled from the [Persians'] elephants. So one of the men undertook the making of a clay elephant and accustomed his horse to its presence, till his horse no longer feared elephants. Thereafter the man drove his horse straight into the elephants. The men cried out: They [the elephants] will kill you! The man replied: There is no harm if I die while opening the way for the Muslims. Likewise at the battle of Yamama, the Hanifa tribe made their forts impregnable. So a Muslim man said: Place me in a sling and hurl me into them. They did so. He fought them alone and opened the gates.

"Sahih Muslim narrates that the Messenger of Allah along with seven of the Ansar faced the Quraish at the battle of Uhud.[8] When the Quraish approached, he [Muhammad] said: 'Whoever repels them from us gains Paradise; he will be my companion in the Garden.' So one of the Ansar advanced and fought till he was slain. This continued till all seven were slain. Thus whoever sacrifices his life in order to enjoin what is good and forbid what is evil attains the highest level of martyrdom. Allah Most High said: '[E]njoin the good and forbid the evil, and bear patiently that which befalls you' [31:17]."

Conclusion: That There Is No Difference Between a Man Killing Himself with His Own Hands or Through the Agency of Another

Based on the above, it becomes clear that there is no difference between the one who causes his own death through his own command (such as in the *hadith* of the youth who ordered his own killing) or through his own actions (such as the people of the ditch who opted to hurl themselves into the pits of flame), or through the actions of another (such as the one who single-handedly attacks a vast army). All of these are praised for their steadfastness in that they sought to benefit and empower the religion. Therefore, this clearly demonstrates that there is no difference whatsoever between the man who kills himself, or who plunges himself into the ranks of the enemy and they kill him, or who commands another to kill him—*provided that this is all done for the good and glory of Islam.*

What confirms this [assertion] is that the converse—the prohibition against the one who kills himself with his own hands as well as the one who commands another to kill him—is also true. For instance, there is no difference between the one who commands another to feed him poison or inject poison into him and the one who kills himself through the agency of another—such as the one who jumps in front of a car or train.

Thus the deciding factor in all these situations is one and the same: the intention—is it to service Islam [martyrdom], or is it out of depression and despair [suicide]?

3. OTHER SITUATIONS WHERE ONE IS PERMITTED TO TAKE HIS OWN LIFE

A. The Superiority of Being Steadfast Against the Enemy and Refusing Surrender to the Point of Death

Abu Hurreira said: "The Messenger of Allah sent out a company made up of ten men headed by Assam bin Thabit al-Ansari. They were eventually tracked down and surrounded by some one hundred men from the tribe of Laheyan. They said to them: Dismount and surrender and we will pledge that not one of you will be slain. So Assam replied: As for me, by Allah I shall never condescend to become a *dhimmi* of an infidel. O Allah, inform your Prophet about us! So the tribesmen slew Assam and seven others with their arrows. The remaining three, however, surrendered and made a pact with the Laheyan. But after they had surrendered, the tribesmen began to treat them harshly, so that one of the three hostages said: This is but the beginning of the[ir] treachery. They tried to appease him but he refused, so they killed him. They took the remaining two hostages and sold them in the market, and one of them was eventually killed. News of this was eventually brought to the Prophet."

Al-Shawkani said in explanation of this *hadith*: "As to the issue of surrender and captivity, there is no reference that the Prophet condemned the three for going into captivity among the infidels, nor did he condemn the seven for refusing surrender and captivity. If either action was illegitimate, surely the Prophet would have informed his Companions of its forbidden status and condemned it."

So this judgement is based on omission?

[Four more *ulema*—al-Khatabi, Ibn Hajar, Ibn Qudama, and al-Mardawi—are quoted making essentially the same conclusion.]

Thus you can see for yourself, O brother *mujahid* of Islam, that the *ulema* are all agreed that it is permissible for a Muslim to refuse to surrender to the foe—even if doing so brings certain death. Indeed, some have made this a duty and a way of escape from the humiliation and authority of the infidels. So this is another example of the legitimacy of destroying oneself—not only in order to benefit the faith, but also to disallow the infidels from lording over and humiliating the Muslim.

B. The Superiority of Being Steadfast to the Point of Death Instead of Giving In to Infidelity

Bukhari narrates in the Book of Coercion, under the title "Whoever preferred to be beaten, killed, and humiliated rather than revert to infidelity," that the Prophet said: "Whoever possesses the following three qualities will have the sweetness of faith: that he love Allah and his Messenger more than anything else; that he loves a fellow human only in Allah; and that he hates reverting back to infidelity just like he hates being hurled into the Fire." Regarding this, Ibn Hajar said: "Some have interpreted this to me that hating infidelity and hell are one and the same. Thus being killed, beaten, and humiliated is far preferable for the believer than going to hell is."

Regarding the verse, "Whoever rejects Allah after having had faith—except for the one who is coerced while his heart remains secure in its faith—earns the wrath of Allah; his will be a dreadful penalty" [16:106], al-Qurtubi said: "The *ulema* have all agreed that the one who chooses death over imposed infidelity receives a greater reward from Allah than the one who gives in."

Khabab bin al-Urt narrates that the Prophet said: "Before your times, they used to take a man, bury him in a hole, place a saw above his head, and split it in two; and they would rake his body with a metal rake till the skin and bones were torn to pieces—and still he would not recant his faith [in Allah]."

He thus describes these men of old with praise for their endurance against coercion and oppression for their faith in Allah, for instead of embracing infidelity, they internalized their faith thereby fending off their torments. Abu Muhammad bin al-Frajj al-Baghdadi narrates: "The aids of Musailima seized two of the Prophet's Companions and brought them before Musailima. The latter asked one of them: Now, then, do you testify that I am the messenger of Allah? The man responded in the affirmative, so he let him be. He then went up to the second man and said: So, do you testify that Muhammad is a messenger of Allah? The man said, Yes. Musailima then asked: And do you testify that I am a messenger of Allah? The man replied: I am deaf and cannot hear. So he advanced toward him and cut off his head. The first man reached the Prophet and said: I am ruined! He asked: What has caused your ruin? So the man relayed the incident, and he said: As for your friend, he had faith, whereas you compromised. Where do you stand now? The man said: I testify that you are the Messenger of Allah! So he said: You are what you are."

C. Permissibility to Kill Oneself in Order to Guard
Against the Exposure of Secrets under Torture
At this juncture, we wish, by the aid of Allah Most High, to point out one of the most important circumstances for one to destroy himself for the general good, and that is, for a hostage to kill himself in order to guard against divulging the secrets of the *mujahidin* to the[ir] enemies. You will note that most who have passed judgment on this issue have grounded their decision in the unadulterated *sunna*, based on the *hadith* of the youth and the king, which we have discussed earlier—for as we said, the *ulema* consider this *hadith* fundamental to these issues.

Regarding this question, Muhammad bin Ibrahim was asked by a group of Algerian *mujahidin* during the liberation war[9] if it was permissible for a hostage to take his own life in order to prevent himself from exposing secrets to the enemy. The question was put thus: "During these last few years, whenever the French have taken hold of an Algerian, they have utilized drugs that make him divulge the whereabouts of hideouts and provision stores. Moreover, some of those taken captive are among the leaders [who know much], and they reveal this place and that. Is it permissible, then, for a person to commit suicide if he knows that they will inject him with the drug, so that he may say, 'Let me die as a martyr,' although they may torture him with various torments?"

[Muhammad bin Ibrahim] responds: "If it is as you say, then yes, it is permissible." Among the evidence he relies on is the *hadith* of the youth and tyrant king, as well as the warriors who drowned themselves instead of allowing themselves and their possessions to be captured by the Crusaders [at Akka].

D. Can a Muslim Kill Himself in Order to Exasperate His Enemy?

Sheikh Hassan Ayub said: "Fundamentally, killing oneself is forbidden and one of the greatest [of sins]. Whoever kills himself will be severely tormented on the Day of Judgment. Such a killing is a great transgression against Allah and an injustice to the self, which Allah forbade from killing, except for reasons legislated by Allah. Such an act reveals a rejection of the will and judgment of Allah, where a man scurries to end his pain. This is what is called 'suicide,' and there is no doubt of its forbidden [status].

"However, there are times when a combatant will fall into the hands of the enemy. His enemy then implements the most painful sorts of torments on him—scorching him with fire, tearing off his flesh bit by bit, inflating him, hanging him upside down, electrocuting him periodically—to the most recent kinds [of torments] that have been utilized by the dogs of the modern world and that were invented by the Nazis and Communists. These [methods] have been implemented by the scum of mankind—they who have no humanity and no mercy in their hearts. So what is the decree if a man falls under such torments: Does he have the right to kill himself or not? I ground my response regarding this critical matter in the texts of the *ulema*, and it is:

"1. If killing oneself has any authentic or strong justification, [it is] when it involves the affairs of Muslims—when it benefits them or brings them harm when not performed. So when this is the situation, it is permitted. For instance, when a person is tortured in order to reveal secrets related to the whereabouts of the [Muslim] combatants, or their names, or exposing the plans of the Islamic army, revealing arms and provision stores, or anything else that, if made known to the enemy, would endanger the Islamic army, individual Muslims, or their women and children. Especially if he knows that he cannot tolerate torture and that he will have no choice but to divulge such secrets, or if he knows that the enemy will inject him with a compound that will make him reveal everything against his will.

"This is demonstrated since all the *ulema* have agreed that it is permissible for one to plunge himself into the enemy knowing full well that he will be killed, if by so doing he services Islam or brings an advantage to the Muslims.

"2. However, if he kills himself due to the sure knowledge that they will kill him but that before doing so they mean to torture him, in order to make an example out of him or aggravate the Muslims—if he commits suicide under such circumstances, then such a killing is disliked. And yet it is not one of the great sins, nor is its permissibility far off [i.e., it is a borderline or "minor" sin]."

PART TWO: THE PERMISSIBILITY OF BOMBARDING
INFIDELS WHEN MUSLIMS AND OTHERS WHO
ARE NOT PERMITTED TO BE KILLED
ARE DISPERSED AMONG THEM

What just passed were proofs of *jihad*'s excellence and the obligation to carry it out. Waging *jihad* against the infidels is the basis of glory and honor, whereas abandoning it results in humiliation and debasement. This is confirmed by the Prophet's assertion: "If you take up a domestic life, hold on to the tails of cattle, are content with farming, and thus abandon *jihad*, Allah will let humiliation lord over you until you return to your religion."

Ibn Omar also relayed that the Prophet said: "Because you have forsaken *jihad*, taking hold of cows' tails and dealing in merchandise, Allah has adorned you with shame and you will never be able to shake it off yourselves until you repent to Allah and return to your original positions."

[Often] mixed among the infidels, whom the *mujahidin* target in warfare, are those whom it is not permitted to kill—such as Muslims, *dhimmis*, women and children, and so forth. So, is *jihad*, which is assigned us, to be abandoned on account of their protected blood, or is killing ones such as these—accidentally, not on purpose—forgiven in face of the highest goods that would be realized from waging *jihad* against the infidels, the enemies of Allah Supreme? This question is the subject of inquiry in this section—so let us speak with Allah's help.

Regarding this question, the *ulema* have disagreed, [resulting] in three views:

THE FIRST VIEW: TOTAL PROHIBITION, RELAYED FROM MALIK AND AL-AWZA'I, AND THE LATER MALIKIS WHO DISAGREED

The Most High said: "[But for the fear that you might have trampled underfoot believing men and women unknown to you and thus incurred guilt unknowingly on their account, Allah would have commanded you to fight it out with them. But He ordained it thus that He may bring whom He will into His mercy.] Had the faithful stood apart from them, We would certainly have punished the infidels among them with a grievous punishment" [48:25].

Regarding this verse, al-Qurtubi said: "This verse demonstrates that if the only way to harm the infidel is by harming the believer, then one should take the [welfare of the] infidel into consideration, in order to guard the sanctity of the believer. Abu Zeid asked Ibn al-

Qassim: 'If a group of idolaters are well protected in their fortification, and they have in their possession a group of Muslim captives,
can the Muslims, while besieging them, burn this fortification or not?'
Ibn al-Qassim said: 'I heard Malik, when they asked him regarding the
legality of firing at a group of idolaters in their warboats, if they have
in their possession [Muslim] captives, say: I don't think so, based on
the Word of the Almighty to the people of Mecca.' ('Had the faithful
stood apart from them, We would certainly have punished the infidels
among them with a grievous punishment' [48:25].) Likewise, if an infidel utilizes a Muslim as a shield, it is not permissible to fire at him.
Whoever does so anyway and destroys one of the Muslims must pay
blood money and make atonement. But if he was unaware [that there
were Muslim hostages], then he need not pay blood money nor make
atonement.

"Ibn Arabi relays that Malik also said: 'We laid siege and encircled
the city of the Romans [Constantinople] so that its water [supply]
was cut off. So they used to let the [Muslim] captives go down and
fetch water for them, and no one could shoot arrows at them, so that
the water reached them against our will.' But Abu Hanifa and his
comrades, as well as al-Thawri, all permitted firing at the idolaters'
fortifications, even if they contain Muslim prisoners and their children—and even if an infidel shields himself with a Muslim child. Firing at an idolater and hitting one of the Muslims, then, does not incur
blood money or atonement. Al-Thawri said that it does require aton-
ing but not the payment of blood money. But for us [Malikis] attempting to accomplish that which is permitted is illegitimate
whenever it takes the soul of a Muslim."

Al-Qurtubi continues: "Yet it is permissible to slay the human
shield without any disagreement—Allah willing—if the advantage
gained is imperative, universal, and certain. 'Imperative' means that
reaching the infidels cannot be attained without killing the human
shield; 'universal' means that the advantage gained by killing the human shield benefits every Muslim—and it is since otherwise the infidels, left untouched, may take over the entire *umma*; and 'certain'

means that the benefit gained by killing the human shield is definite. Our *ulema* have said that this advantage secured through these conditions should not be quarreled over, for either way the human shield is dead for certain—either by the enemy, in which case every Muslim will [eventually] be subjugated, or at the hands of the Muslims, in which case the enemy would be destroyed and every Muslim secured."

The Maliki scholar Sheikh Muhammad Arfa al-Dassuqi [disagreeing with the Maliki consensus] said: "If they use a Muslim as a shield, attack [anyway] and try not to hit him."

It is important to note that those who forbade killing the human shield were speaking about Offensive *Jihads*, where the Muslims target the infidels in their own homes [in order to place them under Islamic rule]. This is evident by Malik's words since he was talking about besieging their fortifications [in Constantinople] or firing at their ships. However, if the good to be gained is imperative, certain, and universal, and this is definitely the case in a Defensive *Jihad*, where Muslims battle those infidels who are attempting to take over Muslim lands, then there is no problem killing those who should not be killed, by accident and not on purpose. For under such circumstances, danger threatens every Muslim if fighting is at any time interrupted. This interpretation is clear from al-Qurtubi's words [that the advantage gained is imperative, universal, and certain]. So this is the view concerning the prohibition against killing the human shield.

THE SECOND VIEW: TOTAL LEGITIMACY TO BOMBARD THE INFIDELS, EVEN IF THERE ARE MUSLIMS AMONG THEM

Al-Jassas has relayed and analyzed the words of Malik and al-Awza'i in detail. He said: "Malik said not to burn the boats of the infidels if they contain Muslim hostages, based on the verse [48:25]. However, the Prophet turned away from them [Meccans] when there were Muslims among them, and if the Muslims were separated from the infidels, he would surely have inflicted a grievous penalty upon them.

Al-Awza'i said: If the infidels shield themselves with the children of the Muslims, do not fire, based on the Word of the Most High [48:25]. So do not burn their ships or catapult their strongholds if they have Muslim hostages therein, and whoever strikes a Muslim errs.

"But the biographers relay that the Prophet besieged the inhabitants of Ta'if[10] [in A.D. 630] and fired at them with catapults, despite his ban on killing women and children. He did so knowing full well that women and children would be struck, for it was not possible to differentiate between them. This demonstrates that if Muslims are intermingled with the people of war, it is still permissible to fire at them, as long as the intended targets are the idolaters. Al-Sa'b bin Jathama said: The Prophet was asked about whether it was permissible to attack the idolaters in the dark even if this led to their women and children being struck. He [Muhammad] replied: 'They [women and children] are from among them [the infidels].' He also used to command that if those whom his armies intended to attack agreed to prayer [i.e., embraced Islam], then they were to be left alone, but if not, then they were to be attacked. This is the course that the righteous caliphs followed. And it is well known that whoever follows such a course, bombarding infidels, will inevitably hit their women and children, who are otherwise forbidden from being killed. Likewise, the same goes if there are Muslims among them. It is compulsory that this [the possibility of hitting women, children, and Muslims] not dissuade the launching of an incursion against them, firing arrows and utilizing other [weapons]—even if one dreads hitting a Muslim.

"As for the verse in question [48:25], what suggests the ban is the portion of the verse that says 'and thus incurred guilt unknowingly on their [Muslims killed accidentally] account.' The exegetes have differed as to what 'guilt' implies in this passage. Some have said that it warrants blood money; others that it requires atonement. Still others have said that it produces sorrow in acknowledging that one has slain a fellow Muslim, for a believer will certainly experience that, even if it was unintentional. Again others have said that it results in shame. And it is told that some have suggested that 'guilt' equates sin. This is false, however, since the Almighty plainly states that it was done 'unknow-ingly'; and one does not sin by doing something out of ignorance."

Sheikh Muhammad al-Sherbani said, in regard to the various views in this matter: "If necessity compels one to fire at them [Mus-lims interspersed among the infidels] one should do so with im-punity—without either blood money or atonement. For if we lay off them, they will emerge triumphant and cause even more harm. Whenever, then, it is necessary to fire upon the idolaters, we should do so while trying not to strike Muslims or *dhimmis* as much as pos-sible. Otherwise, the indignities inflicted on [our] sanctities and honor would be greater than the evils caused by attacking them. It is better that one group [of Muslims or *dhimmis*] bear the burden and be destroyed in order to defend Islam and its territory and the overall welfare [of Muslims]. The other view maintains that firing at infidels is prohibited if a Muslim, *dhimmi*, or some other person who has a pact with Muslims is present."

It is evident from the previous statements that the essence of the *ulema*'s words, whether pro or con, revolves around what the advan-tages are. Therefore, if the good of the people of Islam can be achieved by killing the human shield, then it is permissible; otherwise, it is not. The same applies if the evils produced by not fighting the infidels are greater than the evils produced by killing those among them who should not be killed. The evils produced by attacking impetuously [thereby accidentally killing those who should not be killed] is for-given due to the good of defending Islam and its people and repelling the enemies who wish to take over the sanctities of the Muslims.

All this applies only if the Muslim's presence amid the infidels is due to a legitimate purpose, such as, for instance, business transac-tions. However, if he is with them for some other purpose, such as aiding them against Muslims, going out with them as they battle Mus-lims, or spying on the Muslims and relaying their affairs back to the enemy, then his lot is theirs.

Ibn al-Himam the Hanafi said: "Whether or not holding back from [bombarding] the infidels will result in defeat [for Muslims], there is absolutely nothing wrong with bombarding the strongholds of the infidels, even if there are Muslim hostages or merchants among them—indeed, even if they use the Muslims or their children as human shields. For the intended target is always the infidel."

THE THIRD VIEW: PERMISSIBILITY TO BOMBARD
ONLY UNDER SPECIFIC CONDITIONS

Al-Shafi'i said: "It was asked: How is it possible to bombard a group of idolaters with catapults and fire if among them are women and children who are forbidden from being killed? It was replied: The Prophet launched a raid against the tribe of al-Mustalaq and they fought back. So he commanded to set fire to their fortifications all night long with the widespread knowledge that women and children were in there. This was because it was an idolatrous camp, not exempt [from raiding]. Instead, it was the intentional killing of children and women that was prohibited, whom the Prophet [preferred to] trade and treat as property."

It is important to bear in mind that al-Shafi'i is talking about an Offensive *Jihad*, where the Muslims seek out and pursue the infidels in their own homes and fortifications [in order to offer them the three choices of conversion, taxation and subordination, or death], which is clear from these words of his: "It is permissible for us if there is no Muslim present to make [the area] legitimate without fighting. But if we do decide to engage it, we do so without burning or drowning it. However, if the Muslims begin to grapple in earnest, it is permissible for them to burn it down or drown it."

But when Muslims are defending their religion and their sanctities, and the infidels are surrounding them from every corner, and instead they are the ones who are seeking them out and pursuing them, and whenever they overcome, they torture and murder the Muslims; or when the infidels settle in the lands of Islam trying to impose infidelity by the power of the sword [i.e., by force of arms], making Muslims embrace their laws after first forfeiting the *sharia* of Allah—in these situations it becomes a binding obligation on every Muslim to fight them any way he can. He should never abandon this obligatory duty because some Muslims might be killed mistakenly, not intentionally. Whoever does die is in the hands of Allah, and we trust that he is a martyr.

Ibn Taymiyya said: "Based on the consensus of the *ulema*, those Muslims who are accidentally killed are martyrs; and the obligatory *jihad* should never be abandoned because it creates martyrs."

Ibn Qudama said: "It is not permissible to open the dams in order to drown them [infidels], due to the women and children, who should be guarded against willful destruction; however, if there is no other way, then it is permissible—such as when the Prophet utilized the catapults against the people of Ta'if, or when Amr bin al-As utilized it against the Alexandrians [when Egypt was conquered in A.D. 641]."

Having quoted what applies to us from the various schools of jurisprudence of the *ulema*, regarding bombarding the infidels if either Muslims, women, children, or *dhimmis* are among them or used as shields, we conclude that the views of the *ulema* are condensed into three perspectives:

The first view: total prohibition, based on Malik and al-Awza'i
The second view: total legitimacy with blood money and
    atonement [as the price], based on the words of the Hanafis,
    Ahmad, a number of Hanbalis, and the later Malikis.
The third view: based on the words of al-Shafi'i and the
    Hanbalis, permissibility to bombard the idolaters even if
    Muslims and those who are cautioned against killing are
    intermingled with them as long as there is a need or an
    obligation for Muslims to do so, or if not striking leads to a
    delay of the *jihad*. As for blood money and atonement, these
    are to be judged individually.

This [third] view is the one that we hold to, that is, permitting bombardments in order to expedite the *jihad* and never cause it delay. And based on this, we see that:

1. Bombarding the organizations of the infidels and apostates in this day and age has become an imperative of *jihad* in our war with the idolatrous tyrants, where weakened *mujahidin* battle massive and vigilant armies armed to the teeth: It has become next to impossible to confront them in open warfare.

2. The tyrants and leaders of the infidels shelter themselves in armored vehicles with lots and varied forms of intricate security measures, so that it has become exceedingly difficult to reach them without employing explosives and rockets and other missile weaponry. Therefore, it is permissible to fire at them.

3. The tyrants and enemies of Allah always see to it that their organizations and military escorts are set among the people and populace, making it extremely difficult to hunt them down in isolation. But if we hold off our *jihad* against them for this [reason], the *jihad* would be delayed. Also, take note: It is of course more proper to kill the enemies of Allah Most High in isolation without exposing Muslims or the others [women, children, *dhimmis*] to death. And we endeavor to [find] him isolated and separated far from the people. But expediency makes it so.

4. These means of reaching [them]—explosives and missiles— have proven to be very effective in Egypt, Algeria, Palestine, and Lebanon, wreaking great havoc among the ranks of the enemies of Allah Almighty.

5. The *mujahidin* should see to it that they repeatedly warn the Muslims who are intermixed with the tyrants and their aides to stay away from their centers, offices, and organizations—but this warning should be done in a general way so that the *mujahidin* do not become exposed and suffer losses.

6. There is no question that those [Muslims] who are intermixed with the infidels, apostates, and their aides, of their own free will, are less sacred in the religion than those Muslims who are coerced and used as shields—and even these latter [who are

more sacred], the *ulema* have permitted to be fired upon whenever they are in the midst of the infidels.

7. The only thing *mujahidin* are specifically required to do, should they knowingly kill a Muslim [who is intermixed with the targeted infidels], is make atonement. Blood money, however, is a way out of the dispute altogether. Payment should be made only when there is a surplus of monies, which are no longer needed to fund the *jihad*. Again, this is only if their intermingling with the infidels is for a legitimate reason, such as business. And we assume that those who are killed are martyrs, and believe that what the Sheikh of Islam said about them applies: "[T]hose Muslims who are accidentally killed are martyrs; and the obligatory *jihad* should never be abandoned because it creates martyrs."

As for those dubious persons who say that *jihad* should be abandoned for now due to certain ambiguities, let them know that forfeiting the faith is a much greater harm than forfeiting money or lives. Moreover, we see that the "ambiguities" they speak of have no value in light of what we have meticulously demonstrated here—especially the fact that what the *mujahidin* undertake in many countries has to do with Defensive—not Offensive—*Jihad*.

Just as the Sheikh of Islam said: "Defensive warfare is the most critical form of warfare, [since we are] warding off an invader from [our] sanctities and religion. It is a unanimously accepted duty. After belief, there is no greater duty than to repulse the invading enemy who corrupts faith and the world. There are no rules or conditions for this; he must be expelled by all possible means. Our learned *ulema* and others have all agreed to this. It is imperative to distinguish between repulsing the invading, oppressive infidel [Defensive *Jihad*] and pursuing him in his own lands [Offensive *Jihad*]."

So these people (who complain over particulars)—as well as the government-employed *ulema*, who constantly whisper to them in an effort to keep the Muslims from [waging] *jihad* in order that the infidels dominate them and put them in a vise grip the likes of which can never be broken—should never be heeded. Instead, the obligation is to listen to the *mujahidin ulema*, just as the Sheikh of Islam, Ibn Taymiyya, said: "The obligation is to uphold the correct opinions of the pious persons who are also experienced in the world—not [the opinions] of the worldly persons, who only know religion superficially, nor of those pious persons who have no experience in the world."

PART II

❧

PROPAGANDA

5

The following is an interview with Ayman al-Zawahiri on the four-year anniversary of the 9/11 attacks. It is the most extensive interview with Zawahiri to date. Conducted by al-Sahab ("the clouds") in September 2005, it was released on various Islamist Web sites in December of the same year under the title "Four Years after the New York and Washington Raids."

Zawahiri claims that the "Crusader war," launched in 2001, is a failure—not just in Iraq but also in Afghanistan, where the ousted Taliban have "settled in the villages and mountains, where the real power of Afghanistan lies." Simultaneously, Zawahiri portrays al-Qaeda as growing in strength and numbers.

Most unexpectedly, after explaining to Americans that their culture is defunct, Zawahiri invites them to Islam: "[We call upon Americans] to be honest with themselves and to realize that their current creed—which is composed of materialistic secularism, the distorted Christianity that has nothing to do with Jesus Christ, the hereditary Crusader hatred, and their submission to Zionist hegemony over money and politics—this creed, this mixture, will only lead them to destruction in this world, and torments in the Hereafter."

AYMAN AL-ZAWAHIRI INTERVIEW
FOUR YEARS AFTER 9/11

⟡

INTERVIEWER: We are happy to interview you four years after the New York and Washington raids [of 9/11].

DR. AYMAN AL-ZAWAHIRI: I, too, am happy to address our Muslim *umma* through you during this critical stage of its history. I would like to take this opportunity to thank you, and pray that Allah Almighty will reward you for publicizing the word of truth in the midst of the Crusader campaign and global war that is being waged against Islam and the Muslims.

INTERVIEWER: Dr. Ayman, how do you view the Crusader campaign, four years after it began?

DR. AYMAN AL-ZAWAHIRI: The new Crusader campaign is failing, just like the previous ones, by the grace of Allah. America and its Crusader allies have not accomplished a single thing—except for throwing their armies into the battlefield to take blows on a daily basis, to have their soldiers killed on a daily basis, and to have their economies bled on a daily basis.

What did they accomplish in Afghanistan? They evicted the Taliban government from Kabul, but it centered itself in the villages and mountains—where the real power of Afghanistan lies. Northern Afghanistan and Kabul have become a scene of chaos, pillaging, looting, defiling [women's] honor, and drug trafficking, which have flourished and thrived under the American occupation. Then they held elections, which resembled a masquerade more than anything else—since the country's periphery is controlled by highway bandits and warlords, and since the international committees monitoring the elections—or rather, those who bear false witness—could not (even if they really wanted to) cover more than ten voting districts; and since transferring the ballot boxes takes fifteen days, under the control of the warlords and highway bandits, and then under the control of the occupation forces; and since any resistance, or anything resembling resistance or opposition, is met with bombardment, missiles, the burning of villages, and the killing of hundreds.

Then, after all this, they obtained the false testimony of the U.N. [United Nations], which saw nothing for it to bear witness about—except for a few theatrics in some [voting] districts in the cities. This is but one of many examples of the U.N.'s hypocrisy, which they claim to be the symbol of their international legitimacy.

Now, while the U.N. rejects the elections held in Zimbabwe,[1] for instance, because the time dedicated to voting was insufficient, it is as silent as a cemetery regarding the elections in Afghanistan, which were held under the terrorism of the warlords. For fifteen days! the ballot boxes were passed around among highway bandits and American collaborators, without anyone knowing what happened to them before they [finally] appeared at the ballot-counting centers.

And while the U.N. whines about those killed in Darfur[2] and established an international tribunal for the war crimes committed there, it was as silent as a cemetery regarding the tragedy of one million Iraqi children,[3] who died as a result of the siege on Iraq—the same siege that profited U.N. officials, and the son of Kofi Annan, as the U.N. [itself] admits. The U.N. was recently forced to reveal a part of this scandal, the stench of which spreads far and wide.[4]

And it was as silent as a cemetery when the Taliban, after an agreement was signed with them, were betrayed at the hands of the Americans at Dostum in Qunduz. Then they [the Taliban] were murdered in Qali Jangi, and later they were suffocated in container trucks en route to Shiberghan prison. Then they were treated worse than animals in Shiberghan prison. Yet Lakhdar al-Ibrahimi declares that the issue of Qali Jangi is a "sensitive" one and should not be opened now.[5]

In complete collaboration it [the U.N.] remains silent about what goes on in Abu Ghraib, Guantánamo, and Baghram, and about the way the al-Qaeda and Taliban prisoners are treated.[6] They disappear from the face of the earth! No one knows a thing about them, nor does anyone dare ask where they are, what's been done to them, where they were arrested and tortured, and why, until when, where, and how they will be held in prison.

Where are the international agreements and U.N. treaties? What about human rights—in fact, how about just even *animal* rights?! This is all because the U.N. is part of the Crusader kingdom, over which reigns the Caesar in Washington, who pays the salaries of Kofi Annan and his like.

This is what they have accomplished to this day in Afghanistan. In Kabul, their [allies] are terrified, and their president [Karzai] cannot leave his office. If he goes to Kandahar, he faces assassination attempts. If his plane lands in Gardez, missiles catch up with it.

Forged elections, Crusader forces led by America taking blows on a daily basis, an almost complete media blackout, Pakistani collaboration—yet despite all this, America was forced to admit the strength of the resistance it faces, and admit that the Taliban is still the strongest force in Afghanistan.

And I assure you, O my brothers—nor can the Crusaders and their apostate collaborators deny it—that were it not for the continuous support the Pakistani army gives the Americans, they would have left a long time ago—and they will leave soon, Allah willing!

As for Iraq, what have they accomplished apart from losses and defeats? They established a government through ridiculous elections—boycotted by half the people; fake voters continually flowed in through the borders; while American planes hovered above, eradicating any opposition; and Abu Ghraib and similar prisons that swallow up the free and the honorable.

At the end, the U.N., as is customary, sends its congratulations for the "clean" and "fair" elections. Then the National Guard, the police, and the security forces bear the burden of dealing with the resistance against the Americans. So now there is an independent [Kurdish] state in the north, infiltrated by Jewish intelligence agencies, and which is divided between two collaborating political parties that fight over every little thing. The[ir] agreement is only on secularism and combating Islam, under the American banner.

Had Saladin vanquished them [today], he would have put them to the sword![7] [Shiʿite] movements attempting to sever the south [of Iraq] purport to belong to "Islam," yet they agreed with the Americans, led by the Crusader [George W.] Bush, to occupy Iraq. The government [in Iraq] begs the Americans not to leave, because they know that the day the Americans leave will be their last.

The clear declaration of their failure came one day after the blessed raid on London, when the Americans and English declared they were preparing to leave Iraq. Every day they leak to the press another report about leaving Iraq, in order to calm the terror that has taken hold of their peoples.

INTERVIEWER: Dr. Ayman, what is the situation of Qaedat al-Jihad [the base of *jihad*] after four years of fierce warfare against it?

DR. AYMAN AL-ZAWAHIRI: Qaedat al-Jihad remains a base [*qaeda*] for *jihad*. And all thanks be to Allah alone, its Emir, Sheikh Osama bin Laden, may Allah protect him, still leads the *jihad*.

As for all those lies with which Bush tries to deceive the Americans—that he's wiped out half of al-Qaeda, or three-quarters of al-Qaeda—that's all nonsense that exists only in his mind! by the grace of Allah.

And I proclaim to all Muslims and the *mujahidin* that, by the grace of Allah, al-Qaeda is spreading, growing, and becoming stronger. By the grace of Allah, it has become a popular and trailblazing organization, confronting the new Zionist-Crusader campaign, in defense of all the plundered Muslim lands, and fighting all the apostate and collaborating regimes that rule our Muslim *umma*.

And people from every region of Islam rally around it [al-Qaeda], as they confront the infidels, apostates, traitors, and collaborators, wherever they may be, with weapons, with fighting, with calls [to Islam], and with argumentation. All praise be to Allah.

INTERVIEWER: How do you view the *jihad* movement in general?

DR. AYMAN AL-ZAWAHIRI: The *jihad* movement is growing and rising. It reached its peak with the two blessed raids on Washington and New York. And now it is waging a great historic battle in Iraq, Afghanistan, Palestine, and even within the Crusaders' own homes.

The latest raid on the Crusaders' homes was the blessed raid against London, which was a slap to the face of British Crusader arrogance—and this after the *mujahid* lion of Islam, Sheikh Osama bin Laden had offered the peoples of the West a treaty, if they leave the countries of Islam [see p. 234]. But their arrogance drove them to crime, and [their] foreign secretary, the arrogant Jack Straw, said that these proposals should be treated with contempt. So let them pay the price!—of their government's filth and arrogance.

Whoever strikes us—with the help of Allah—we chop off his hand; and whoever acts with insolence toward us will pay the price for his audacity.

The Crusader West has decided to follow Bush and [British prime minister Tony] Blair in their aggression against the Muslims. So let them pay the price for this aggression. And let them be patient and endure, for the battle is still in its first stages.

INTERVIEWER: How do you view the situation in Afghanistan?

DR. AYMAN AL-ZAWAHIRI: In Afghanistan, America is being dragged down the same abyss into which the U.S.S.R. fell—though much faster. America keeps silent over most of its losses [casualties] in Afghanistan, although the simple media of the *mujahidin* exposes their lies and publicizes their losses. America will leave Afghanistan, just like the Soviets left; and it will be afflicted by the same disasters that afflicted the Soviet Union after it left Afghanistan.

INTERVIEWER: Dr. Ayman, after the recent operations of the Pakistani army in north Waziristan,[8] after the kidnapping of civilians and the killing of more than eighteen women and children from those who fled, and after the siege on the religious schools, and the killing of their students—what is your message to the Muslim *umma* in Pakistan in general and to anyone with a trace of faith remaining in his heart, in the Pakistani army in particular?

DR. AYMAN AL-ZAWAHIRI: Well, I say to them that Pakistan is the main supporter of the Crusader campaign against Afghanistan.

The Pakistani army today plays the same role that the British Indian army used to play in the aggression against the Muslims in India and in quelling the Muslim uprisings in the British colonies. Today, the Pakistani army operates as a private institution, serving the interests of Bush while [Pakistani president Pervez] Musharraf pockets the reward. The Pakistani army has abandoned the mission of defending Pakistan and is devoting itself to killing the Muslims in Waziristan, in defense of the American army.

As for the defense of Pakistan—Musharraf has claimed that America would defend him, if the Pakistani army devotes itself to serving Bush's interests. Therefore, if this policy continues, we won't be surprised to see the Pakistani army surrendering to the Indian army in Islamabad, as it surrendered in Dhaka.

Musharraf wants a Pakistan without Islam. This is why they destroyed the Islamic schools; and they are inventing a new religion, which they composed for him in America. They call this fairy tale "enlightened moderation" [Zawahiri pronounces this in English].

INTERVIEWER: More than four years have passed since America began its campaign to destroy al-Qaeda and the Taliban. So far, despite all America's capabilities and despite all aid rendered by Pakistan, America has not succeeded in capturing Mulla Muhammad Omar [deposed leader of the Taliban] or Sheikh Osama bin Laden, may Allah protect them both. What is the reason, in your opinion?

DR. AYMAN AL-ZAWAHIRI: The main reason is the protection of Allah Most High, the Exalted, which is *incomprehensible* to the Americans and to the materialistic Crusader West. The second reason, which stems from the first, is that the Muslim masses opened their hearts and home to the *mujahidin*, gave them refuge and protected them, exposed their children, families, property, and homes to bombings and burning and risked being killed or captured—all for the sake of Allah, in support of Islam, and in defense of the *mujahidin*.

Jihad in the path of Allah is greater than any individual or organization. It is a struggle between Truth and Falsehood, until Allah Almighty inherits the earth and those who live on it. Mullah Muhammad Omar and Sheikh Osama bin Laden are merely two soldiers of Islam in the journey of *jihad*, while the struggle between Truth and Falsehood transcends time.

I call upon the *mujahidin* to focus their campaigns on the stolen petroleum of the Muslims. Most of its revenue goes to the enemies of Islam, and what's left [behind] is plundered by the thieves who rule our countries. *This is the greatest theft in the history of mankind.* The enemies of Islam are consuming this vital resource with unparalleled greed. It is incumbent upon us to stop this theft any way we can, in order to save this resource for the sake of the Muslim *umma*.

If the only way to repel these thieves is by killing them, then let them be killed—without dignity.

INTERVIEWER: How are you [al-Qaeda] connected to the London incident?

AYMAN AL-ZAWAHIRI: The blessed London raid is one of the raids that the Qaedat al-Jihad [i.e., al-Qaeda] organization had the honor of carrying out against the British Crusader arrogance—as well as the British Crusader aggression toward the Muslim *umma* for more than one hundred years; and against Britain's historic crime of establishing Israel; and against the continual crimes the English perpetrate against Muslims in Afghanistan and Iraq.

In the last wills of the heroic brothers, the horsemen of *tawhid* in the London raids—may Allah have mercy upon them, may He place them in Paradise, and may He accept their good deeds—in these wills there are important lessons for the Muslim *umma* in general and for Muslims in Pakistan and the West in particular: about renouncing tyrants; about exposing the lies of the *ulema* of evil, who conceal much of the *sharia*, preferring the fleeting things of this life; and about the determination of the *mujahidin* and lions of Islam to take revenge upon the Crusaders and Jews, for the crimes and sins perpetrated by their hands, which are drenched with Muslim blood.

This blessed raid, along with similar raids, has revealed the true, hypocritical face of Western civilization, which sings [the praises of] "human rights" and "liberties"—as long as such singing serves *its* interests and benefits *it*.

And after the London raid, the British government started legislating a number of new laws that reveal Britain's despicable imperialistic face. It also revealed that British freedom is, in fact, the freedom to be hostile to Islam. They began talking about secret trials, and brought to mind the issues of secret evidence, secret witnesses, and unlimited detention, which contradict the most basic principles of fair trial. The only explanation for this contradiction is Britain's hostility to Islam.

Then Britain initiated measures to deport the political refugees to their countries. Britain used to claim it was protecting them from their countries' oppression. The only explanation for this contradiction is Britain's hostility to Islam.

British freedom was broad enough to include Salman Rushdie,[9] who published an article in *The Times*—finally—in which he calls upon Muslims to reach harmony with Western culture. He casts doubt upon the Divine Entity and the Koran; he calls upon Muslims to accept Western values—such as homosexuality. However, its [Britain's] freedom was not broad enough to include Sheikh Abu Qatada,[10] whom it arrested, along with nine others, on the *very same day*, after signing extradition treaties with Jordan and Pakistan, knowing full well that members of the Muslim factions extradited to these countries would be subject to torture and possible death. The only explanation for this contradiction is Britain's hostility to Islam.

The British liberties, which permitted Salman Rushdie to insult Islam and the Muslims, were not broad enough to include the Islamic libraries and Internet sites that sympathize with the *mujahidin*, and they threaten to shut them down; nor to include the preachers who sympathize with the *mujahidin*, and they threaten to shut down their mosques and arrest them or deport them. The only explanation for this contradiction is Britain's hostility to Islam.

Britain's "sensitive conscience" could not tolerate the killing of civilians in the center of London yet it tolerated the killing of *a million children* in the siege of Iraq, and the killing of *tens of thousands of children* in Afghanistan and Iraq, due to the bombings of the English and their allies. The only explanation for this contradiction is Britain's hostility to Islam.

Britain's "open-mindedness" could not tolerate the suspicion that the fictional weapons of mass destruction existed in Iraq, and so it destroyed Iraq under the false pretext of searching for them. Yet Britain's open-mindedness tolerates Israel's huge arsenal of all types of these weapons, which Britain *itself* helped to manufacture in Israel. The only explanation for this contradiction is Britain's hostility to Islam.

There are *lots* of other examples of Britain's and the Crusading West's hypocrisy, but time does not permit addressing them. Yet they all point to the contradiction arising out of the Crusader claims of protecting freedom and human rights. The only explanation for this contradiction is the Crusader's hostility to Islam.

INTERVIEWER: Dr. Ayman, how do you respond to the announcements made by both the British and American governments—one day after the London incident—that they would withdraw most of their forces from Iraq?

AYMAN AL-ZAWAHIRI: This is the confusion that precedes defeat. Bush and Blair are concealing the truth about the catastrophe that they are facing in Iraq and in Afghanistan. And they know better than anyone else that they have no hope of victory. The specter of Vietnam blocks all—all their exits.

They were forced to make this declaration, in order to alleviate the terror and despair that afflicted their peoples. Yet what they witnessed on the screens is but a *tiny fraction* of what goes on in Iraq and Afghanistan. So they watched the destruction in London, which was punishment and retribution for the crimes that these Crusader nations perpetrated against the Muslims.

INTERVIEWER: Dr. Ayman, how do you respond to Bush's response to your [al-Qaeda's] latest message?

AYMAN AL-ZAWAHIRI: I say to him: O you pathological liar! you were lying when you entered Iraq, you are lying as you are being defeated in Iraq, and you will be lying when you leave Iraq. You entered Iraq under the pretext of "weapons of mass destruction," and you are being defeated today in Iraq under the pretext of achieving "freedom and security." And you will be leaving it soon enough—Allah willing—under the pretext that your mission has been accomplished. But you will leave behind tens of thousands of dead, wounded, and crippled.

INTERVIEWER: And how do you respond to Blair's insistence that what occurred in London has nothing to do with his foreign policy?

AYMAN AL-ZAWAHIRI: Blair considers his people to be fools, and they, for their part, act like fools for his sake. He's become like a madman, repeating over and over again, "The London incidents have nothing to do with Iraq!"

And so we address them in the only language they understand; and if they don't understand the lesson the first time around, we will repeat it until they understand it completely.

They claim to be democratic and to have an elected government. This elected government kills our children, and our
women, and desecrates what is sacred to us. So if they really oppose it, then let them depose it; but if they are satisfied with it,
then they should pay the price for this satisfaction.

INTERVIEWER: Dr. Ayman, how do you [al-Qaeda] view the calls for
reform currently being promoted?

AYMAN AL-ZAWAHIRI: There is no reform without *jihad* in the path of
Allah. And every call seeking reform without *jihad* condemns itself to death and failure. We need to appreciate the nature of the
battle and the nature of the struggle—for our enemies will not
grant us our rights without *jihad*.

No one should be deceived by what happened in Georgia, the
Ukraine, Kyrgyzstan, Ajbahiya [sic], and so on, for these were
changes that America wanted and encouraged. It allowed them to
happen, and prevented the Russians from interfering.

The Americans will never permit any Islamic organization to
assume rule in the heart of the Islamic world, unless it collabo-
rates with them, as is happening now in Iraq. And here's [Egyp-
tian president Hosni] Mubarak preparing himself for a *fifth*
term—only after the Americans gave him permission to do so.
Look at [Saudi king] Abdallah bin Abd al-Aziz ascending the
throne—only after the Americans organized it for him. And all
the demonstrations, appeals, protests, and initiatives were to no
avail, for they were depending on America.

And so the very same abhorrent regimes still practice the
very same abominable policies, with the blessing of America and
in defense of its interests, and the interests of Israel—against the
real enemy, that is, the resisting *mujahid* Islam, and not the fake
Islam, an Islam of begging and pleading.

Isn't it America that's sending prisoners from Guantánamo
and Baghram to Egypt and Jordan, where they are tortured by the
very same regimes that America insists should respect human
rights? Brother Ibn al-Sheik al-Libi was placed in a coffin and

shipped from Baghram to the National Security Department in Cairo, where he was severely tortured and held for one year, after which he was sent back once again to Baghram. This is one of *thousands* of examples.

Muslim brothers, reform will never be realized through endless talk and chatter about the corruptions of America, or through hoarse shouting at demonstrations: everybody is talking about the corruptions of America and its collaborators—even America's own collaborators and the people who have profited from their relations with it talk about its oppression and its leaders' corrupt practices!

There is no way of achieving reform except by [first] uprooting these corrupt and corrupting regimes, and by establishing a Muslim government that will protect rights, defend sanctities, institute justice, spread [the principle of] consultation, raise the banner of *jihad*, and confront the invaders, the foes of Islam. There will be no reform without all this. Whoever calls for a different path deceives himself before anyone else.

INTERVIEWER: Dr. Ayman, what is your take on America's call for spreading freedom around the world?

AYMAN AL-ZAWAHIRI: America does not want to spread freedom. Rather, it aims at occupying our countries, spreading corruption and promiscuity, encouraging missionary activity for the distorted Christianity, and calling for the spread of a new Islam that will facilitate its assault and promote its corrupt and corrupting collaborators—an Islam without *jihad*, without resistance, and without [the principle of] enjoining good and forbidding evil.

But instead of all this nonsense, we call the Americans to join Islam. Instead of waging failed wars against the Muslims and continuing to oppress and attack them, we call upon them to listen to the voice of truth. [We call upon them] to be honest with themselves and to realize that their current creed—which is composed of materialistic secularism, the distorted Christianity that has nothing to do with Jesus Christ, the hereditary Crusader hatred,

and their submission to Zionist hegemony over money and politics—this creed, this mixture, will only lead them to destruction in
this world, and torments in the Hereafter.

So we call upon every rational American and Westerner to
conduct a personal soul-search, and ask themselves several clear
and honest questions: "Are we really calling for freedom, justice,
equality, human rights, environmental preservation, and an end
to the killing, the destruction, the war of pillaging and plundering? Are our governments being honest in the reasons they give
for our wars against others, and especially the Muslims? Are we
really being just when we enable Israel to maintain its occupation
of Palestine, to kill Palestinians, destroy the Aqsa Mosque, and ju-
daicize Palestine?

"Are the Muslims really terrorists, a crazy bunch, or are they
honorable defenders of their religion, freedom, and sanctities?
Why did the Muslims attack us in particular? Why didn't they
attack the Swiss or Vietnamese, for instance? Are the Muslims
enemies of the People of the Book [Christians and Jews], or do
they exalt all the prophets, including Abraham, Moses, and Jesus? Are the Muslims indeed hostile to the Torah and the
Gospels, or do they hold them sacred?—only that they [Mus-
lims] have been requesting for fourteen centuries [since the
dawn of Islam] that we provide the original and authentic versions of these books, and it is we, the Crusaders, who are unable
to comply.[11]

"Do you Muslims really have a Book [the Koran] that has not
been distorted or altered, the likes of which mankind cannot produce? Is there any reality or truth to all these claims, which are being poured into our ears day and night, or are they lies, which
have been exposed and shattered by reality?"

In closing, I take this opportunity to address our captives,
who are being held in Crusader jails, and especially our *mujahid*
Sheikh Omar Abd al-Rahman,[12] as well as our captives in America, in Guantánamo, in Abu Ghraib, in Baghram, in the secret

American jails around the world, and in the prisons of the tyrants of Egypt, the Peninsula, Syria, Jordan, Tunisia, Morocco, Algeria, and in Palestine and elsewhere—I say to them: We have not forgotten you. We are still committed to the debt of your salvation. And with Allah's strength, we will continue to deliver blows to America and its allies, until we shatter your shackles.

MESSAGES TO THE AMERICANS

6

On October 7, 2001, nearly one month after the 9/11 strikes, President George W. Bush announced that the United States had launched a military campaign—"Enduring Freedom"—against al-Qaeda and Taliban targets in Afghanistan. Two weeks earlier the U.S. president had made a series of demands of the Taliban, including the extradition of al-Qaeda leaders: "None of these demands were met. And now the Taliban will pay a price." Hours later, Prime Minister Tony Blair confirmed that British forces were also engaged in the bombardment of Afghanistan.

On the same day, and on the heels of Blair's announcement, bin Laden appeared on al-Jazeera. Apparently he had taped this message earlier and asked that it be aired whenever the inevitable U.S.-led air strike against the Taliban occurred.

The main focus of his message is to show the disparity in the world's response when Americans are killed as opposed to when they kill others. He also portrays the U.S. strike on Afghanistan as an official declaration from the West that it is at war with Islam: "I say to you that these events have divided the entire world into two separate camps—one of faith, where there is no hypocrisy, and one of infidelity."

Finally, bin Laden takes his famous oath that no American will ever know safety until Muslims in Palestine first know it and Western forces completely withdraw from all Muslim territory.

"OSAMA BIN LADEN'S
OATH TO AMERICA"

❧

Praise be to Allah; we beseech His help and forgiveness. We seek refuge in Allah from our own evils and bad deeds. Whoever is guided by Allah will not go astray, and whoever is led astray has no guidance. And I testify that there is no god but Allah—alone, partnerless—and that Muhammad is His slave and Messenger.

Allah Most High has struck America in its most vulnerable spot, destroying its mighty buildings, praise be unto Him. Look at America—filled with terror from north to south, east to west—all praise be to Allah! What America is tasting today is but a fraction of what we have been tasting for decades: Our *umma* has been tasting this humiliation and contempt for over eighty years.[1] Its sons have been slain, its blood has been shed, and its sacred places have been defiled—all in opposition to what has been revealed by Allah. Despite this, no one has listened or responded. Thus did Allah Most High bestow success upon a convoy of Muslims—the vanguard of Islam—allowing them to devastate America utterly. I pray that Allah Almighty may raise them up to the highest [level of] Paradise. When these men retaliated [via the operations of 9/11] on behalf of their oppressed sons, brothers, and sisters in Palestine and elsewhere in the lands of Islam, the whole world cried out. And the infidels cried out, followed by the hypocrites [i.e., secular Arab governments and moderate Muslims].

Up until now, one million innocent children have been killed in Iraq,[2] though they were guilty of nothing. Despite this, we have not heard anyone condemn this, nor have the official *ulema* issued a *fatwa* [against it]. As I speak, Israeli tanks and bulldozers are entering Palestine—in Jenin, Ramalla, Rafa, Beit Jala, and elsewhere—[in order to] wreak havoc, and yet we hear no voices raised nor moves made. But after eighty years, when the sword falls down on America, the hypocrites stand up to lament these murderers who have scorned the blood, honor, and holy places of Muslims. The very least one can say about these people [Muslim "hypocrites"] is that they are morally depraved and dissolute apostates, who assist the butcher against his victim and help the oppressor against the innocent child. May Allah Most High protect [us] against them, and may He mete them the punishment they have earned.

I tell you, the matter is very clear: in the aftermath of this event, and now that the senior officials of America have spoken—beginning with that head of international infidelity, [U.S. president George W.] Bush and his associates—all Muslims should rise and hurry to the defense of their religion. In arrogance, they came out with their men and their horses instigating against us until even the lands [that belong to] Islam joined ranks with them against this group [al-Qaeda] who declared their faith in Allah Most High and refused to abandon their religion.

They came to fight Islam and its people under the pretext of "fighting terrorism." Hundreds of thousands, both young and old, were killed in the farthest region on earth—Japan[3]—and yet [for them] this is not considered an atrocity, but rather a "debatable issue." The same goes for Iraq: after bombing it, they consider it a debatable issue. Yet when a few of them were killed in Nairobi and Dar al-Salam,[4] they bombed Afghanistan and Iraq, and all the hypocrites stood behind the head of global infidelity—behind the Hubal[5] of the modern era—America and its supporters. I say to you that these events have divided the entire world into two separate camps—one of faith, where there is no hypocrisy, and one of infidelity, may Allah protect us from it. Every Muslim must give what he can to strengthen the religion. The winds of faith and change have blown to remove falsehood from the [Arabian] Peninsula of Muhammad.

As for America and its people, I share with them these few words: I swear by Allah Most High, who raised the heavens without pillars, that neither America, nor anyone living there, will ever enjoy safety until we can first see it as a reality in Palestine and before all the infidel armies quit the land of Muhammad. Allah is Great! Glory to Islam!

Peace be upon you, and Allah's mercy and blessings.

7

Sometime in February 2002, sixty American thinkers drafted a letter ("What We're Fighting For"), declaring America's resolve to combat Islamic terrorism. In response, 153 prominent Saudi scholars drafted their own letter ("How We Can Coexist") published in May in Riyad. This response, signed by many important figures in the Saudi establishment, incurred the wrath of al-Qaeda, which resulted in the critical essay "Moderate Islam Is a Prostration to the West" (see p. 22).

After chastising the Saudis for what al-Qaeda considered to be a theologically invalid and cowardly response, one typified by "prostrations" to the West, bin Laden took it upon himself to personally respond to the American letter by composing an open letter to the American people titled "Why We Are Fighting You," which was posted on the Internet in October 2002.

Arabic copies of this essay have proven difficult to find. This translation has been taken directly from the *Guardian*'s Web site, altered slightly for consistency: http://observer.guardian.co.uk/worldview/story/0,11581,845725,00.html.

" 'WHY WE ARE FIGHTING YOU':
OSAMA BIN LADEN'S LETTER
TO AMERICANS"

In the Name of Allah, the Compassionate, the Merciful.

"Permission to fight is given to those who are attacked, for they have been wronged and surely Allah is able to give them victory" [22:39].

"Those who believe, fight in the cause of Allah, and those who disbelieve, fight in the cause of evil. So fight you against the friends of Satan; ever feeble indeed is the plot of Satan" [4:76].

Some American writers have published articles under the title "What We're Fighting For." These articles have generated a number of responses, some of which adhered to the truth and were based on the *sharia*, and others which have not [the Saudis' "How We Can Coexist"]. Here we wanted to outline the truth—as an explanation and warning—hoping for Allah's reward, seeking success and support from Him.

While seeking Allah's help, we form our reply based on two questions directed at the Americans:

1. Why are we fighting and opposing you?
2. What are we calling you to, and what do we want from you?

As for the first question—Why are we fighting and opposing you?—the answer is very simple:

1. Because you attacked us and continue to attack us.
    A. You attacked us in Palestine:
        i. Palestine, which has sunk under military occupation for more than eighty years. The British handed over Palestine,

with your help and your support, to the Jews, who have occupied it for more than fifty years[1]—years overflowing with oppression, tyranny, crimes, murders, expulsion, destruction, and devastation. The creation and continuation of Israel is one of the greatest crimes, and you are the leaders of its criminals. And of course there is no need to explain and prove the degree of American support for Israel. The creation of Israel is a crime that must be erased.[2] Each and every person whose hands have become polluted in the contribution toward this crime must pay its price—and pay for it heavily.

ii.   It brings us both laughter and tears to see that you have not yet tired of repeating your fabricated lies that the Jews have a historical right to Palestine, as it was promised to them in the Torah.[3] Anyone who disputes with them on this alleged fact is accused of anti-Semitism. This is one of the most fallacious, widely circulated fabrications in history. The people of Palestine are pure Arabs and original Semites.[4] It is the Muslims who are the inheritors of Moses and the inheritors of the real Torah that has not been changed. Muslims believe in all of the prophets, including Abraham, Moses, Jesus, and Muhammad. If the followers of Moses have been promised a right to Palestine in the Torah, then the Muslims are the most worthy nation of this.

When the Muslims conquered Palestine and drove out the Romans [in A.D. 638], Palestine and Jerusalem returned to Islam, the religion of all the prophets. Therefore, the call to a historical right to Palestine cannot be raised against the Islamic *umma* that believes in all the prophets of Allah, and we make no distinction between them.

iii.   The blood pouring out of Palestine must be equally avenged. You must know that the Palestinians do not cry alone; their women are not widowed alone; their sons are not orphaned alone.

B. You attacked us in Somalia; you supported the Russian atrocities against us in Chechnya, the Indian oppression against us in Kashmir, and the Jewish aggression against us in Lebanon.

C. Under your supervision, consent, and orders, the governments of our countries—which act as your agents—attack us on a daily basis:

   i. These governments prevent our people from establishing *sharia* law, using violence and lies to do so.

   ii. These governments give us a taste of humiliation, placing us in a large prison of fear and submission.

   iii. These governments steal our Islamic *umma*'s wealth and sell them to you at a paltry price.

   iv. These governments have surrendered to the Jews and handed them most of Palestine, acknowledging the existence of their state over the dismembered limbs of their own people.

   v. The removal of these governments is an obligation upon us, and a necessary step to free the Islamic *umma*, make *sharia* law supreme, and regain Palestine. Our fight against these governments is one with our fight against you.

D. You steal our wealth and oil at paltry prices because of your international influence and military threats. This theft is indeed the biggest theft ever witnessed by mankind in the history of the world.

E. Your forces occupy our countries; you spread your military bases throughout them. You corrupt our lands, and you besiege our sanctuaries, to protect the security of the Jews and to ensure the continuity of your pillage of our treasures.

F. You have starved the Muslims of Iraq, where children die every day. More than 1.5 million Iraqi children have died as a result of your sanctions, and you amazingly did not show concern.[5] Yet when three thousand of your people died [in the events of 9/11], the entire world jumped up and has not yet sat down.

G. You have supported the Jews in their idea that Jerusalem is their eternal capital and agreed to move your embassy there.

With your help and under your protection, the Israelis are planning to destroy the Aqsa Mosque. Under the protection of your weapons, [Israeli prime minister Ariel] Sharon entered the Aqsa Mosque, to pollute it as a preparation to capture and destroy it.[6]

2. These tragedies and calamities are only a few examples of your oppression and aggression against us. It is commanded by our religion and intellect that the oppressed have a right to return the aggression. Do not expect anything from us except *jihad*, resistance, and revenge. Is it in any way rational to expect that, after America has attacked us for more than half a century, we will then leave her to live in security and peace?!!

3. You may then dispute that all the above does not justify aggression against civilians, for crimes they did not commit and offenses in which they did not partake:

    A. This argument contradicts your continual repetition that America is the land of freedom, and freedom's leaders in this world. The American people are the ones who choose their government by way of their own free will [through democratic elections]—a choice that stems from their agreement to its policies. Thus the American people have chosen, consented to, and affirmed their support for the Israeli oppression of the Palestinians, the occupation and usurpation of their land, and the continual killing, torture, punishment, and expulsion of the Palestinians. The American people have the ability and choice to refuse the policies of their government and even to change it if they want.

    B. The American people are the ones who pay the taxes that fund the planes that bomb us in Afghanistan, the tanks that strike and destroy our homes in Palestine, the armies that occupy our lands in the Arabian Gulf, and the fleets that ensure the blockade of Iraq. These tax dollars are given to Israel for it to continue to attack us and penetrate our lands. So the American people are the ones who fund the attacks against us, and they are the ones who oversee the expenditure of these monies in the way they wish, through their elected candidates.

C. Moreover, the American army is part of the American people. It is this very same people who are shamelessly helping the Jews fight against us.

D. The American people are the ones who employ both their men and their women in the American forces that attack us.

E. This is why the American people are not innocent of the innumerable crimes committed by the Americans and Jews against us.

F. Allah Most High legislated the permission and option to take revenge. Thus, if we are attacked, we have the right to attack back. Whoever has destroyed our villages and towns, we have the right to destroy their villages and towns. Whoever has stolen our wealth, we have the right to destroy their economy. And whoever has killed our civilians, we have the right to kill theirs.

The American government and press still refuse to answer the question:

Why did they [9/11 hijackers and their accomplices] attack us in New York and Washington?

If Sharon is a man of peace in the eyes of [President George W.] Bush, then we too are men of peace!!! America does not understand the language of manners and principles, so we address it using the language it does understand [i.e., a language of force].

As for the second question that we want to answer: What are we calling you to, and what do we want from you?

1. The first thing that we are calling you to is Islam.

A. The religion of *tawhid* ; of freedom from associating partners with Allah Most High, and rejection of [such blasphemy]; of complete love for Him, the Exalted; of complete submission to His *sharia*; and of the discarding of all the opinions, orders, theories, and religions that contradict with the religion He sent down to His Prophet Muhammad. Islam is the religion of all the prophets and makes no distinction between them.

It is to this religion that we call you—the seal of all the previous religions.[7] It is the religion of the *tawhid* of Allah, sincerity, the best of manners, righteousness, mercy, honor, purity, and piety. It is the religion of showing kindness to others, establishing justice between them, granting them their rights, and defending the oppressed and the persecuted. It is the religion of enjoining the good and forbidding the evil with the hand, tongue, and heart. It is the religion of *jihad* in the way of Allah, so that Allah's Word [Koran] and religion [*sharia* law] reign supreme. And it is the religion of *tawhid* and agreement in obedience to Allah, and total equality between all people, without regard to their color, sex, or language.

B. It is the religion whose Book—the Koran—will remain preserved and unchanged, after the other divine books and messages have been changed. The Koran is the miracle until the Day of Judgment. Allah has challenged anyone to bring a book like the Koran or even ten verses like it.

2. The second thing we call you to is to stop your oppression, lies, immorality, and debauchery that has spread among you.

A. We call you to be a people of manners, principles, honor, and purity; to reject the immoral acts of fornication, homosexuality, intoxicants, gambling, and usury.

We call you to all of this that you may be freed from that which you have become caught up in; that you may be freed from the deceptive lies that you are a great nation, which your leaders spread among you in order to conceal from you the despicable state that you have attained.

B. It is saddening to tell you that you are the worst civilization witnessed in the history of mankind:

i. You are the nation who, rather than ruling through the

sharia of Allah, chooses to invent your own laws as you will and desire. You separate religion from your policies, contradicting the pure nature that affirms absolute authority to the Lord your Creator. You flee from the embarrassing question posed to you: How is it possible for Allah the Almighty to create His creation, grant them power over all the creatures and land, grant them all the amenities of life, and then deny them that which they are most in need of: knowledge of the laws [i.e., the *sharia*] that govern their lives?

ii. You are the nation that permits usury, though it has been forbidden by all the religions. Yet you build your economy and investments on usury. As a result of this, in all its different forms and guises, the Jews have taken control of your economy, thereby taking control of your media, and now control all aspects of your life, making you their servants and achieving their aims at your expense—precisely what Benjamin Franklin warned you against.[8]

iii. You are a nation that permits the production, spread, and usage of intoxicants. You also permit drugs, and only forbid the trade of them, even though your nation is the largest consumer of them.

iv. You are a nation that permits acts of immorality, and you consider them to be pillars of "personal freedom." You have continued to sink down this abyss from level to level until incest has spread among you, in the face of which neither your sense of honor nor your laws object.

Who can forget your President Clinton's immoral acts committed in the official Oval Office?[9] After that you did not even bring him to account, other than [by saying] that he "made a mistake," after which everything passed with no punishment. Is there a worse kind of event for which your name will go down in history and be remembered by nations?

v.   You are a nation that permits gambling in its all forms. The companies practice this as well, resulting in the investments becoming active and the criminals becoming rich.

vi. You are a nation that exploits women like consumer products or advertising tools, calling upon customers to purchase them. You use women to serve passengers, visitors, and strangers to increase your profit margins. You then rant that you support the "liberation of women."

vii. You are a nation that practices the trade of sex in all its forms, directly and indirectly. Giant corporations and establishments are built on this [commodity], under the name of "art, entertainment, tourism, and freedom," and other deceptive names you attribute to it.

viii. And because of all this, you have been described in history as a nation that spreads diseases that were previously unknown to man. Go ahead and boast to the nations of man that you brought them AIDS as a Satanic American Invention![10]

ix. You have destroyed nature with your industrial waste and gases more than any other nation in history. Despite this, you refuse to sign the Kyoto agreement[11] so that you can secure the profit of your greedy companies and industries.

x.   Your law is the law of the rich and wealthy people, who hold sway in their political parties and fund their election campaigns with their gifts. Behind them stand the Jews, who control your policies, media, and economy.

xi. What you are most singled out for in the history of mankind, however, is that you have used your power to destroy more people than any other nation in history— not to defend principles and values, but to hasten to secure your interests and profits. You who dropped a nuclear bomb on Japan, even though Japan was ready to negotiate an end to the war.[12] How many acts of oppression, tyranny, and injustice have you carried out, O you "callers to freedom"?

xii. Let us not forget one of your major characteristics: your
double standard in both manners and values; your
hypocrisy in manners and principles. All manners, principles, and values have two scales: one for you and one for
the rest [of the world].

c. The freedom and democracy that you call to is for yourselves
and the white race only; as for the rest of the world, you impose upon them your monstrous, destructive policies and
governments, which you call "America's Allies." Yet you prevent them from establishing democracies. When the Islamic
party in Algeria wanted to practice democracy and they won
the election, you unleashed your agents in the Algerian army
on them, attacking them with tanks and guns, imprisoning
them and torturing them—a new lesson from the "American
book of democracy"!!!¹³

D. Your policy of prohibiting and forcibly removing weapons of
mass destruction to ensure world peace applies only to those
countries that you do not permit to possess such weapons. As
for the countries you consent to—such as Israel—they are allowed to keep and use such weapons to defend their security.
Anyone else who you suspect might be manufacturing or
keeping these kinds of weapons, you call them criminals and
you take military action against them.

E. You are the last ones to respect the resolutions and policies of
International Law, yet you claim to want to selectively punish
anyone else who does the same. Israel has for more than fifty
years been pushing U.N. resolutions and rules against the
wall with the full support of America.¹⁴

F. As for the war criminals whom you censure and form criminal courts for—you then shamelessly ask that your own are
granted immunity!! However, history will not forget the war
crimes that you committed against the Muslims and the rest
of the world; those you have killed in Japan, Afghanistan, Somalia, Lebanon, and Iraq will remain a shame that you will
never be able to escape. It will suffice to remind you of your

latest war crimes in Afghanistan, in which densely populated innocent civilian villages were destroyed; bombs were dropped on mosques causing the roof of the mosque to come crashing down on the heads of the Muslims praying inside. You are the ones who broke the agreement with the *mujahidin* when they left Qunduz, bombing them in Jangi Fort, and killing more than one thousand of your prisoners through suffocation and thirst.[15] Allah alone knows how many people have died by torture at your hands and those of your agents. Your planes remain in the Afghan skies, looking for anyone remotely suspicious.

G. You have claimed to be the "vanguards of human rights," and your Ministry of Foreign Affairs issues annual reports containing statistics of those countries that violate any human rights. However, all these things vanished when the *mujahidin* hit you [9/11], and you proceeded to implement the same methods of those governments you used to curse. In America, you captured thousands of Muslims and Arabs, took them into custody without a cause or even a court trial—without even disclosing their names. You issued newer, harsher laws.[16]

What happens in Guantánamo [Bay][17] is a historical embarrassment to America and its values, and it screams in your faces—you hypocrites: What is the value of your signature on any agreement or treaty?

3. We call you to take an honest look at yourselves—and I doubt you will do so—to discover that you are a nation without principles or manners, and that values and principles for you are something that you merely demand from others—not something that you yourselves practice.

4. We also advise you to stop supporting Israel, and to end your support of the Indians in Kashmir, the Russians against the Chechens, and to also cease supporting the Manila government against the Muslims in southern Philippines.

5. We also advise you to pack your luggage and get out of our

lands. We desire for your goodness, guidance, and righteousness, so do not force us to send you back as cargo in coffins.

6. We call upon you to end your support of the corrupt leaders in our countries. Do not interfere in our politics and method of [Islamic] education. Leave us alone, or else expect us in New York and Washington.

7. We also call you to deal with us and interact with us on the basis of mutual interests and benefits, rather than the policies of submission, theft, and occupation, and to end your policy of supporting the Jews—for this will result in more disasters for you.

If you fail to respond to all these conditions, then prepare to fight with the Islamic *umma*. The *umma* of *tawhid*, which puts complete trust in Allah alone and fears none other than Him. The *umma* that is addressed by its Koran with the words: "Do you fear them? Allah has more right that you should fear Him if you are believers. Fight against them so that Allah will punish them by your hands and disgrace them and give you victory over them and heal the breasts of believing people. And remove the anger of their [Muslims'] hearts. Allah accepts the repentance of whom He wills. Allah is All-Knowing, All-Wise" [9:13–14].

The *umma* of honor and respect:

"But honor, power, and glory belong to Allah, and to His Messenger [Muhammad], and to the believers" [63:8].
   "So do not become weak [against your enemy], nor be sad; you will overcome if you are indeed true believers" [3:139].

The *umma* of Martyrdom—the *umma* that desires death more than you desire life:

"Think not of those who are killed in the way of Allah as dead. Nay, they are alive with their Lord, and they are being provided for. They rejoice in what Allah has bestowed upon

them from His bounty and rejoice for the sake of those who
have not yet joined them, but are left behind [not yet mar-
tyred] for on them no fear shall come, nor shall they grieve.
They rejoice in a grace and a bounty from Allah, and Allah
will not waste the reward of the believers" [3:169–171].

The *umma* of victory and success that Allah has promised:

"It is He who has sent His Messenger [Muhammad] with
guidance and the religion of truth [Islam], to make it victorious over all other religions, even though the idolaters hate it"
[61:9].
   "Allah has decreed that 'Verily it is I and my messengers
who shall be victorious.' Verily Allah is all-powerful, all-
mighty" [58:21].

The Islamic *umma* that was able to dismiss and destroy previous
evil empires like yourself [18]; the *umma* that rejects your attacks, wishes
to remove your evils, and is prepared to fight you. You are well aware
that the Islamic *umma*, from the very core of its soul, despises your
haughtiness and arrogance.
   If the Americans refuse to listen to our advice and the goodness,
guidance, and righteousness that we call them to, then beware that
you will lose this Crusade Bush began, just like the other previous
Crusades in which you were humiliated by the hands of the *mujahidin*, fleeing to your home in great silence and disgrace. If the
Americans do not respond, then their fate will be that of the Soviets
who fled from Afghanistan to deal with their military defeat, political
breakup, ideological downfall, and economic bankruptcy.
   This is our message to the Americans, as an answer to theirs. Do
they now know why we fight them and over which form of ignorance,
by the permission of Allah, we shall prevail?

8

On October 18, 2003, some seven months after the U.S.-led invasion of Iraq, al-Jazeera released a message from Osama bin Laden directed to the American people regarding the war in Iraq. (That same day al-Jazeera also released a message from bin Laden directed to the Iraqi people; see p. 243.)

In this brief message, bin Laden singles out President George W. Bush and his administration by name, accusing them of widespread corruption and subservience to the "Zionist" lobby. In connection, bin Laden also tries to make it clear to the American people that the war in Iraq is being waged solely to guarantee Israel's interests and dominate the oil fields: "This gang and their leader enjoy lying, war, and looting—[all] in order to serve their own ambitions. . . . They have fooled you and deceived you into invading Iraq for a second time."

Historical allusions are also made here—from the dignity and grandeur of the city of Baghdad, home of the Abbasid Caliphate, which "will never fall to you," to the United States' transgressions against the Native Americans.

"ISRAEL, OIL, AND IRAQ"

This is a message from Osama bin Muhammad bin Laden to the American people regarding your aggression in Iraq. Peace to whoever follows [right] guidance.

Some have the impression that you are a reasonable people—yet the majority of you are base, lacking sound ethics or good manners. You elect the wicked from among you, the greatest liars and most depraved, and you are enslaved to the wealthiest and most influential [among you], especially the Jews—who direct you through the lie of "democracy" to support the Israelis and their machinations and in complete antagonism toward our religion [Islam].

These machinations are paid for in our blood and land—but also in your blood and economy.

This has been proven by recent events: the war on Iraq, which does not concern you, demonstrates as much.

[U.S. president George W.] Bush and his gang, with their heavy sticks and cruel hearts, are an evil to [all] mankind. They have stabbed into the truth, until they have killed it altogether in the eyes of the world.

With this behavior they have encouraged hypocrisy spreading corruption and [political] bribes shamelessly to the level of heads of state.

This gang and their leader enjoy lying, warring, and looting—[all] in order to serve their own ambitions. The blood of the children of Vietnam, Somalia, Afghanistan, and Iraq still drips from their teeth. They have fooled and deceived you into invading Iraq for a second time, [all while] lying to you and the whole world.

Nations are nothing without sound ethics and morals. So if these depart, the nations [too will] depart.

Bush has sent your sons into the lion's den—to slaughter and be slaughtered—claiming that this act was in defense of international peace and America's security, thereby concealing the facts [from you].

On the one hand he is carrying out the demands of the Zionist lobby that helped him into [the office of] the White House—that is, annihilate the military might of Iraq because it is too close to the Jews in occupied Palestine, regardless of the harm that will come to your people and your economy.

On the other hand, he is concealing his own ambitions and the ambitions of the Zionist lobby in their desire for oil. He is still following the policy of his ancestors who slew the American Indians in order to seize their land and wealth. He thought that this [venture] would be easy—a lie that would not be exposed.

But Allah sent him to Baghdad, the seat of the Caliphate,[1] the land of people who prefer death to honey. They [the Iraqis] turned his profits into losses, his happiness into misery, and now he is merely looking for a way [to go] back home.

Thanks be to Allah Most High, who has exposed the lies of George Bush and made his term as president a term of continual disaster.

To Bush I say, you are begging the [whole] world to come to your aid, begging mercenaries from every corner of the world, even from the small states. This begging has shattered your pride and revealed how trivial and weak you are after claiming [that you will] defend the [whole] world.

Now you are like the knight who was trying to protect the people from the Sword of Malik, but ended up begging someone to protect him.

We have the right to retaliate at any [given] time and place against [any and] all countries involved—particularly England, Spain, Australia, Poland, Japan, and Italy,[2] including those Muslim states that took part [in the raid against Iraq], especially the Gulf states, and in particular Kuwait, which has become a launching pad for the Crusading forces.

To the American soldiers in Iraq I say, now that all the lies have been exposed and the greatest liar revealed, your presence on Iraqi land multiplies the oppression and is great folly.

It shows that you sell your lives for the lives of others. You are spilling your blood to swell the bank accounts of the White House gang and their fellow arms dealers and the proprietors of great companies. Surely the greatest folly in life is to sell your [own] life for the lives of others!

In conclusion, I say to the American people: we will continue to fight you and continue to conduct martyrdom operations inside and outside America until you depart from your oppressive course, abandon your follies, and rein in your madmen.

Know that we are counting our dead, especially in Palestine, where your allies the Jews murder them. We are going to take revenge for them from your blood, as we did on the day of New York [9/11]. Remember what I said to you about that day regarding our security and your security. Baghdad—the seat of the Caliphate—will never fall to you, by Allah's grace, and we will fight you as long as we carry our guns. If we fall, our sons will replace us.

May our mothers become barren if we leave any of you alive on our soil.

9

In late October 2004, a few days before the U.S. presidential elections, the image of Osama bin Laden resurfaced again on al-Jazeera. This lengthy message focused on a number of issues, including the "true" reasons for the war in Iraq (which includes remarks about the controversial military contractor Halliburton); al-Qaeda's hope that, like the Soviet Union before it, the United States will economically bleed to death; and the "best way" to cease hostilities—which culminates with a simple statement of reciprocity: "Every action produces a reaction."

This message also marks the first time bin Laden publicly acknowledged his role in the 9/11 strikes; previously he had insisted that he was merely an "inciter" and that it was the Muslim *umma* in general who had retaliated in defense of their faith.

"YOUR FATE IS IN YOUR HANDS ALONE"

Praise be to Allah, who created the world for his worship, commanding them [mankind] to be just, while permitting whoever is wronged to retaliate against the oppressor in kind.

Peace to whoever follows [right] guidance.

O people of America, I address these words to you regarding the best way to avoid another Manhattan [i.e., 9/11], as well as the war, its causes and consequences.

From the start, I tell you that security is an indispensable pillar of human life; free men do not underestimate their security—contrary to [President George W.] Bush's claim that we hate freedom.[1] If so, let him explain to us why we have not attacked Sweden, for instance. Moreover, it is well known that whoever hates freedom does not possess a defiant spirit, such as the nineteen [9/11 hijackers]—may Allah have mercy on them.

No, we have been fighting you precisely because we are free men who will not remain silent in the face of injustice. We want to restore freedom to our Islamic *umma*. Thus, as you violate our security, so [shall] we violate yours. Only a stupid thief could persuade himself that he can meddle with the security of others while he himself remains secure. However, intelligent people, whenever disaster strikes, make it a priority to discover its causes, in order to prevent it from happening again.

But you amaze me! Though we are in the fourth year after the events of September 11, Bush is still misleading you with his campaign of distortion and deception, concealing from you the true causes. Consequentially, the motives for another [terrorist attack] remain. So I will now explain to you the causes underlying these events, and I will tell you the truth[2] about the moment in which these decisions were taken, to allow you to ponder.

With Allah as my witness, I say to you that we had never considered striking the [twin] towers; however, after things became unbearable, and we witnessed the oppression and atrocities perpetrated against our people in Palestine and Lebanon by the American-Israeli coalition—it was then that I got the idea.

The events that directly affected me, weighing heavily on my soul, commenced in 1982 and continued thereafter—when America permitted the Israelis to invade Lebanon with the aid of the American Sixth Fleet. They started a bombardment, killing and wounding many, while others were terrorized and displaced.[3] I still recall those distressing scenes—blood, severed limbs; women and children massacred. Everywhere there were homes being destroyed and high-rises collapsing over their residents, while bombs ruthlessly rained down on our homes. It was just like a crocodile devouring a child who could do nothing but scream! (And does a crocodile understand any language other than that of arms?) The whole world saw and heard what happened, but did nothing.

During these difficult moments, many nebulous notions surged in me, culminating in a powerful urge in me to reject oppression and retaliate against the oppressors. Thus as I looked upon those crumbling towers in Lebanon, I was struck by the idea of punishing the oppressor in kind by destroying towers in America—giving them a taste of their own medicine and deterring them from murdering our women and children. It was on that day that I became convinced that oppression and the premeditated murder of innocent women and children is an established American policy: terrorism is [called] "freedom" and "democracy," while resistance to this is [called] "terrorism" and "intolerance." Imposing brutal sanctions on millions of people [in Iraq], as [former U.S. president George] Bush Sr. did, thereby resulting in the mass slaughter of children, is the worst thing mankind has ever witnessed. While [current U.S. president] Bush Jr. dropped millions of pounds of bombs and explosives on millions of children[4] in Iraq in order to remove a former agent [of the United States, Sad-

MAKE MISCHIEF

dam Hussein] and install a new one who will help steal Iraq's oil along with [committing] other outrages.

So against this backdrop and these images, and in response to these terrible crimes, the events of September 11 came. Shall a man be blamed for protecting his own? Self-defense and punishing the wicked in kind—are these shameful [acts of] "terrorism"? And even if it is, we have no other option. This is the message that time and time again I tried communicating to you, by both word and deed, years prior to September 11. Note my interview with Scott [MacLeod] in *Time* magazine in 1996, or with Peter Arnett on CNN in 1997, or John Weiner in 1998; note the events of Nairobi, Tanzania, and Aden[5]; note my interviews with Abdul Bari Atwan and with Robert Fisk (the latter being one of your own [a Westerner] and coreligionist [Christian], but one whom I consider neutral).

But would those who claim to stand for freedom in the White House and the media that supports them ever interview him [Fisk] in order that he convey to the American people what he has gathered from us to be the reasons for our fight against you? Because if you could avoid these reasons you would lead America right back to the security it enjoyed prior to September 11. So much for the war and its causes.

As for the consequences [of the "War on Terror"], these have been, thanks be to Allah Most High, very positive, and have far exceeded all standards of expectation, for many reasons—particularly because we encountered no difficulty leading Bush and his administration on, since they so resemble the regimes in our countries, half of whom are ruled by the military, the other half by the sons of kings and presidents. Our experience with them is a long one. And both types [military/hereditary dictatorships] are replete with those who are known for their haughtiness, conceit, greed, and the misappropriation of wealth.

This resemblance goes back to Bush Sr.'s visit to the region [i.e., Arabian Peninsula]. While many of our people were dazzled by America, hoping these visits would make an impression on our countries, the opposite occurred: he was the one impressed by the monarchic and military regimes. He grew envious of the fact that they could remain in power for decades, embezzling the public wealth of the nation without ever being held accountable. So he brought [and bequeathed] to his son tyranny and the suppression of freedoms—and this they called the "Patriot Act,"[6] implemented under the pretext of combating terrorism.

Moreover, Bush Sr. understood the benefits of installing his sons as state governors; nor did he forget to import into Florida—straight from our region's leaders—the idea of election fraud, to be used at critical times.[7] Thus as previously mentioned, it has been easy for us to provoke and lure this administration. All we had to do was send two *mujahidin* to the farthest east to raise aloft a piece of rag with the words "al-Qaeda" written on it, and the [U.S.] generals came a-scurrying—causing America to suffer human, economic, and political damages, while accomplishing nothing worth mentioning aside from providing business [contracts] for their private corporations. On the other hand, we have gained experience in guerrilla and attritional warfare in our *jihad* against that great and wicked superpower, Russia, which we, alongside the *mujahidin*, fought for ten years until, bankrupt, it was forced to withdraw [out of Afghanistan in 1989]—all praise be to Allah! And so we are continuing the same policy: to make America bleed till it becomes bankrupt—Allah willing. Nothing is too great for Allah.

Even so, it would not be wholly accurate to say that al-Qaeda has triumphed over the White House administration, or that the White House administration has lost this war: upon close scrutiny, it is impossible to say that al-Qaeda is the only cause for these spectacular gains. In fact, the White House policy of creating war fronts in order to give business to their various corporations—whether in the field of armaments, oil, or construction—has also helped al-Qaeda achieve these remarkable results. Indeed, it has even appeared to some analysts and diplomats that the White House and we are playing as one team toward the [economic] goals of America, even if our intentions differ. Such notions and their like were referred to by a British diplomat during a lecture at the Royal Institute for International Affairs—for instance, that while al-Qaeda spent $500,000 on the events [of 9/11], America lost more than $500 billion, due to the events and their aftermath. In other words, for every dollar spent by al-Qaeda, America lost 1 million—thanks be to Allah Almighty—along with an enormous number of jobs lost. As for the [federal/economic] deficit, it reached astronomical figures estimated to be more than a trillion dollars.

Even more critical for America was the fact that the *mujahidin* have recently forced Bush to resort to an emergency budget[8] in order to continue the fighting in Afghanistan and Iraq—evidence of the bleed-till-bankrupt plan, Allah willing. While this all demonstrates that al-Qaeda has made gains, so too does it demonstrate that the Bush administration has equally profited. Anyone who sees the enormity of contracts acquired by large and dubious corporations, such as Halliburton[9] and others connected to Bush and his administration, can be sure of this. Thus it is you, the American people and your economy, who are the real losers [in this war].

Incidentally, we had agreed with the commander-general [of the 9/11 operations] Muhammad Atta that all operations were to be carried out within twenty minutes, before Bush and his administration could react: we were not aware that the commander in chief of the American armed forces would abandon 50,000 of his citizens in the twin towers to face those great horrors alone, just when they needed him most. Apparently a little girl's story about a goat[10] and its "butting" was more important than paying attention to planes and their butting into skyscrapers [Arabic for skyscraper: cloud butting]. This allowed us three times the amount of time needed to carry out the operations.

It should also be clear to you that American thinkers and intellectuals warned Bush before the war [with Iraq, telling him]: all that you want for securing America and removing weapons of mass destruction [from Iraq]—assuming they exist—is at your disposal; the nations of the world are with you regarding inspections, and it is in the interests of America not to be thrust into an unjust war with an unknown outcome.

But the black gold blinded him; he gave priority to private interests over American public interest. So war commenced, many were slain, and the American economy bled. And thus Bush has become embroiled in the quagmire of Iraq, which threatens his future. His situation is akin to the parable of the cantankerous goat, which used its hoofs to dig up a knife from under the earth [and which was later used to slaughter it].

I tell you: More than fifteen thousand of our people have been killed and tens of thousands injured, while more than a thousand of yours have been killed and tens of thousands injured. Bush's hands are stained with the blood of all those murdered on both sides—and all for the sake of oil and more business for his private companies.

Know that you behave like a nation that punishes a weak man who has profited from the deaths of one of its sons, while absolving a man from a privileged background for profiting from the deaths of a thousand of its sons. In like manner your allies in Palestine terrorize women and children, and murder and imprison men.

Bear in mind that every action produces a reaction.

Finally, it behooves you to reflect on the testaments of those thousands who left you on September 11, waving their hands in despair: these are inspiring testaments, which should be published and closely studied. One of the most notable things I have read was some prose in their gesticulations before they dropped, saying: "We were wrong to let the White House's aggressive foreign policies go unchecked against oppressed people." It's as if they were saying to you: "People of America, hold accountable those responsible for our deaths." Happy is he who learns from the experience of others. Their signals of desperation also remind me of a verse of poetry:

> *Evil slays those who perpetrate it, and the pastures of iniquity*
> *are fatal.*

It's been said: An ounce of prevention is better than a pound of cure. Know that a return to what is right is preferable than to persist in that which is wrong. No sensible person would ever forfeit their security, property, or home—all for the sake of the liar in the White House.

In conclusion, I tell you in all honesty that your security lies not in the hands of [former presidential candidate John] Kerry, Bush, or al-Qaeda. No, it lies in your own hands; and any state that does not encroach upon our security automatically guarantees its own.

Allah is our Guardian and Helper—while you have none.

Peace to whoever follows [right] guidance.

Late in January 2006, an audiotaped message from bin Laden—his first public utterance in over a year—was broadcast on al-Jazeera. In it, bin Laden cites U.S. opinion polls, which show an increased majority of people disapproving of the war in Iraq as his reason for communicating with the Americans at this time.

In light of the opinion polls, bin Laden offers a long-term truce: "For we are the *umma* that Allah has forbidden from double-crossing and lying" (see p. 224 for an analysis of this offer). This would be the second time al-Qaeda had offered a truce to the West; nearly two years earlier bin Laden had offered a truce to Europe (see p. 234). And as the Europeans rejected the truce offer, the White House summarily rejected this offer: "We do not negotiate with terrorists. We put them out of business."

"BIN LADEN'S TRUCE OFFER TO THE AMERICANS"

※

In the name of Allah, the Compassionate, the Merciful.

Peace to whoever follows [right] guidance.

My message to you is about the war in Iraq and Afghanistan and the way to end it. I did not intend to speak to you about this [anymore] since this issue has already been settled upon among us. "Only steel breaks steel," and our situation, by Allah's grace, is only getting better and better, while your situation is the opposite of that.

Yet what has roused me to speak are the continual mistakes your President Bush commits regarding his comments over the results of your opinion polls, which indicate that an overwhelming majority of you wish [to see] American forces withdraw from Iraq. But he opposed this wish and said that withdrawing the forces would send a wrong message to the rivals, and that it is better to fight them [terrorists] on their land than for them to fight us on our [American] land. Between my hands I hold the answer to these mistakes:

I say that the war in Iraq is raging without end [in sight]; the operations in Afghanistan are continually escalating in our favor—praise be to Allah. Pentagon figures show an increase in your casualties and wounded—let alone the massive economic losses, the destruction of the soldiers' morale there, and an increase [in cases] of suicide among them.

Try to picture the state of psychological breakdown that afflicts the soldier while he gathers the remains of his fellows after they step on a land mine and are blown apart. Thereafter, the soldier is caught up between a rock and a hard place: either he refuses marching out on patrols (leaving [the safety of] the military camps behind) and earn-ing himself a severe chastisement from the "butcher of Vietnam" [usual epithet for former U.S. defense secretary Donald Rumsfeld], or else he goes forth and is utterly annihilated by mines. So he has but two choices—both of which place extreme psychological pressure on him [and lead to] fear, humiliation, and defeat. All the while his people are unmindful of him. Thus he finds no other solution than to commit suicide. And this is what you hear about him and his suicide—a strong message he writes to you with his soul, blood, and anguish, to save what can be saved from this inferno. The solution is in your hands, if you care about them [U.S. troops].

As for news surrounding our *mujahidin* brothers, this differs from what the Pentagon propagates, since they notify the[ir] media outlets to portray only that which does not accord with reality. But what casts even greater doubt over the White House administration's information is the fact that it targets those media outlets that *do* report some of the reality as it occurs. And it has recently appeared, supported by documents, that the butcher of freedom in the world [epithet for President George W. Bush] was bent on bombing the headquarters of the al-Jazeera network in Qatar, after bombing its offices in Kabul and Baghdad,[1] [the network] that is above all one of your own creations.

From another angle, *jihad* is ongoing, by the grace of Allah, despite all the suppressive measures adopted by the American army and its agents—to a point that there is no mentionable difference between these crimes and [former Iraqi leader] Saddam [Hussein's] crimes. The[ir] crimes have reached a degree to where women are raped and seized as hostages in place of their husbands—and there is no power save in Allah!

As for the torturing of men, this has reached a point to where burning chemical acids and electric drills to dismember them are utilized. And whenever they [the Americans] give up on [interrogating] them, they sometimes kill them by drilling them in the head. Read, if you will, the humanitarian reports that enumerate the horrors [committed] in the Abu Ghraib, Guantánamo, and Baghram prisons.[2]

So I say that, despite all the barbarous methods, the resolve of the resistance is unbroken. The *mujahidin* are increasing in number and strength. Indeed, the reports indicate the growing defeat and failure of the unlucky quartet of Bush, [Vice President Dick] Cheney, Rumsfeld, and [World Bank president Paul] Wolfowitz. Announcing this defeat and making it public is just a matter of time; [it will be revealed] according to how well the American people know of this tragedy. Sensible people know that Bush does not have a plan to realize his alleged victory in Iraq.

And if you compare the small number of dead on the day that Bush announced the end of major operations in that fake and immature performance aboard the aircraft carrier[3] with the tenfold number of dead and wounded who were killed in the smaller operations, you would know the truth of what I say: that Bush and his administration possess neither the desire nor the intention to get out of Iraq, due to their own private, dubious interests.

And so to return to what I spoke of at the start: I say that the poll results please those who are sensible and that Bush's opposition to them is a mistake. Reality proves that the war against America and its allies has not been limited to Iraq, as he claims. On the contrary, Iraq has become a point of attraction and restorer of [our] energies. At the same time, the *mujahidin* have been able to penetrate time and time again all security measures adopted by the oppressive alliance. The proof of this is the explosions you have seen in the most important capitals of the European nations [that are] in this hostile coalition. As for the delay of similar operations occurring in America, this has not been because of failure to break through your security measures. The operations are under preparation and you will see them in your own homes once they are readied.

Based on all the above, it becomes evident that what Bush says is false. Yet the statement that slipped his lips—which is represented by the opinion polls calling for withdrawing the troops—is that it is better if we [Americans] don't fight Muslims on their land and that they don't fight us on our land.

So we have no qualms in offering you a long-term truce on fair conditions that we adhere to. For we are the *umma* that Allah has forbidden from double-crossing and lying.[4] Both sides would be able to enjoy security and stability under this truce so we can build Iraq and Afghanistan, both of which have been devastated by the war. There is no shame in this solution, which prevents the wasting of billions of dollars that have gone to those with influence and the merchants of war in America, who have supported Bush's election campaign with billions of dollars. And from here we can [begin to] comprehend Bush and his gang's insistence to continue the war.

If you [Americans] are sincere in your desire for peace and security, so here it is—we have answered you. And if Bush decides to carry on with his lies and oppression, then it would be useful for you to read the book *Rogue State* [written by William Blum], which states in its introduction: "If I were president, I would stop the attacks of the United States: First I would give an apology to all the widows and orphans and those who were tortured. Then I would announce that American interference in the nations of the world has ended once and for all."

In closing, I tell you that the war will be either ours or yours. If it is the former, it will mean your loss and your shame forever—and the winds are blowing in that direction, by Allah's grace. But if it is the latter, then read history! for we are a people who do not stand for injustice, and we strive for vengeance all [the days of] our lives. And the days and nights will not pass until we avenge [ourselves] as [we did] on September 11. Your minds will be troubled, your lives embittered, and the course of events will lead to that which is hateful to you. As for us, we have nothing to lose: one who swims in the sea does not fear rain.

You have occupied our lands, transgressed against our manhood and dignity, spilled our blood, plundered our wealth, destroyed our homes, dislocated us, and played with our security—*and we will give you the same treatment.*

You have tried preventing us from leading an honorable life, but you will not be able to prevent us from a noble death. Neglecting *ji-had*, which is prescribed in our religion, is a grievous sin. The best death for us is under the shadow of swords [Paradise]. Do not let your strength and modern arms fool you, for they but win a few battles yet lose the war. Patience and steadfastness are greater, and the end result is the most important thing. With patience and crude weapons we battled the Soviet foe for ten years. We bled their economy and by the grace of Allah they are now nothing. In that there is a lesson for you. Steadfast shall we fight you, until our strongest die, and we shall never quit the struggle until our weapons quit.

I have sworn to not die except as a free [man]. Even if I find bitter the taste of death—let me not die humiliated or deceived.

Peace to whoever follows [right] guidance.

11

On January 13, 2006, a U.S. air strike targeting Ayman al-Zawahiri missed its target, killing eighteen people in Pakistan's remote tribal regions. Not surprisingly, it was not long before an irate and apparently unscathed Zawahiri appeared before the world condemning the attacks (which were formally condemned by many, including the Pakistani government). He singled out President Bush in particular, taunting him: "Bush, do you know where I am? I am among the Muslim masses."

The second half of his message is directed to the American people, whom Zawahiri castigates for continuing to "drown in illusions" and allowing their leaders to reject bin Laden's truce offer. This message also echoes bin Laden's threat that soon Americans will be seeing terrorist operations in their very own homes (see p. 223).

"I AM AMONG THE MUSLIM MASSES"

❖

With the collaboration of [Pakistani president Pervez] Musharraf the traitor and his security agencies, the servants of the Crusaders and the Jews, American airplanes launched an [air]strike against the village of Damdula, in Bajuar, shortly after the Feast of the Sacrifice [i.e., 1/13/06]. Eighteen Muslims—men, women, and children—were killed in their war against the *jihad*, which they call "terrorism," claiming that they were attempting to kill this weak individual [Zawahiri] and four of my brothers. The whole world has discovered the extent of American lies and failures, as well as [the extent of] its savagery in its war against Islam and the Muslims.

In response to this event, I have some messages to deliver:

I direct my first message to the butcher of Washington, Bush, to whom I say: Bush, not only are you a defeated liar but, by Allah's help and strength, you are also a failure and loser. You are the bane of your nation. You have brought—and will bring—to it disasters and tragedies. And know [this], O Bush, you failed Crusader, that your conflict is with the *umma* of *tawhid*—we who believe in one god, the One, He who begets not, nor is begotten, and none is like unto Him; He who sent His Prophet to us with a secure Book [Koran], which has never been altered or perverted like the books before it [Torah and Gospels]—a miraculous book that challenges all mankind to produce another like it. Allah Most High the Almighty has informed us, in His eternal and miraculous Book, that "every soul shall taste death," and that the day of death is predetermined and set. So I will meet my predestined death, according to the will of Allah Exalted. However, if my end is not yet come, neither you nor all the forces of the world—indeed! not all of creation—can hasten my death even by a single second.

Bush, do you know where I am? I am among the Muslim masses—enjoying the grace Allah has bestowed upon me, by way of their support, generosity, protection, *and their participation in the* ji-had *against you*, till we defeat you, by the help and strength of Allah.

As for my second message, it is to the American people, who are drowned in illusions. I say to them that Bush and his gang are shedding your blood and wasting your money in failed adventures. They have in-volved you in a struggle—*which you cannot win*—against the Muslims, [in order to] increase their wealth. They are drawing up a future for you that is painted with the color of blood, the smoke of explosions, and the oppression of terror. The *mujahid* lion of Islam, Sheikh Osama bin Laden, had offered you an honorable way out of your dilemma [truce offer, see p. 221]. But your leaders—due to their desire to accumulate wealth—insist on casting you into perdition and destroying your souls, in Iraq and Afghanistan—no, even more: in your own homes, Allah willing. Your leaders responded to Sheikh Osama's initiative by saying that they do not negotiate with terrorists and that they are winning the war on terror. I say to them: O you greedy liars, you merchants of war! *Who is withdrawing from Iraq and Afghanistan, we or you? And whose soldiers are committing suicide out of despair, ours or yours?*

O you American mothers, if the Department of Defense phones you saying that your son will be returning to you in a coffin—remem-ber George Bush. O you British wives, if the Ministry of Defense phones you saying that your husband will return paralyzed, chopped into pieces, or burned—remember Tony Blair.

MESSAGES TO THE
EUROPEANS

12

October 2002 was incredibly busy for Islamic terrorists: four notable acts of terrorism occurred around the world during this month. One month later, in November, bin Laden praised these attacks on an audiotape, along with two others that occurred earlier in the year. The victims of these separate attacks included British, German, French, Australian, and Russian citizens—all citizens of nations allied with the United States to varying degrees.

Again, the overall message is one of reciprocity: "Why should fear, killing, destruction, displacement, orphaning, and widowing continue to be our lot, while security, stability, and happiness is yours?"

It is unclear, however, to what degree the perpetrators of these six attacks were affiliated with al-Qaeda or if the attacks were carried out under its leadership. Bin Laden's words are ambiguous; he declares that all the attacks were "carried out by the zealous sons of Islam in defense of their faith and in response to the order of their Lord and Prophet."

"TO THE ALLIES OF THE UNITED STATES"

✧

In the name of Allah, the Merciful, the Compassionate.

From the slave of Allah, Osama bin Laden, to the nations allied to the tyrannical American government:

Peace to whoever follows [right] guidance. The road to safety begins by eliminating the aggression. Reciprocal treatment is part of justice.

The events that have taken place since the attacks on Washington and New York [9/11]—such as the killing of Germans in Tunisia, the French in Karachi, the bombing of the giant French tanker in Yemen, the killing of marines in Failaka, of British and Australians in the Bali explosions, the recent operation in Moscow,[1] and various other sporadic operations—are all reactions of reciprocity, carried out by the zealous sons of Islam in defense of their faith and in response to the order of their Lord and Prophet.

What [U.S. president George W.] Bush, the Pharaoh of the age, has been doing—murdering our sons in Iraq—and what America's ally, Israel, has been doing—bombing houses sheltering old men, women, and children with American airplanes in Palestine—was sufficient to prompt the sane leaders among you to distance themselves from this gang of criminals. Our people in Palestine have been suffering murder and torture in Palestine for nearly a century. But right as soon as we defend them [via the attacks of 9/11], the world becomes agitated and joins forces against the Muslims, unjustly and falsely— under the pretext of "fighting terrorism."

What do your governments want by allying themselves against the Muslims with that gang of criminals at the White House? Are they unaware that this gang is [composed of] the greatest butchers of our age?

This [former U.S. defense secretary Donald] Rumsfeld, the

butcher of Vietnam, is responsible for the deaths of 2 million, as well as wounding many others.

As for [U.S. vice president Dick] Cheney and [former U.S. secretary of state Colin] Powell, they have reaped more death and destruction in Baghdad than did Hulegu[2] the Tatar.

So why are your governments—particularly those of Britain, France, Italy, Canada, Germany, and Australia—allying themselves with America in its attacks on us in Afghanistan?

We had warned Australia beforehand not to participate [in the war] in Afghanistan, as well as its despicable attempts to separate East Timor—but it ignored the warning till it woke up to the sounds of explosions in Bali. Thereupon its government falsely claimed that Australians were not targeted.

If it pains you seeing your victims and your allies' victims in Tunisia, Karachi, Failaka, Bali, and Amman, bear in mind that our children are murdered daily in Palestine and Iraq; remember our victims in Khost and the deliberate slaying of our people in weddings in Afghanistan.[3] If it pains you seeing your victims in Moscow, then remember ours in Chechnya.

Why should fear, killing, destruction, displacement, orphaning, and widowing continue to be our lot, while security, stability, and happiness is yours?

This is injustice. The time to settle accounts has arrived: just as you kill, so shall you be killed; just as you bomb, so shall you be bombed. Expect more to come.

By Allah's will, the Islamic *umma* has begun to strike back with its own beloved sons—who have pledged to Allah that they will continue waging *jihad*, by both word and deed, as long as they have eyes to see and blood coursing in their veins, in order to establish right and expose falsehood.

In conclusion, I call upon Allah to help us achieve the triumph of His religion and to continue *jihad* in the path of Allah until we meet Him and He be satisfied with us—for He guarantees as much and is capable.

And our final call is, Praise be to Allah, Lord of the Worlds.

On March 11, 2004, Spain experienced its own version of 9/11: simultaneous explosions in the trains of Madrid killed 191 people and injured approximately 1,460. Certain Islamic extremist groups affiliated with al-Qaeda were believed to be responsible. Three days later, the Spanish Socialist Worker's party—which was opposed to Spain's participation in the war in Iraq—won the election.

One month after these events, the following audiotaped message from bin Laden was delivered. Like the messages directed to the Americans, this message, addressed to the Europeans, stresses the importance of reciprocal treatment, making an analogy between the events of 9/11 and 3/11 on one hand and the oppression against the Palestinians and Iraqis on the other. Also, as in the messages to the Americans, bin Laden insists that all these hostilities and counterhostilities are due to the greed and malice of a few—"the merchants of war."

Citing opinion polls and "positive interactions," bin Laden concludes by offering the Europeans a peace treaty. It is rejected. However, the day after winning the elections, the prime minister of Spain's newly elected government, José Zapatero, promised to withdraw Spain's 1,300 troops from Iraq, saying, "The war [in Iraq] has been a disaster [and] the occupation continues to be a disaster. It has only generated violence." One month later the last of Spain's troops left Iraq.

"OSAMA BIN LADEN'S PEACE TREATY
OFFER TO THE EUROPEANS"

❧

Praise be to Allah Most High.

Peace to whoever follows [right] guidance.

This is a message to our neighbors north of the Mediterranean, containing a peace proposal[1] in response to positive reactions. Evil slays its perpetrators and the pastures of iniquity are fatal.

There is a lesson [to be learned] regarding what happens in occupied Palestine and what happened on September 11 and March 11 [Madrid train bombings, killing 191 and injuring 1,460]: These are your goods returned to you. It is well understood that security is a vital necessity for all of mankind—though we do not agree that you should monopolize it for yourself. Nor do sensible people allow their leaders to compromise their security.

Having said as much, we inform you that your description of us as "terrorists" and our actions as "terrorism" necessarily means that you and your actions must be defined likewise. Our actions are merely reactions to yours—represented by the murder and destruction of our people in Afghanistan, Iraq, and Palestine.

Look, for instance, at the event that terrified the whole world: the murder of the old and wheelchair-bound Sheikh Ahmad Yassin.[2] We pledge to Allah Most High that we will avenge his death on America, Allah willing.

Which creed considers your dead innocent while our dead are considered worthless? And which rationale counts your blood real while our blood is counted as water? Reciprocal treatment is part of justice; and he who initiates aggression is the unjust one.

As for your leaders and their followers, who insist on ignoring the real problem—the occupation of all of Palestine—who engage in lies and deceptions regarding our right to self-defense and resistance, these have no self-respect. Through such deceptions, they reveal their contempt for the blood and minds of people—which only means that your blood will continue to be shed.

By merely looking to the murders that still take place in our lands—and yours—an important fact becomes clear, namely that we both suffer injustices by your leaders, who send your sons, despite objections [made], to our countries, to kill and be killed. Thus it is in both our interest to stop the ones who shed their own people's blood, for both their own narrow, personal interests and the interests of the gang residing at the White House.

This war is profiting the major corporations—both arms manufacturers and reconstruction firms, such as Halliburton[3] and its offshoots and sister companies—with billions of dollars.

It is readily apparent, then, who benefits most from igniting war and bloodshed: the warlords and bloodsuckers who direct world policy from behind a curtain. As for President Bush, other leaders similar to him, big media, and the United Nations—all these are agents of deception and exploitation, and pose a fatal threat to the entire world. And the most dangerous and difficult of these groups is the Zionist lobby. Allah permitting, we are determined to continue the fight and build atop what we have already achieved. But in response to the positive interactions that have been reflected in recent events, and the opinion polls[4] that demonstrate that most people in Europe want peace, I call upon just men—especially *ulema*, media, and businessmen—to form a permanent commission to enlighten the European peoples of the justice of our causes, particularly Palestine. [To this end] they can make great use of the media.

I therefore offer them this peace treaty, which essentially is a commitment to cease operations against every country that pledges not to attack Muslims or interfere in their business—including the American conspiracy against the greater Islamic world. This peace treaty can be renewed at the end of a government's term [the one that agrees to the treaty] and the beginning of a new one, if both sides consent. It [the peace treaty] will commence with the departure of its last soldier from our lands; it is available for a period of three months starting from the day this statement is issued.

But whoever chooses war over peace will discover us prepared for battle. And whoever chooses peace can see that we have responded favorably. Stop shedding our blood and thereby save your own. The solution to this equation—both easy and hard—lies in your hands. As you know, the situation will only grow worse the longer you delay—though you will have but yourselves to blame. Rational people do not compromise their security, property, and families in order to satisfy the liar in the White House. If Bush's call for peace had been sincere, he would not describe the man who tore open the bellies of pregnant women in Sabra and Shatila,[5] the architect of the "surrender process" [pun on the "peace process"], as a "man of peace" [a reference to Israeli prime minister Ariel Sharon]. Nor [would Bush] declare that we hate freedom and kill for the sake of it.[6] Reality demonstrates our truthfulness and his deception. The Russians were killed only after they invaded Afghanistan and Chechnya; the Europeans were killed only after they invaded Afghanistan and Iraq; the Americans were killed in New York [9/11] only after they supported the Jews in Palestine and invaded the Arabian Peninsula, and after they invaded Somalia in Operation Restore Hope[7]—wherein we restored [i.e., repulsed] them to hopelessness, praise be to Allah.

It is said that a penny spent on prevention is preferable to a fortune on cure. Blessed is he who has offered warning; heeding the truth is preferable to persisting in falsehood.

Peace to whoever follows [right] guidance.

14

The following message, from Ayman al-Zawahiri, praises the July 7, 2005, bombings in London and calls England "one of the severest enemies of Islam." Zawahiri also condemns British Muslim *ulema* for being in league with the Queen. This speech was broadcast in a film by al-Sahab Media Productions titled *Wills of the Knights of the London Raid*. (This text was taken directly from the BBC News Web site: http://news.bbc.co.uk/go/pr/fr/-/2/hi/middle_east/4443364.stm. Published: 2005/11/16 18:09:39 GMT.)

"AYMAN AL-ZAWAHIRI BERATES THE QUEEN OF ENGLAND"

❧

I speak to you today about the blessed raid[1] on London that came as a blow to the insolent British Crusader pride and made it take a sip from the same glass from which it had long made the Muslims drink.

The blessed raid that, like its illustrious predecessors in New York, Washington [9/11], and Madrid [3/11], took the battle to the enemy's own soul [soil?].

After long centuries of his taking the battle to our soil and after his hordes and armed forces occupied our lands in Chechnya, Afghanistan, Iraq, and Palestine, and after centuries of his occupying our land while enjoying security at home.

This blessed raid, like its illustrious predecessors, came to pass thanks to the racing of the vanguards of Islam to achieve martyrdom in defense of their religion and sanctities and security.

These vanguards compete for the pleasure of their Lord and follow in each other's footsteps to punish the new Zionist Crusade.

So rejoice, people of the Crusader alliance! rejoice at the disasters that the policies of [U.S. president George W.] Bush and [U.K. prime minister Tony] Blair and those who march behind them have brought upon you and—Allah willing—will continue to bring upon you.

O People of the Crusader alliance, we have alerted you and warned you, but it appears that you want us to make you taste death in all its horribleness.

So taste some of what you have made us taste.

Didn't the lion of Islam, the Mujahid Sheikh Osama bin Laden—may Allah protect him—offer you a peace treaty so that you might depart from the Islamic lands?

But you were obstinate and were led by arrogance to more crime and your foreign secretary Jack Straw said that these proposals "deserve to be met with our contempt."[2]

So taste the consequences of the insolence of your governments.

Blair has brought disaster to his people in the middle of their capital and shall bring more, Allah willing.

He continues to exploit the heedlessness and negligence of his people and obstinately insists on treating them as if they are idiots incapable of understanding by repeatedly telling them that what occurred in London had no connection to the crimes he has committed in Palestine, Afghanistan, and Iraq.

People of the Crusader alliance, Blair isn't only taking lightly Muslim blood in Iraq, Palestine, Chechnya, and Afghanistan—he's also taking lightly your blood, because he is taking you to the inferno in Iraq and exposing you to death and killing your own homeland because of his Crusade against Islam.

Let Bush, Blair, and those that march behind their Crusader-Zionist banner know that the honorable *mujahidin* of Islam have made a covenant with their Lord to fight them until victory or martyrdom.

Allah Most High said: Can you expect for us any fate other than one of two glorious things? But we can expect for you either that Allah will send his punishment from Himself or by our hands. So wait expectant; we too will wait with you.

As for the *ulema* of beggary who gathered in front of the British parliament to demonstrate their support for Blair and attack the *mujahidin* and seekers of martyrdom, I say to them: Why didn't you gather in front of the British parliament when the sanctions murdered a million children in Iraq?

Why didn't you gather in front of the British parliament when the mosques in Afghanistan were bombed with the worshippers inside?

Why did you not gather in front of the British parliament when the Zionist missiles killed Sheikh Ahmad Yassin?[3]

Why did you not gather in front of the British parliament when the Crusader bombers pulverized the women and children in Fallujah?

Why did you not gather in front of the British parliament when America desecrated the Holy Koran?[4]

Why didn't you issue a *fatwa* after each of these crimes declaring Blair a criminal who fights Islam, and that every Muslim must oppose him and refuse to follow or submit to his Crusader regime?

On the contrary, a group of you colluded with the Crusader armies and issued a *fatwa* allowing Muslims to join the Crusader armies in their attack on Iraq.

Here are the *ulema* of beggary, O Muslims, working to please [Queen] Elizabeth, head of the Church of England, blindly imitating her and issuing *fatwas* according to her views.

They say: We are British citizens subject to Britain's Crusader laws and we carry its passports and are proud of our submission to Sultan Blair, who fights against Islam, and Elizabeth, head of the Church of England.

The *ulema* of beggary put forward their usual contradictory misconceptions and say: We must obey our governments, observe their laws, serve in its army, police, and security services, and pay our taxes to our governments so that they can spend them on killing our sons, daughters, and women in Iraq, Palestine, and Afghanistan.

They say that responding to the Crusaders' crimes inside their countries will harm the Muslims living there.

Those who issue *fatwas* according to the views of the head of the Church of England pretend they forget that England is one of the severest enemies of Islam and the Muslims; that England toppled the Ottoman empire; that the English commander Allenby said when he entered Jerusalem: "Now the Crusades have finished"[5]; that England created Israel and killed thousands of Palestinian *mujahidin*; that England killed tens of thousands of Muslims from Delhi to Dinshawai [a village in Egypt] and that it participated in the sanctions against Iraq that killed more than 1 million Iraqi children[6]; and that it participated in the Crusader campaign against Afghanistan and Iraq.

MESSAGES TO THE
IRAQIS

15

Toward the end of 2002, it became increasingly clear that the United States was preparing to lead an invasion into Iraq under the assumption that Saddam Hussein was building up weapons of mass destruction. In that context Osama bin Laden issued the following message to the Muslims of Iraq.

Overall, the message is a primer exhorting the Iraqis to prepare themselves for *jihad* in the path of Allah. To do this, Muslims must first repent of their sins and rededicate their lives to Allah, while staying clean from everything un-Islamic—in the tradition of Loyalty and Enmity (see p. 66). In addition, based on his experiences in Tora Bora—which at once portray him as a military authority and hero— he recommends that Muslims build and utilize trenches against U.S. air strikes.

"TO THE MUSLIMS OF IRAQ"

In the name of Allah, the Compassionate, the Merciful.

Peace be upon you, with the mercy and blessing of Allah.

"O you who have believed! Fear Allah as He ought to be feared, and do not allow yourselves to die except in a state of submission [to Allah]" [3:102].

We are with great interest and concern keeping watch over the Crusaders' war preparations in order to occupy a former capital[1] of Islam, plunder the wealth of Muslims, and establish a puppet government over you that gets its cue from its masters in Washington and Tel Aviv [Israel]—just like the other traitorous and puppet Arab governments—all in preparation for the creation of Greater Israel.[2] "For us, Allah suffices; He is the best disposer of affairs" [3:173].

In the midst of this unjust war—a war of profligates and infidels led by America, its allies and agents—we wish to confirm a number of key points:

1. Sincerity of will: let all fighting be [grounded] in the path of Allah alone, unassociated with anything else—not the championing of a particular ethnic group, nor the championing of any non-Islamic government, which are prevalent in all Arab states, such as in Iraq. Allah Most High said: "Those who have believed fight in the cause of Allah, but those who reject [faith] fight in the cause of evil. So fight the friends of Satan—for feeble indeed is the cunning of Satan!" [4:76].

2. We affirm that victory is given from Allah Most High alone; all we need do is make preparations and incite the *jihad*. Allah

Most High said: "O you who have believed! If you aid Allah, He will aid you, and plant your feet firm" [47:7].

And it behooves [us] to fervently repent of [our] sins before Allah Most High—especially the great ones, as the Prophet said: "Avoid the seven deadly sins: idolatry against Allah, sorcery, suicide—which Allah forbade, except when done for a just cause [i.e., martyrdom operations][3]—usury, seizing orphans' money, fleeing the battle scene, and slandering innocent, female believers." Likewise, [avoid] the other great sins: alcohol, adultery, rebellion toward parents, and perjury. It behooves [us] to strive to obey [Allah] in all things—especially repeatedly invoking the name of Allah in battle. Abu al-Darda said: "Perform a good deed before battle commences, for you fight with naught but your deeds."

3. It has become clear to us from our defense and engagement with the American foe that, in war, they chiefly depend on psychological warfare, evidenced by the enormous propagandist media machine they possess. Moreover, they greatly depend on massive air strikes in order to conceal their weak points, which are fear, cowardice, and a total lack of fighting spirit in the American soldier. For these soldiers are totally convinced of the injustices and lies of their government; nor do they possess a just cause to defend. Instead, they fight only for the sake of capitalists, the lords of usury, and arms and oil dealers—such as that gang of criminals at the White House.

Add to this [former U.S. president George] Bush Sr.'s Crusader hatred and personal grudges.[4]

It has also been demonstrated to us that one of the most effective and readily available means of rendering the Crusader air force ineffective is to dig large numbers of roofed and disguised trenches—something I pointed out in a previous statement issued last year during the battle of Tora Bora.[5]

In that great and terrible battle, by holding fast to principles, faith overcame all the materialistic forces of the people of evil, by Allah Exalted's grace. I will recount to you a part of this great battle to demonstrate both the extent of their cowardice and how effective trenches are at wearing them down.

Now, our ranks consisted of approximately three hundred *mujahidin*.[6] We dug up a hundred trenches spread out over an area not to exceed one square mile, one trench for every three brothers, in order to avoid large human casualties from the bombardment. From the first hour of the American campaign on October 7, 2001, our center was exposed to concentrated bombardments. Later, these bombardments became sporadic till about mid-Ramadan. Then, on the seventeenth morning of Ramadan [November 3, 2001], a severe and fierce bombardment began, especially after the American commanders became sure that a number of al-Qaeda leaders were present in Tora Bora—including this poor servant [of Allah, bin Laden himself] and the brother *mujahid*, Dr. Ayman al-Zawahiri. The bombardment was round-the-clock; not one second passed without warplanes hovering over our heads, day and night. The control room of the leaders of America's defense ministry [i.e., the Pentagon], along with all its allied forces, exhausted all efforts to blow up and annihilate this tiny spot—wiping it out altogether. The warplanes were pouring their fire above us, especially after concluding their central mission in Afghanistan. And the American forces were bombarding us with smart bombs, bombs weighing thousands of pounds, cluster bombs, and bunker-busters. B-52–type bombers—each one hovering above our heads for more than two hours at a time—dropped anywhere from twenty to thirty bombs. Modified C-130 planes bombed us all night long with carpet bombs and other sorts of modern bombs.

But despite this massive bombardment and wild propaganda [surrounding it], unprecedented for such a tiny, besieged area, along with the additional forces of the hypocrites [Afghani allies of the United States] that they [Americans] prodded on to fight us for two weeks nonstop—despite all this, we blocked their daily attacks, sending them back defeated, bearing their dead and wounded—thanks be to Allah the Exalted, Most High. And not once did the American forces dare storm our positions! What clearer proof of their cowardice, fear, and lies concerning the myths of their alleged power is there?!

The battle, in conclusion: a resounding and utter failure for the international alliance of evil, with all its forces, against a small group of *mujahidin*—three hundred *mujahidin* inside trenches scattered over a square mile, in temperatures reaching as low as ten degrees below zero. The battle resulted in a 6 percent casualty loss; we ask Allah to accept them as martyrs. As for our trenches, only 2 percent were damaged—all praise be to Allah!

Now, if all the forces of international evil were unable to exercise their will against one square mile containing a tiny amount of *mujahidin* with very limited capabilities, how then can these evil forces prevail against the Islamic world? This is an impossibility—Allah willing—so long as the people stay firm in the faith and insist on *jihad* in its way.

So, our *mujahidin* brothers in Iraq: do not fear the lies propagated by America regarding their power and their smart or laser-guided missiles. For smart bombs—which require clear targets—have no effect worth mentioning in the midst of mountains and trenches, plains and forests. Thus neither smart—nor stupid—bombs can penetrate well-disguised trenches; only random strikes that deplete the enemy's munitions and resources [are possible]. A large number of trenches will serve you well, as Omar [the second caliph] said: "Use the ground as a shield." That is to say, take the ground for a shelter, thereby ensuring the complete exhaustion of the enemy's missile supply within months. As for their daily production [of ammunition], that's a small matter, easily borne.

We also point out the importance of luring the enemy forces into a protracted, close, and exhausting battle, utilizing the camouflaged, defensive positions in plains, farms, mountains, and cities. The enemy's greatest fear is urban and street warfare—warfare that the enemy knows would produce grave and costly human losses. We also stress the importance of martyrdom operations against the foe—operations that have inflicted harm on America and Israel the likes of which have never before been witnessed in their history.

Furthermore, we clearly declare that if any of Iraq's hypocrites or the rulers of Arab countries or those who approve of them aid America; [if any] helps them in this Crusader war, whether by fighting for them or providing bases and administrative support, or any other sort of support—even if it be by one word—to kill Muslims in Iraq, he should beware that he is an apostate, an outcast from the [Islamic] *umma*. His blood and money are forfeit. Allah Most High said: "O you who have believed! Do not take the Jews and Christians as friends and protectors: they are but each other's friends and protectors. And whoever among you turns to them for friendship and protection is one of them. Truly, Allah does not guide an unjust people" [5:51].

And we also stress to honest Muslims that, in the midst of such momentous events and [in this] heated atmosphere, they must move, incite, and mobilize the Muslim *umma* to liberate itself from being enthralled to these unjust and apostate ruling regimes, who themselves are enslaved to America, and to establish the *sharia* of Allah on earth.

The regions most in need of liberation are Jordan, Morocco, Nigeria, Pakistan, the land of the Two Holy Sites [Saudi Arabia], and Yemen.[7]

Moreover, it is no secret that this Crusader war is primarily directed against the people of Islam—whether the Socialist party[8] and Saddam [Hussein] remain [in power] or not. Thus Muslims in general, Iraqis in particular, must brace themselves for *jihad* against this unjust campaign, and be vigilant in acquiring ammunition and weapons. This is a prescribed duty upon them. Allah Most High said: "[L]et them take precautions and bear arms; for the infidels desire that you may be careless of your arms and your luggage, so that they may then turn upon you with a sudden united attack" [4:102].

It is well known that fighting in order to avail the banners of *jahiliyya* [i.e., fighting on behalf of a non-Islamic cause] is not permitted. Therefore, it behooves the Muslim to make his creed and banner visible when fighting in the path of Allah—as was spoken by the Messenger of Allah: "Whoever fights in order to make the Word of Allah reign supreme—he [walks] in the path of Allah."

However, in circumstances such as these, there is no harm if the interests of the Muslims coincide with those of the socialists [Baathists] in the fight against the Crusaders—despite our firm belief in the infidelity of socialists. For the socialists and these rulers lost their authority a long time ago. And socialists are infidels, wherever they may be—whether in Baghdad or Aden.[9] This current battle and the fighting that will take place in the coming days are reminiscent of the battles that Muslims engaged in previously.

Nor did shared interests adversely affect the Muslims' battles with the Romans [Byzantines]: their interests converged with the Persians' [Sassanians'] interests—and this posed no harm to the Companions.

Before concluding, we also stress the importance of high morale and guarding against false rumors, defeatism, uncertainty, and discouragement. The Messenger of Allah said: "Bring forth good tidings, and do not discourage [others]." He also said: "The [war-]bellow of Abu Talha amid the soldiers is preferable to a thousand men."

The biographies also mention that a man said to Khalid bin al-Walid at the battle of Yarmuk[10]: "How many are the Byzantines, how few the Muslims!"

Khalid responded: "Shame on you! Armies do not become victorious from an increase in numbers [of men]. Instead, [the spirit of] defeatism defeats them"—or something to that effect.

And let the Word of Allah Most High remain ever before your eyes: "It is not fit for a Prophet to take captives before he has thoroughly subdued the land" [8:67]. And the Word of the Most High: "When you come upon infidels, smite at their necks [i.e., decapitate them]" [47:4].[11]

Let your reprimand to the Crusaders be as was spoken by the poet: "The only thing between us is gut-stabbings and head-choppings."

In closing, I urge us all to fear Allah, both covertly and overtly, and to be patient in the *jihad*—for victory requires patience. I also advise myself and yourselves to remember and call [upon Allah]. Allah Most High said: "O you who have believed! When you encounter a force, be firm and call upon Allah, ever mindful [of Him], that you may prevail" [8:45].

O Allah, who sent down the Book, guider of clouds, defeater of factionalism—defeat them and let us prevail over them.

O Allah, who sent down the Book, guider of clouds, defeater of factionalism—defeat them and let us prevail over them.

O Allah, who sent down the Book, guider of clouds, defeater of factionalism—defeat them and let us prevail over them.

O Lord! provide us with goodness in this world and the Hereafter, and guard us from the torments of the Fire [hell].

And may Allah's prayers and blessings be upon Muhammad and all his family and Companions.

Unlike bin Laden's first message to the Iraqis, which is best character-ized as an exhortation, this second message sounds more like a victory speech. Relying on the same language and imagery that Western crit-ics of the U.S. invasion of Iraq use, bin Laden portrays the United States as being "entangled in the quagmires of the Tigris and Eu-phrates."

In an effort to rally the *umma*'s Muslims to Iraq's defense by way of *jihad*, he also presents the war in Iraq as merely the first phase of the West's aggression toward the Islamic *umma*: "And know this: This war is a new Crusader campaign for the Islamic world; it is a war over the destiny of the entire *umma*. Allah only knows what sort of ramifi-cations it holds for Islam and its people."

Finally, bin Laden depicts the United States as waning in power and authority—especially thanks to the 9/11 strikes he orchestrated, thereby reinforcing his heroic status among Iraqis.

"TO THE MUSLIMS OF IRAQ II"

Praise be to Allah—and again, Praise be to Allah!

Praise be to Allah, who said: "O Prophet! [Wage] *jihad* against the infidels and hypocrites and be harsh with them. Their abode is hell— and evil is the destination" [9:73].

And prayers and blessings be upon our Prophet Muhammad, who said [in a *hadith*]: "He who is killed for [defending] his possessions is a martyr; he who is killed for [defending] his blood is a martyr; he who is killed for [defending] his religion is a martyr; he who is killed for [defending] his households is a martyr."

This is our second message to our Muslim brothers in Iraq.

O scions of Sa'id and al-Muthani, and Khalid and Ma'na—O you scions of Saladin.[1]

Peace be upon you, and the mercy and blessing of Allah.

I salute you, your efforts, and your blessed *jihad*—for, by Allah, you have massacred the enemy and ushered in joy to the hearts of Muslims everywhere, Palestinians particularly. Allah has bestowed upon you the best reward, and your *jihad* is well appreciated. Allah has made you stand firm and guided your fire.

Rejoice! for America has become entangled in the quagmires of the Tigris and Euphrates. Bush had thought that Iraq and its oil were easy prey—but here he is in an embarrassing and critical situation, by Allah Most High's grace. Here stands America today—hollering out in its loudest voice as it crumbles before the whole world. So thanks be to Allah, who has deflected its foul deeds, forcing it to beg for assistance from both Eastern and Western mercenaries.

What you have done to America—bringing down upon them

such an exemplary punishment—comes as no surprise, for you are the sons of those mighty horsemen[2] who bore Islam eastward till they reached China.

And know this: this war is a new Crusader campaign for the Islamic world; it's a war over the destiny of the entire *umma*. Allah only knows what sort of ramifications it holds for Islam and its people.

O you youths of Islam everywhere—especially in the bordering countries [of Iraq] and Yemen![3] *Jihad* is your responsibility, so roll up your sleeves and follow the truth. And don't you dare associate with those men who follow their own whims and desires, who are a burden on the earth; or those who have bowed before the oppressors, spreading lies about you, and holding you back from this blessed *jihad*.

Voices have been raised in Iraq—just like voices were raised before in Palestine, Egypt, Jordan, Yemen, and elsewhere—calling for a peaceful and democratic solution in regard to dealing with apostate governments, or with the Jewish and Crusader invaders, instead of fighting in the path of Allah. It is necessary to war, in brief, against the dangers of this unenlightened—and unenlightening—path that contradicts the *sharia* of Allah and prevents fighting on its behalf.

So how can you obey those who never once fought in the path of Allah? Have you never considered?! These are the people who sapped the energies of the *umma* from the righteous men, following instead worldly whims—that is, democracy: a faith of *jahiliyya*.[4] By entering the legislative councils, they have gone astray and misled many.

How can they enter councils of idolatry, the legislative council of representatives, which Islam had destroyed? By so doing, they destroy the essence of the religion. What's left for them?! Then they claim that they're in the right! They commit a grievous sin. Allah knows that Islam is clean of their deeds.

Thus: Islam is the religion of Allah, while the legislative council of representatives is the religion of *jahiliyya*. So whoever obeys the rulers and *ulema* in making permissible what Allah forbade—such as entering legislative councils—or forbidding what Allah allowed—such as *jihad* in his path—takes them for lords in place of Allah. There is no power or ability save in Allah alone!

Now, then, I direct the call to Muslims in general, Iraqis in particular, and I say to you: see that you do not assist America's Crusading forces and their supporters. For all who cooperate with them—under whatever name and title—are apostates and infidels.

Likewise for all those who assist the infidel [political] parties—such as the Arab Socialist Baath party [Saddam Hussein's former party], the democratic Kurdish parties, and their like.

And it is no secret, any government established by America is a puppet and treasonous government—like the rest of the governments in the region, such as Karzai's government and Mahmoud Abbas', which were formed to put an end to *jihad*.[5]

The "Road Map"[6] is nothing but a new link in the long chain of conspiracies to end the blessed uprising [i.e., the "intifada"].

Jihad must endure until an Islamic government ruling according to Allah's *sharia* is established.

So, O you Muslims: this is a serious matter and no joke. Whoever has endurance, or ideas, or principles, or courage, or money—this is the time for it. It's at times like these that people are put to the test—the true find out who is false and the religious zealots find out who are indifferent.

The free and noble Muslim women must likewise hold fast to their roles.

And I say to my *mujahidin* brothers in Iraq: by Allah, I share your concerns and feel what you feel—yet I envy your *jihad*. And Allah knows if I could find a way to your battlefields I would not delay.

How could I remain idle, when our Prophet, our model and example, said [in *hadith*]: "Muhammad himself, with his own hand, would participate in every single battle in the path of Allah, if it were not a burden for Muslims." And he said: "I hoped to fight in the path of Allah, and be killed, fight and be killed, fight and be killed." Such, then, is the *sunna* of our Prophet Muhammad. Such is the *sunna* to make the faith triumphant. To establish a Muslim state, this [*sunna*] must be strictly adhered to—and only the righteous will adhere to it.

So to all you Muslims, to you people of Rabi'a and Mudir, and you Kurds: raise up your banner—may Allah raise you up—and never fear those thugs and their weapons. For Allah has weakened their schemes and rendered them ineffectual. Nor be startled by their vast numbers—for their hearts are empty and their rule has begun to wane, both militarily and economically, thanks to that blessed day in New York [9/11], by the grace of Allah.

After that strike and its aftermath, their [economic] losses reached more than a trillion dollars. Moreover, they have recorded a budget deficit for the third consecutive year; this year alone the deficit reached a record peak of more than 4.5 billion—praise and blessings be to Allah.

In conclusion: To our *mujahid* brothers in Iraq, to the heroes in Baghdad—the home of the Caliphate—and all around it; to the supporters of Islam,[7] the sons of Saladin; to the free peoples of Baquba, Mosul, and al-Anbar[8]; to those who have emigrated in the path of Allah, forsaking fathers and sons, families and countries, in order that they may fight and die for the victory of their religion; to all of these—

I extend my greetings and peace to you all, and I say to you: you are the soldiers of Allah, the arrows of Islam—the first line of defense for this *umma* today. For the Romans[9] have begun mustering under the banner of the cross to battle the *umma* of beloved Muhammad. So consider well your *jihad*. I hope destruction is not brought upon the Muslims because of you. Allah bless you with what I entrust you, and—after Allah—greatest hopes rest upon you. So do not shame the Muslims today, but take up the example of Sa'id at the battle of the Trench,[10] where he said:

> *He stood fast but a little*
> *battle comes swiftly*
> *Death is not feared—*
> *should its time come*

O Allah! This day is one of your days, so take hold of the hearts of the youth of Islam and commit them to *jihad* in your way.

O Allah! Bind them to their creed and let them stand fast; direct their fire and unite their hearts in harmony.

O Allah! Send down your victory to your slaves the *mujahidin* in every place—in Palestine, Iraq, Chechnya, Kashmir, the Philippines, and Afghanistan.[11]

O Allah! Give comfort to our brothers who are held hostage in the tyrants' prisons, in America, Guantánamo [Bay],[12] occupied Palestine, in Riyad [capital of Saudi Arabia], and everywhere—for you are capable of all things.

O Allah our Lord! Extend to us patience, make us stand firm, and make us victorious over the infidel peoples.

"Allah is victorious over all, though most people are unaware."

May Allah's peace be upon our Prophet Muhammad, his family, and all his Companions.

In closing, we assert that all praise belongs to Allah, Lord of the Worlds.

THEMES

The *mujahid* victory over the once-mighty Soviet Union; the obligation of all Islamic youth to wage *jihad* and conduct "martyrdom operations" in defense of their faith; the belief that a democratic United States is leading a Crusade against Islam; and the belief that Jews are conspiring with the Crusaders in order to destroy Islam: all of these themes form the heart of al-Qaeda's propaganda campaign.

The following excerpts are from various bin Laden statements over the years and are structured around the aforementioned four themes. Excerpts from al-Jazeera were translated from the original Arabic; the rest were copied directly from their host Web sites and altered slightly for syntactical consistency.

Al-Qaeda, and especially bin Laden, often present the Afghan-Soviet war as a paradigm for the war against the United States. Time and time again al-Qaeda has insisted that since the *mujahidin* were able to defeat one superpower, then surely they can defeat the other.

THE AFGHAN-SOVIET PARADIGM

The Myth of the Superpower and U.S. Cowardice

❧

May 1998

After our victory in Afghanistan and the defeat of the oppressors who had killed millions of Muslims, the legend about the invincibility of the superpowers vanished. Our boys no longer viewed America as a superpower. So, when they left Afghanistan, they went to Somalia and prepared themselves carefully for a long war. They had thought that the Americans were like the Russians, so they trained and prepared. They were stunned when they discovered how low was the morale of the American soldier. America had entered with thirty thousand soldiers in addition to thousands of soldiers from different countries in the world. . . . As I said, our boys were shocked by the low morale of the American soldier, and they realized that the American soldier was just a paper tiger. He was unable to endure the strikes that were dealt to his army, so he fled, and America had to stop all its bragging and all that noise it was making in the press after the Gulf War in which it destroyed the infrastructure and the milk and dairy industry that was vital for the infants and the children and the civilians and blew up dams that were necessary for the crops people grew to feed their families. Proud of this destruction, America assumed the titles of "world leader" and "master of the new world order." After a few blows, it forgot all about those titles and rushed out of Somalia in shame and disgrace, dragging the bodies of its soldiers. America stopped calling itself world leader and master of the new world order, and its politicians realized that those titles were too big for them and that they were unworthy of them. I was in Sudan when this happened.

I was very happy to learn of that great defeat that America suffered, so was every Muslim. . . .

Source: http://www.pbs.org/wgbh/pages/Frontline/shows/binladen/who/interview.html

December 1998

We believe that those who waged *jihad* in Afghanistan did more than their duty. They found out that with meager resources—a few RPGs, a few antitank mines, and a few Kalashnikovs—the myth of the mightiest military known to mankind was annihilated: the greatest military machine was annihilated, and with it the myth of the so-called superpowers. Moreover, we are convinced that America is much weaker than Russia, especially from the news that reached us from our brothers who [waged] *jihad* in Somalia: they were amazed beyond their wildest belief at the weakness and cowardice and mockery of the American soldier. [After] a mere eighty [*sic*: eighteen] of them were slain, they slipped out in the darkness of night, never [once] looking back—this after [they had] filled the world with talk about the "New World Order."

Source: http://www.aljazeera.net

January 1999

INTERVIEWER: Can you describe the U.S. air strikes on your camps?

BIN LADEN: The American bombardment had only shown that the world is governed by the law of the jungle. That brutal, treacherous attack killed a number of civilian Muslims. As for material damage, it was minimal. By the grace of Allah, the missiles were ineffective. The raid proved that the American army is going downhill in its morale. Its members are too cowardly and too fearful to meet the young people of Islam face-to-face.

Source: http://www.time.com/time/asia/news/interview/0,9754,174550-3,00.html

June 1999

Nowadays, *jihad* needs to be waged by the *umma*. The obligation to engage in *jihad* may be dropped if people suffer from disability. But we believe that those who participated in the *jihad* in Afghanistan bear the greatest responsibility in this regard, because they realized that with insignificant capabilities, with a small number of RPGs, with a small number of antitank mines, with a small number of Kalashnikov rifles, they managed to crush the greatest empire known to mankind [U.S.S.R.]. They crushed the greatest military machine. The so-called superpowers vanished into thin air. We think that the United States is very much weaker than Russia. Based on the reports we received from our brothers who participated in *jihad* in Somalia, we learned that they saw the weakness, frailty, and cowardice of U.S. troops. Only eighty [*sic*: eighteen] U.S. troops were killed. Nonetheless, they fled in the heart of darkness, frustrated, after they had caused great commotion about the New World Order.

> Source: http://web.archive.org/web/20021213085956/www.terrorism.com/ terrorism/BinLadinTranscript.shtml

October 2001

INTERVIEWER: Al-Qaeda is facing now a country that leads the world militarily, politically, technologically. Surely, the al-Qaeda organization does not have the economic means that the United States has. How can al-Qaeda defeat America militarily?

BIN LADEN: This battle is not between al-Qaeda and the U.S. This is a battle of Muslims against the global Crusaders. In the past when al-Qaeda fought with the *mujahidin*, we were told, "Wow, can you defeat the Soviet Union?" The Soviet Union scared the whole world then. NATO used to tremble from fear of the Soviet Union. Where is that power now? We barely remember it. It broke down into many small states and Russia remained.

Allah, who provided us with his support and kept us steadfast until the Soviet Union was defeated, is able to provide us once more with his support to defeat America on the same land and with the same people. We believe that the defeat of America is possible, with the help of Allah, and is even easier for us, Allah permitting, than the defeat of the Soviet Union was before.

INTERVIEWER: How can you explain that?

BIN LADEN: We experienced the Americans through our brothers who went into combat against them in Somalia, for example. We found they had no power worthy of mention. There was a huge aura over America—the United States—that terrified people even before they entered combat. Our brothers who were here in Afghanistan tested them, and together with some of the *mujahidin* in Somalia, Allah granted them victory. America exited dragging its tail in failure, defeat, and ruin, caring for nothing.

America left faster than anyone expected. It forgot all that tremendous media fanfare about the new world order, that it is the master of that order, and that it does whatever it wants. It forgot all of these propositions, gathered up its army, and withdrew in defeat, thanks be to Allah. We experienced combat against the Russians for ten years, from 1979 to 1989, thanks be to Allah. Then we continued against the Communists in Afghanistan. Today, we're at the end of our second week. There is no comparison between the two battles, between this group and that. We pray to Allah to give us his support and to make America ever more reluctant. Allah is capable of that.

Source: http://archives.cnn.com/2002/WORLD/asiapcf/south/02/05/binladen.transcript/index.html

March 2003

Like these exalted heroes I say: O people, do not fear America and its army. By Allah, we have struck them time and time again, and they have been defeated time after time. In combat they are the most cowardly of people. Our defense and our war against the American enemy have shown that [America's] warfare is mainly psychological in nature, because of the vast propaganda apparatus at its disposal. It is also based upon intensive bombing from the air, which is designed to conceal its most obvious weakness: cowardice and the American soldier's lack of fighting spirit. Were it not for the need for brevity, I would tell you almost unbelievable stories of this from our fighting against them in Tora Bora and Shahi-Khot in Afghanistan. May Allah make it possible to go into this in detail [in the future].[1]

First of all I should like to remind you of the defeats suffered by a number of the great powers at the hands of the *mujahidin*. I want to remind you of the defeat of the former Soviet Union, of which nothing remained after ten years of hard fighting by the Afghans and those Muslims who came to their aid, by the grace of Allah. Similarly, the Russian defeat in Chechnya, where the *mujahidin* displayed the finest examples of self-sacrifice. The Chechen *mujahidin*, together with their Muslim brethren, deflated the Russians' pride and caused them loss after loss. Beaten, they withdrew after the first war. Later the Russians returned with American support, and Russia is still suffering heavy losses because of a small group of believers, whom, we pray, Allah will support and make victorious.

I should also like to remind you of the defeat of the American forces in the year 1402 of the Muslim calendar [1982], when the Israelis invaded Lebanon. The Lebanese resistance sent a truck full of explosives to the American marines' center in Beirut and killed over 240 of them, may they go to hell and to a bitter end.

Later, after the second Gulf War, the Americans sent their forces into Somalia, where they killed thirteen thousand Somalis. There is no power and no strength save in Allah.

Then the lions of Islam awoke among the Afghan Arabs and they came to the aid [of the Somalis] and, together with their brothers in that country, they dragged America's pride through the mud. They killed them, they destroyed their tanks and brought down their planes. America and her allies fled under cover of night, each one avoiding the others' glances. Praise and thanks be to Allah!

At the same time, young *mujahidin* prepared explosive charges [for use] against the Americans in Aden. When they went off, the cowards had no choice but to flee within twenty-four hours. Later, in the year 1415 of the Muslim calendar [1994], there was an explosion in Riyad in which four Americans were killed. This sent a clear message that the local people were opposed to the American policy of support for the Jews and the occupation of the Land of the Two Holy Places.

The following year there was another explosion in al-Khobar [Saudi Arabia], in which nineteen people were killed and over four hundred wounded. As a result, the Americans were forced to move their large bases from the towns to the desert. In the year 1418 of the Muslim calendar [1997], the *mujahidin* publicly threatened America, [hoping this] would cause it to stop supporting the Jews and to depart the Land of the Two Holy Places. The enemy rejected the warning and the *mujahidin* managed, through the grace of Allah, to deliver two tremendous blows in east Africa. Later America was warned again, but paid no heed, and Allah sent success to the *mujahidin* who, in a tremendous act of self-sacrifice, annihilated the American destroyer *Cole* in Aden. This was a resounding slap in the face for the American military establishment. This operation also revealed the fact that the Yemeni government, like that of the other countries in the region, had collaborated [with the United States].

Source: http://www.memri.org/bin/articles.cgi?Area=sd&ID=SP47603

18

Al-Qaeda has made it abundantly clear that their call to arms is directed primarily to the youth of Islam. Almost every single interview geared toward the Arab and Muslim worlds ends with a call for those youth to come to Islam's defense. Bin Laden even gives an age range: fifteen to twenty-five.

THE YOUTH OF ISLAM

Jihad *and Martyrdom*

December 1998

As is well known, from birth till the age of fifteen, people are incapable [of taking care of themselves]; nor are they aware of great events. After the age of twenty-five and above, people enter into family commitments; they graduate from college and commit themselves to work, in order to support their wives and children. So while his mind grows in maturity, his ability to give grows weaker. Who shall I leave my children to? Who will support them? Etc. In reality, then, we find that the only age group capable of giving and waging *jihad* is the fifteen to twenty-five age bracket. This we noticed in the *jihad* in Afghanistan. . . . I say that the Crusader world has combined to eat up the Islamic world; the nations have rallied up against us. After Allah Almighty, the Most High, all we have left [to cope with them] are the youth who have not been weighed down by the filth of the world.

Source: http://www.aljazeera.net

December 2001

They [nineteen hijackers of the 9/11 strikes] performed a very great and heroic deed. Allah reward them, and we pray that their parents are proud of them: they raised Muslim heads high, teaching America a lesson not soon forgotten—Allah willing. . . . From Saudi Arabia, fifteen youths set out from the Land of Belief. . . . Another two came from the eastern Peninsula, from the Emirates; one from the Levant, Ziad al-Jarra; and one from the land of Egypt—Muhammad Atta. May Allah receive them all as martyrs. By their very deeds they produced a great sign, demonstrating that it was the belief in their hearts that urged them to such things, giving their souls to [the affirmation] "There is no god but Allah." Through their actions they opened a doorway for goodness and truth. Those we hear in the media saying that martyrdom operations should not be performed merely repeat the desires of the tyrants, America, and its agents. . . . There is a clear moral in the *hadith* of the youth, king, sorcerer, and monk—of people offering themselves up for [the proclamation] "There is no god but Allah."[2]

Source: http://www.aljazeera.net

December 2001
Osama bin Laden's Message for the Youth of the Muslim Umma
KANDAHAR (Islam News): What follows is the message that Osama bin Laden conveyed to the youth of the Muslim *umma*.

My beloved brothers in Islam,
We have been struggling right from our youth; we sacrificed our homes, families, and all the luxuries of this worldly life in the path of Allah (we ask Allah to accept our efforts). In our youth, we fought with and defeated the (former) U.S.S.R. (with the help of Allah), a world superpower at the time, and now we are fighting the U.S.A. We have never let the Muslim *umma* down.

We should realize that this life is temporary and eventually we have to return to Allah, the lord of the heavens and the earth.

Truly to Allah we belong and truly to Allah we shall return.

Muslims are being humiliated, tortured, and ruthlessly killed all over the world, and it is time to fight these satanic forces with the utmost strength and power. Today, the whole of the Muslim *umma* is depending (after Allah) upon the Muslim youth, hoping that they would never let them down.

The *jihad* has become an obligation upon each and every Muslim. We advise the Muslim youth not to fall victim to the words of some *ulema* who are misleading the *umma* by stating that *jihad* is still a communal duty [as in an Offensive *Jihad*]. The time has come when all the Muslims of the world, especially the youth, should unite and soar against infidelity and continue *jihad* till these forces are crushed to naught, all the anti-Islamic forces are wiped off from the face of this Earth, and Islam takes over the whole world and all the other false religions.

"And fight them until there is no more seduction and the religion will all be for Allah alone. But if they cease (worshipping others besides Allah), then certainly Allah is All-Seer of what they do" [8:39].

We ask Allah to rank us among His truthful slaves.

Your brother,

Osama bin Laden

Source: http://www.ict.org.il/spotlight/det.cfm?id=716

October 2002

America has made many accusations against us and many other Muslims around the world. Its charge that we are carrying out acts of terrorism is an unwarranted description [though bin Laden later admitted to it; see pp. 214–15].

We never heard in our lives a court decision to convict someone based on a "secret" proof it has. The logical thing to do is to present a proof to a court of law. What many leaders have said so far is that America has an indication only, and not a tangible proof. They describe those brave guys [the nineteen hijackers] who took the battle to the heart of America and destroyed its most famous economic and military landmarks [i.e., 9/11].

They did this, as we understand it, and this is something we have incited for before, as a matter of self-defense, in defense of our brothers and sons in Palestine, and to liberate our sacred religious sites/things. If inciting people to do that is terrorism, and if killing those who kill our sons is terrorism, then let history be witness that we are terrorists.

Source: http://archives.cnn.com/2002/WORLD/asiapcf/south/02/05/binladen
.transcript/index.html

March 2003

I instruct the young people to exert every effort in *jihad*, for it is they upon whom this duty primarily devolves. . . .

You should know that seeking to kill Americans and Jews everywhere in the world is one of the greatest duties [for Muslims], and the good deed most preferred by Allah, the Exalted.

I also bid them [the young people] to rally round the honest *ulema* and the sincere preachers, that is, those who practice what they teach; I also counsel them to manage their affairs in secrecy, especially the military affairs of *jihad*.

I am happy to inform all of you—and our brothers in Palestine in particular—that your brethren who are engaged in *jihad* continue to pursue the way of *jihad*, targeting the Jews and the Americans. The Mombasa operation[3] is just the first drop that heralds the approaching rain, Allah willing, may He be praised and exalted. We shall never abandon you. Go on, continue the fighting with Allah's blessing, and we too, with you, will continue to fight, Allah willing.

Source: http://www.memri.org/bin/articles.cgi?Area=sd&ID=SP47603

January 2004

I urge the youth of Islam to [wage] *jihad*, especially in Palestine and Iraq. . . . In closing, I would like to say a few words to the Muslim youth—words uttered by your grandfathers who were put to the test through many years in Palestine, and who witnessed many initiatives, conspiracies, disasters, and calls for peace. Let me remind you of these words: "My son, they will talk to you of peace. Do not listen to such appeals, for though I once believed them, I still live in a tent."

Source: http://www.aljazeera.net

19

Al-Qaeda maintains that the West is ultimately waging a Crusade against the Islamic world that is no different from the Crusades of nearly a thousand years ago. To prove this, bin Laden has been quick to quote President Bush's remark—which he was criticized for even in the United States—that the War on Terror is a "crusade" (see pp. 285–86, n. 7).

A CRUSADE

October 2001

Our goal is for our nation to unite in the face of the Christian Crusade. This is the fiercest battle. Muslims have never faced anything bigger than this. Bush said it in his own words: "crusade." When Bush says that, they try to cover up for him, then he said he didn't mean it. He said "crusade." Bush divided the world into two: "either with us or with terrorism." Bush is the leader; he carries the big cross and walks. I swear that everyone who follows Bush in his scheme has given up Islam and the word of the Prophet. This is very clear. The Prophet has said, "Believers don't follow Jews or Christians." Our *ulema* have said that those who follow the infidels have become infidels themselves. Those who follow Bush in his crusade against Muslims have denounced Allah. . . . This is a recurring war. The original crusade brought Richard [the Lionhearted] from Britain, Louis from France, and Barbarus from Germany [the kings of the original Crusade of the twelfth century]. Today the crusading countries rushed as soon as Bush raised the cross. They accepted the rule of the cross. What do the Arab countries have to do with this Crusade? Everyone that supports Bush, even with one word, is an act of great treason.

Source: http://archives.cnn.com/2002/WORLD/asiapcf/south/02/05/binladen .transcript/index.html

November 2001

Bush has used the word "crusade." This is a crusade declared by Bush. It is no wisdom to barter off blood of Afghan brethren to improve

Pakistan's economy. He will be punished by the Pakistani people and Allah.

Source: http://www.dawn.com/2001/11/10/top1.htm

January 2004
Didn't Bush say that this war is a Crusade? Didn't he say that the war will last for many years, and target sixty states? Are you unaware?

Source: http://www.aljazeera.net

20

While Jews are constantly castigated in al-Qaeda's messages, it is interesting to note how often bin Laden has relied on a historically Western charge—that there is a Zionist conspiracy bent on world domination—to further magnify the Jews' role.

THE ZIONIST LOBBY

May 1998

American politicians have painted a distorted picture of Islam, of Muslims and of Islamic fighters. We would like you to give us the true picture that clarifies your viewpoint. . . .

The leaders in America and in other countries as well have fallen victim to Jewish Zionist blackmail. They have mobilized their people against Islam and against Muslims. These are portrayed in such a manner as to drive people to rally against them. The truth is that the whole Muslim world is the victim of international terrorism, engineered by America at the United Nations. We are a nation whose sacred symbols have been looted and whose wealth and resources have been plundered. It is normal for us to react against the forces that invade our land and occupy it. . . .

> Source: http://www.pbs.org/wgbh/pages/frontline/shows/binladen/who/ interview.html

December 1998

Since the time that Iraq became a force to be reckoned with in the region, becoming the greatest Arab power to threaten Jewish and Israeli security, America has been digging up issues. . . . It is clear today that any attack on any Islamic country is initiated by the true aggressor: Israel. . . . The Jews have succeeded in obligating American and British Christians to strike Iraq. America claims to be bringing Iraq to account and justice. But the fact is that the Israeli authority and the Jewish authority, which are powerful in the White House as is plainly seen—the Defense Minister is Jewish, the Secretary of State is Jewish, the CIA and National Security officials are Jewish, all the biggest officials are Jews—have led the Christians to clip the wings of the Islamic world.

Source: http://www.aljazeera.net

October 2001

I tell you freedom and human rights in America are doomed. The U.S. government will lead the American people and the West in general will enter an unbearable hell and a choking life because the Western leadership acts under the Zionist lobby's influence for the purpose of serving Israel, which kills our sons unlawfully in order for them to remain in their leadership positions. . . . We swore that America wouldn't live in security until we live it truly in Palestine. This showed the reality of America, which puts Israel's interest above its own people's interest. America won't get out of this crisis until it gets out of the Arabian Peninsula and until it stops its support of Israel. This equation can be understood by any American child, but Bush, because he's an Israeli agent, cannot understand this equation unless the swords threatened him above his head.

Source: http://archives.cnn.com/2002/WORLD/asiapcf/south/02/05/binladen
.transcript/index.html

November 2001

The Muslims were massacred under the U.N. patronage in Bosnia. I am aware that some officers of the State Department had resigned in protest. Many years ago the U.S. ambassador in Egypt had resigned in protest against the policies of President Jimmy Carter. Nice and civilized [people] are everywhere. The Jewish lobby has taken America and the West hostage.

Source: http://www.dawn.com/2001/11/10/top1.htm

March 2003

One of the most important objectives of the new Crusader attack is to pave the way and prepare the region, after its fragmentation, for the establishment of what is known as the Greater State of Israel, whose borders will include extensive areas of Iraq and Egypt, through Syria, Lebanon, Jordan, all of Palestine, and large parts of the Land of the Two Holy Places.

Come let me tell you what is meant by "Greater Israel" and what disasters will beset the region. What is happening to our people in Palestine is merely a model that the Zionist-American alliance wishes to impose upon the rest of the region: the killing of men, women and children, prisons, terrorism, the demolition of homes, the razing of farms, the destruction of factories. People live in perpetual fear and paralyzing terror, awaiting death at any moment from a missile or shell that will destroy their homes, kill their sisters, and bury their babies alive. What response shall we make to Allah tomorrow [on the Day of Judgment]? What is happening there is unbearable [even] for able-bodied men—is it not even harder for the enfeebled mothers who see their children killed before their very eyes? We come from Allah, and unto Him we shall return. We put our trust in Allah. Allah, I beg you [to save us] from the actions of the Jews, the Christians, the treacherous rulers and their ilk, and I apologize to you for the actions of those who fail to take part in the struggle for Islam.

The founding of "Greater Israel" means the surrender of the countries of the region to the Jews. Come let me tell you who the Jews are. The Jews have lied about the Creator, and even more so about His creations. The Jews are the murderers of the prophets, the violators of agreements, of whom Allah said: "Every time they make a promise under oath, some of them violated it; most of them are infidels." These are the Jews: usurers and whoremongers. They will leave you nothing, neither this world nor religion. Allah said of them: "Have they a share in [Allah's] dominion? If they have, they will not give up so much [of it] as would equal a spot on the stone of a date" [4:52]. Such are the Jews who, in accordance with their religion, believe that human beings are their slaves and that those who refuse [to recognize this] should be put to death. Allah said of them: "They said: 'We need not fulfill any undertaking to these unlettered people [i.e., non-Jews]. They deliberately attributed falsehood to Allah' " [3:75].

These are some of the Jews' qualities, of which you must beware, and these are some of the features of the Crusader plot, which you must resist.

Source: http://www.memri.org/bin/articles.cgi?Area=sd&ID=SP47603

21

Bin Laden often justifies his violence against U.S. citizens by repeatedly pointing out that since the United States (and other Western nations) is a democracy, the people are ultimately responsible for the actions of their government.

THE PRICE OF AMERICAN DEMOCRACY

✦

May 1998

If the people have elected those governments in the latest elections, it is because they have fallen prey to the Western media that portray things contrary to what they really are. And while the slogans raised by those regimes call for humanity, justice, and peace, the behavior of their governments is completely the opposite. It is not enough for their people to show pain when they see our children being killed in Israeli raids launched by American planes, nor does this serve the purpose. What they ought to do is change their governments, which attack our countries. The hostility that America continues to express against the Muslim people has given rise to feelings of animosity on the part of Muslims against America and against the West in general. Those feelings of animosity have produced a change in the behavior of some crushed and subdued groups who, instead of fighting the Americans inside the Muslim countries, went on to fight them inside the United States of America itself.

The Western regimes and the government of the United States of America bear the blame for what might happen. If their people do not wish to be harmed inside their very own countries, they should seek to elect governments that are truly representative of them and that can protect their interests. . . . I say to them that they have put themselves at the mercy of a disloyal government, and this is most evident in Clinton's administration. . . . We believe that this administration represents Israel inside America. Take the sensitive ministries such as the Secretary of State and the Secretary of Defense and the CIA, you will find that the Jews have the upper hand in them. They make use of

America to further their plans for the world, especially the Islamic world. American presence in the Gulf provides support to the Jews and protects their rear. And while millions of Americans are homeless and destitute and live in abject poverty, their government is busy occupying our land and building new settlements and helping Israel build new settlements in the point of departure for our Prophet's midnight journey to the seven heavens [based on the Koran and Islamic tradition]. America throws her own sons in the land of the two Holy Mosques for the sake of protecting Jewish interests. . . .

The American government is leading the country toward hell. . . . We say to the Americans as people and to American mothers, if they cherish their lives and if they cherish their sons, they must elect an American patriotic government that caters to their interests, not the interests of the Jews. If the present injustice continues with the wave of national consciousness, it will inevitably move the battle to American soil, just as Ramzi Yousef [one of the planners of the 1993 World Trade Center bombing] and others have done. This is my message to the American people. I urge them to find a serious administration that acts in their interest and does not attack people and violate their honor and pilfer their wealth. . . .

> Source: http://www.pbs.org/wgbh/pages/frontline/shows/binladen/who/ interview.html

December 1998
Every American man is an enemy—whether he fights us directly or pays his taxes. And perhaps you have heard these days that the number of those [Americans] who support Clinton's strike against Iraq is some three-quarters of the population! This is a people whose votes are won when he kills innocents; a people who, after their president commits adultery and great [sins], sees only his popularity rise—a depraved people who can never understand the meaning of values.[4]

> Source: http://www.aljazeera.net

November 2001

The American people should remember that they pay taxes to their government, they elect their president, their government manufactures arms and gives them to Israel and Israel uses them to massacre Palestinians. The American Congress endorses all government measures, and this proves that all of America is responsible for the atrocities perpetrated against Muslims. All of America, because they elect the Congress.

I ask the American people to force their government to give up anti-Muslim policies. The American people had risen against their government's war in Vietnam. They must do the same today. The American people should stop the massacre of Muslims by their government.

Source: http://www.dawn.com/2001/11/10/top1.htm

NOTES

PREFACE

1. http://archives.cnn.com/2002/WORLD/asiapcf/south/02/05/binladen.transcript/
   index.html.

NOTE ON TEXT AND TRANSLATION

1. Abd al-Rahim Ali, *Hilf al-Irhab,* Cairo: Merkez al-Mahrussa l-il Nashr we al-
   Khadimat al-Sahifiyya we al-Ma'lumat: 2004.

FOREWORD AND AL-QAEDA'S DECLARATION OF WAR AGAINST AMERICANS

1. Montasser al-Zayyat, a former close associate of Ayman al-Zawahiri, has written a biography of the latter revealing much about Zawahiri's role as ideologue
   and his relationship with bin Laden, including the following statements: "Many
   people have drawn a distinction between Zawahiri's skills in oration and
   rhetoric and those of his close ally Osama bin Laden. They said that bin Laden
   has the ability to reach to the hearts of people with simple words, and is a much
   better orator than Zawahiri. . . . However, Zawahiri is gifted in individual per-
   suasion and in recruiting new cadres, because his ideas are very organized and
   his aims very clear" (p. 51). "Zawahiri managed to introduce drastic changes to
   Osama bin Laden's philosophy after they first met in Afghanistan in the middle
   of 1986, mainly because of the friendship that developed between them. Zawahiri convinced bin Laden of his *mujahid* approach, turning him [bin Laden]
   from a fundamentalist preacher whose main concern was relief work, into a
   mujahid, clashing with despots and American troops in the Arab world" (p. 68).
   "I am convinced that he [Zawahiri] not bin Laden is the main player in these
   events [9/11]" (p. 98). Montasser al-Zayyat, *The Road to Al-Qaeda: The Story of
   Bin Laden's Right-Hand Man,* trans. Ahmed Fekry (London: Pluto Press, 2004).
2. Contrary to popular opinion, *fatwas,* which today are little more than nonbind-
   ing legal opinions, can be issued by virtually any Muslim, since with the dissolution of the Ottoman empire, there is no longer an official *mufti* to speak on

behalf of Islam. Also contrary to popular opinion, *fatwas* can deal with any legal question in dispute and are not just limited to being "death warrants," as in the famous case of Salman Rushdie. The value of any *fatwa* ultimately depends on how well rooted it is to the teachings of Islam.

3. By referring to this group of messages as "propagandistic" I am not implying that they are necessarily fake, which the word "propaganda" seems to connote. Rather, I have Webster's definition of "propaganda" in mind: "ideas, facts, or allegations spread deliberately to further one's cause or to damage an opposing cause."

4. *Ijtihad*—that is, the process of independently grappling with the Koran and *sunna* in order to derive a ruling—was a recognized method of jurisprudence. In fact, it was one of the methods utilized by the earliest *ulema*, especially the founders of the four schools of jurisprudence (*madhhabs*). However, since the beginning of the tenth century, after all four schools had reached a level of development where almost everything had been codified, the doors of *ijtihad* are said to have closed.

5. Like any careful exegete, Zawahiri gives precedence to the *hadith* collections of Bukhari and Muslim, both of which are considered highly authentic by Sunnis. (Bukhari is practically unquestioned.) Moreover, he quotes only the most recognized and authoritative *ulema*—from the early founders of the various schools of jurisprudence (not just Ibn Hanbal), to prominent figures of the Middle Ages (such as al-Qurtubi, Ibn Taymiyya, Ibn Kathir, and Ibn Qayyim), to the authoritative writings of modern-day *muftis*, sheikhs, and imams.

6. This declaration was written a little over five years before the March 2003 U.S. invasion of Iraq. It is discussing the negative consequences Iraqis have suffered from the 1991 Gulf War and its subsequent economic sanctions.

7. About his signature in the declaration, Abu Yasir Rifa'i Ahmad Taha has said "that he was informed by telephone about the intention of the group [al-Qaeda] to issue a statement expressing their support to the Iraqi people against the aggression they were suffering. He agreed to the inclusion of his name in the statement. He was surprised to discover later that the statement referred to the establishment of a new front, and that it included a very serious *fatwa* that all Muslims would be required to follow." Al-Zayyad, *The Road to Al-Qaeda: The Story of Bin Laden's Right-Hand Man* (London: Pluto Press, 2004), 89.

PART I: THEOLOGY

1. "MODERATE ISLAM IS A PROSTRATION TO THE WEST"

1. Originally published under the title "Al-Qaeda's Declaration in Response to the Saudi Ulema: It's Best You Prostrate Yourselves in Secret."

2. There are four reasons to believe that this essay was written by bin Laden. First, it is always attributed to bin Laden wherever found in *jihadi* Arabic books. Second, it is written to the Saudis, with a certain familiar tone. This fact also indicates that the author is the Saudi bin Laden. (The other top al-Qaeda figure, al-Zawahiri, is Egyptian and historically has been concerned only with Egypt's politics.) Third, the essay is the perfect counterpart to bin Laden's "Letter to the Americans: Why We Are Fighting You" (see p. 197), which almost every expert agrees was written by bin Laden. Finally, the original title of the declaration begins with "al-Qaeda's declaration," and the first person "I" is used, several times in the essay: Who else but bin Laden has the honor or curse to conflate himself with that organization? Since it is in fact "al-Qaeda's declaration" and bin Laden is the unquestioned leader of al-Qaeda, it seems reasonable to treat the essay as bin Laden's own.

3. Aside from the familiar adjectives applied to Muslims like al-Qaeda—"radical," "extremist," "fundamentalist"—academics also tend to use terms such as "Salafi" (i.e., Muslims who consider the first three generations of Islam as ideal and to be literally emulated) and "Wahhabis" (i.e., followers of eighteenth-century Islamic reformer Ibn al-Wahhab, who sought to purge Islam of the many innovations that attached themselves to it throughout the centuries). To Muslims such as bin Laden and Zawahiri, however, such adjectives and terms are meaningless. They simply consider themselves to be faithful Muslims, understanding and practicing Islam the same way that the original Muslims of Muhammad's time did.

4. "What We're Fighting For" and an English translation of "How We Can Coexist," as well as the second American letter and David Blankenhorn's analysis, can be read in their entirety at the Web site of the Institute of American Values, http://www.americanvalues.org.

5. The exclamation "There is no power or ability save in Allah!" (and other variants) is very common in the Arab world and is meant to express utter dismay.

6. Islam is the world's second largest faith (20 percent of the world's population), second to Christianity (33 percent of the world's population). It is, however, the fastest-growing religion. It is believed that this is due more to the higher birthrates in Muslim countries than it is to mere conversion: six out of the top ten countries in the world with the highest birthrates have a Muslim majority.

7. By relying on the Americans' own words—"[T]his movement [al-Qaeda] now possesses . . . the capacity and expertise . . . to wreak massive, horrific devastation on its intended target"—bin Laden magnifies al-Qaeda's role and power to the Muslim world, which is used to perceiving their secular leaders as totally helpless vis-à-vis the United States.

8. On September 16, 2001, Bush asserted: "This crusade, this war on terrorism, is going to take a while." This statement created much controversy, and since then the president has dropped "crusade" from his rhetoric. The historic Crusades, which occurred between the eleventh and thirteenth centuries, were a series of wars waged mostly by western Europe (then known as Christendom) in order to recapture the Holy City, Jerusalem, from the Muslim *umma*. Revisionist history has portrayed the Crusades as a wholly unprovoked attack against Islam. In fact, it was a counterattack, since the Muslims themselves were the first to initiate an unprovoked attack against Jerusalem some five hundred years earlier, seizing it from the Christian empire of Byzantium. Nonetheless, Muslims since have understandably developed a great aversion to the word and its history; and al-Qaeda often points to President Bush's remark as evidence that the war on terror is essentially a war on all of Islam waged by malicious Christians.

    Thus, even though Bush was in all likelihood using the word "crusade" to denote a righteous enterprise undertaken with zeal, bin Laden and many other Muslims understand by that word only the Crusades of the Middle Ages. To reflect this, "Crusade" here is capitalized, since that is how it would be appreciated in the original Arabic.

9. There are two sorts of *jihad* in Islam, Defensive and Offensive. In the footsteps of Muhammad and his successors, Offensive *Jihad* is the original and historically predominant form of *jihad*, waged solely in order to convert people to Islam or place their territories under Islamic rule.

10. During the battle of the Trench (627), when Muhammad and the Medinians were surrounded by several hostile tribes led by the Meccans, the Muslim Prophet contemplated bribing the numerically imposing tribe of Ghatafan with one-third of Medina's date harvest.

11. These "legal paths" are most likely a reference to the doctrine of *taqiyya*, which permits dissembling in order to preserve one's life or empower the faith. For a more complete treatment of the subject, see "The Difference Between Befriending and Dissembling" in Ayman Zawahiri's "Loyalty and Enmity" (p. 72).

12. On February 7, 2002, Muslim extremists allegedly set fire to an Indian passenger train. This incident sparked massive religious riots between the Hindus and the Muslim minority. All in all, some 1,000 Muslims were killed and nearly 100,000 were dislocated in the Indian district of Gujarat.

13. The "Orientalists" were the European scholars—mostly French, British, and German—of the eighteenth and nineteenth centuries who made the (Near) East their specialty. Today the term possesses negative connotations, in part due to Edward Said's controversial book *Orientalism*, which depicts Orientalists as little more than racist and propagandist tools of the age of Western imperialism.

14. The popular and indispensable reference aid *Concordance et Incides de la Tradi-*

tion Musulmane (New York: Brill, 1997), compiled by A. J. Wensinck and J. P. Mensing.

15. Though Muhammad is spoken of in third person here, this assertion—oft quoted by radicals—is in fact a verbatim quote of one of Ahmad's (4869) *hadiths* attributed to the Prophet and originally spoken in the first person, "*I* have been sent in the final hours with the sword . . ."

16. For instance, the famous *hadith* relayed by Ibn Omar where the Muslim Prophet says: "Because you have forsaken *jihad*, taking hold of cows' tails and dealing in merchandise, Allah has adorned you with shame and you will never be able to shake it off yourselves until you repent to Allah and return to your original positions."

17. Theologically speaking, the essence of both Judaism and Islam is belief in one indivisible God, worshipped alone. While Christians consider themselves monotheists, the issue of the trinity and Christ's divinity in general are at great odds with the strict monotheism of both Judaism and Islam. Bin Laden is saying that, though the Christians are depicted as being "closer" to Muslims than Jews in the Koran, that is only because when they heard the message of Muhammad, they converted to Islam—not because of anything intrinsic to Christianity.

18. Traditionally, Offensive *Jihad* targets idolaters (Hindus, Buddhists, animists, etc.) before the People of the Book (Jews and Christians), since the former are seen as completely deluded and more in need of Islam's guidance.

19. While Jesus (Isa) is referred to as the "Christ" (Messiah) in the Koran, the followers of Christ are consistently referred to as "Nazarenes" (al-Nassara).

20. In accordance to this ban, Muslim women are forbidden from marrying non-Muslim men; however, despite this seemingly straightforward ban, Muslim men, under *sharia* law, are permitted to marry non-Muslim women.

21. Bin Laden is saying here that the issue of abrogation regarding verse 2:256 is controversial only in that some exegetes believe that forced conversion (as in the cited "sword" verses) actually is acceptable. However, says bin Laden, there is no contradiction in the mainstream interpretation that forced conversion is not acceptable while the imposition of *sharia* law and *dhimmi* (i.e., "second-class") status on the People of the Book is.

22. The issue of abrogation—whereby a particular verse in the Koran cancels out others—is common in Islamic theology and is acknowledged in the Koran: "Whenever We exchange one verse for another—and Allah knows best what He reveals—they say 'You [Muhammad] are a fraud.' But most of them are ignorant" (16:101; see also 2:106 and 13:39). The basic logic behind the theory of abrogation is that whenever Koranic verses contradict, those revealed later in Muhammad's life (Medinan period) have precedence over those revealed earlier in his life (Meccan period). Bin Laden is pointing out that the "verses of the

sword"—especially 9:5 and 9:29—are held by the *ulema* as having abrogated earlier, more peaceful verses, such as 60:8. (Bin Laden also discussed the issue of abrogation regarding verse 2:256, "There is no compulsion in religion"; see p. 40.

23. Eleven days after the attacks of 9/11, in an address to a joint session in Congress and the American people, President Bush said, "Tonight we are a country awakened to danger and called to defend freedom." "Defending freedom" has been a prominent theme for the Bush administration, often in association with the "War on Terror."

24. The Copts are the original Christian inhabitants of Egypt, who now exist as a minority (approximately 12 percent of Egypt's population). Prior to Egypt's conquest in A.D. 641 by the Muslim Prophet's Companion Amr bin al-As, Egypt was mostly Christian. The Coptic church is one of the oldest Christian churches in the world.

25. The "pact of Omar" is the treaty (of *dhimmitude*) that was made between the People of the Book and the second caliph, Omar. In order to continue practicing their faiths, Jews and Christians had to agree to several social conditions enumerated in the pact that, among other things, were meant to induce humiliation and debasement in accordance with the verse cited (9:29). For instance, they were to rise from their seats if a Muslim wanted it; they were forbidden from riding on saddles or bearing any arms; they were forbidden from publicly showing their crosses or worshipping too loudly, lest Muslim eyes or ears be offended; they were forbidden from building new churches or even repairing old ones. Regarding this last point, Egypt's secular government—a U.S. ally—still upholds some of the severe restrictions that apply to Christian churches. See http://www.copts.net/detail.asp?id=919. Some apologists maintain that these conditions were not strictly enforced at all times. However, what is important here is that *dhimmitude,* as bin Laden asserts, is in fact a basic tenet of Islam and thus should be enforced under *sharia* law.

26. Abu Sayyaf is an Islamist group fighting to establish an Islamic theocracy in Mindanao, an island in the southern Philippines. The Abu Sayyaf group— which translates to "Father of the Sword"—has known ties to a number of Islamic fundamentalist organizations around the world, including al-Qaeda. Hamas—or "Zeal"—is an Arabic acronym for "Islamic resistance movement," the largest Palestinian resistance party. Created in 1987, it has since been labeled a terrorist organization by Israel and the United States. Unexpectedly, it won a majority of house seats (76 out of 132) in the Palestinian elections held on January 26, 2006.

27. Following twelve days of secret negotiations at the U.S. presidential retreat that they were named after, the Camp David Accords were signed on September 17,

1978, by Egyptian president Anwar Sadat and Israeli prime minister Menachem Begin. President Jimmy Carter oversaw these negotiations. By signing a peace treaty with Israel (1979) and not demanding greater concessions for the Palestinians, Sadat was seen by many Muslims and Arabs as a traitor. He was assassinated in 1981 by Islamic radicals. One of the thousands who were rounded up and incarcerated during this time was Ayman al-Zawahiri, who was jailed and tortured for over two years.

28. In fact, Sheikh Abdullah Azzam (1941–1989), the highly influential Islamic scholar, *mujahid*, and bin Laden's onetime mentor and hero, often boastfully referred to the Prophet of Islam as not only a terrorist but as the first terrorist: "We are terrorists. Every Muslim must be a terrorist. Terrorism is an obligation as demonstrated in the Koran and *sunna*. Allah Most High said: 'Muster against them [infidels] all the men and cavalry at your command, so that you may strike terror into the heart of your enemy and Allah's enemy' (8:60). Thus terrorism is a [religious] obligation. And the Messenger of Allah is the first terrorist and the first menace" (*al-Hijra wa al-I'dad*, i.e., "Emigration and Preparation"). Some have accused bin Laden of falling out with and assassinating Azzam in order to assume control of the then nascent base ("al-Qaeda").

2. "LOYALTY AND ENMITY"

1. See pp. 285–86, n. 7.

2. The Murji'ites, or "Postponers," were an early Muslim sect, subsequently deemed heretical, who believed that all judgment should be postponed and that believers were answerable only to Allah and thus need not hold to the principles or be subjected to the penalties of the *sharia*. Moreover, faith alone was enough to safeguard against the fires of hell even if believers led sinful lives.

3. Along with the profession of the faith, fasting, praying, pilgrimaging, and giving alms make up the traditional Five Pillars of Islam.

4. Waged in 624, the battle of Badr was one of Muhammad's first and most decisive battles against his Meccan foes, the Quraish tribe.

5. Regarding Cain and Abel, the Koran states that after Allah accepted Abel's sacrifice and rejected Cain's, the latter threatened to kill the former, to which Abel replied: "If you stretch your hand to kill me, I shall not stretch mine to kill you, for I fear Allah, Lord of the Worlds. I would rather you should add your sin against me to your other sins and thus become an inmate of the Fire—the reward of the wicked" (5:28–29).

6. Starting with the discussion of Ibn Taymiyya above until this point, Zawahiri is apparently aiming his words at the soldiers and military commanders of the

many "apostate" regimes in the Islamic world, exhorting them to not fight the *mujahidin* but instead help them overthrow tyranny.

7. Zawahiri is saying here that all Islamist factions around the world should work together regardless of whether they treat each other justly.

8. From the time of the Islamic conquests, especially during the Middle Ages, and arguably until now, Jewish and Christian *dhimmis* living in Muslim lands, especially Egypt, the Levant, and Mesopotamia, have often held important posts, such as scribes, due to their higher literacy rates.

9. In Islam, the Abode of Islam represents all those lands where Islamic rule prevails—the *umma*; the Abode of War represents all those lands inhabited by infidels who refuse to submit to Allah and embrace Islam. Under Islamic jurisprudence, absolute peace will occur once the Abode of War is subsumed into the Abode of Islam, that is, once the whole world submits to Islam.

10. This particular verse—quoted in full three times on the same page—is one of the primary sources that validate the *hadith* as a fundamental source of jurisprudence. The *hadith* contains countless thousands of sayings and actions attributed to Muhammad regarding countless religious and mundane matters (which are often perceived as one and the same). See the Foreword for a complete treatment on Islamic jurisprudence.

11. The great Mongol conqueror Genghis Khan (r. 1206–1227) promulgated a set of laws encompassing everyday life known as the *yasiq* (usually translated as "the Great Code"). After the Mongol conquests, the *yasiq* was enforced in many eastern Islamic lands. Not much is known about this code, as only fragments have survived. What is clear, however, is that it affected Muslims' everyday life, often in direct contradiction to Islam's *sharia*. Many Muslims, especially after Ibn Taymiyya's famous *fatwa* condemning the *yasiq*, rose up against their Mongol overlords, who were eventually defeated by Egypt's Mamluks (themselves of Mongol descent).

12. Since Medina literally means "city," Zawahiri is probably punning to make an analogy between the praiseworthy Medinians, who sheltered Muhammad, and today's city dwellers (i.e., civilians), who should emulate the Medinians by providing shelter to the *mujahidin*.

13. By stressing this *hadith*, Zawahiri is saying that all those who have erred against Allah by befriending the Jews and Christians can now atone for this great sin by joining the ranks of *jihad* and battling the infidels.

14. The 1949 Armistice Agreements were signed between Israel and the Arab states of Egypt, Syria, Lebanon, and Jordan, ending the first Arab-Israeli war of 1948. Geared toward a lasting peace process, the 1993 Oslo Accords were the culmination of secret and public negotiations between Israel and the Palestine Liberation Organization. Focusing on another peace initiative, this time set forth by Saudi Arabia (which normally plays a less conspicuous role vis-à-vis Israel), the

Beirut Summit of 2002 was yet another attempt at diffusing the Palestinian-Israeli conflict.

15. The use of medical imagery here reminds one of Zawahiri's profession and the meticulousness it exacts, as demonstrated in this and his other treatises.

16. More sarcasm on Zawahiri's part: *dhimmis* are guaranteed protection after paying tribute (the *jizya*) to Islam and recognizing its laws. Many Muslims rationalized the "Crusaders'" presence in Muslim lands through this prism—that they are *dhimmi* "guests" who should be guaranteed protection. Zawahiri is saying that, in fact, those Muslims are living like *dhimmis*, paying tribute to and recognizing the authority of the Crusaders.

17. The doctrine of *irja'* ("postponement") was a heresy in early Islamic history (late seventh century), upheld by the Murji'ites ("Postponers"). In essence, it maintained that all censure and punishment should be postponed until the Last Day, when Allah would judge. Thus it placed no emphasis on works or upholding *sharia* law but stressed only faith.

18. The Kharijites were another extreme sect that arose just decades after Muhammad's death. They maintained the exact opposite of the Murji'ites—that those who do not meticulously follow the *sharia* are no Muslims at all and can be killed with impunity. One such sect, the Azraqi, ritually killed Muslims whom they did not deem "pious" enough. Among some of their more barbarous practices, new recruits, to prove their sincerity, would have to slit the throats of enemy captives and engage in "religious murder" (*ist'arad*), whereby men, women, and children (all professed Muslims) were slaughtered. Zawahiri is saying that the secular regimes are acting like the Kharijites by vilifying, persecuting, and killing the truest of all Muslims, the *mujahidin*.

19. See p. 288, n. 26.

20. Founded in 988, the al-Azhar Islamic school of theology in Cairo is one of the oldest universities in the world and has one of the most authoritative voices in Islam—even though it is often accused of being a puppet of the government, as Zawahiri is doing here.

21. A seasoned veteran and hero of the Soviet-Afghan war, Osama bin Laden had offered his and his *mujahidin*'s military services to the Saudi crown to expel Saddam's forces from the peninsula. His offer was rejected; the Saudis preferred the U.S. military to defend them. This event—the Saudis opting for infidels to defend the land of the Prophet after Muslim forces had offered their services—is perhaps the main complaint bin Laden has had against the Saudi crown and his strongest evidence that they are acting against the *sharia*: the *sharia* expressly forbids non-Muslims from setting foot on the sacred grounds of the peninsula, especially when they are armed. See also p. 292, n. 24.

22. This treatise was written approximately three months before the second U.S.-led invasion of Iraq.

23. On October 8, 2002, while U.S. war games were being conducted on the Kuwaiti island of Failaka, two Kuwaitis walked up to U.S. troops and opened fire, killing one and wounding two.

24. This injunction is based on an authoritative *hadith* (found in both Bukhari and Muslim), where Muhammad said: "There shall not be two religions together in the Arabian Peninsula."

25. "Greater Israel" represents the belief shared by many opponents of Israel that the latter seeks to fulfill the biblical promise made by Yahweh to Abraham: "In the same day Yahweh made a covenant with Abra[ha]m, saying, 'Unto thy seed have I given this land, from the [Nile] river of Egypt unto the great river, the river Euphrates [in Iraq]" (Genesis 15:18). Many opponents of Israel maintain that the two blue stripes above and beneath the Star of David on the Israeli national flag symbolize the two rivers, the Nile and the Euphrates, which demarcate Israel's purported territorial ambitions. Israelis maintain that the blue lines are based on the design of the Jewish prayer shawl and are not portents.

26. The words "tyrant" and "idolatry" are etymologically related: *tagha* and *taghut*, respectively. Zawahiri is likening the tyrants to the idolatry and Satan in the verses that follow.

3. "SHARIA AND DEMOCRACY"

1. These are the five categories of Islamic jurisprudence used by all four schools (*madhhabs*). Under the *sharia*, any action whatsoever falls into one of these categories. See pp. 7–10 of Foreword ("Determining Right and Wrong in Islam") for more information.

2. The word *jahiliyya* is important in Islamic history. It is often used to refer to the time before the Koran was revealed to the Arabs; prior to the seventh century, they were pagans living in ignorance. Thus when Zawahiri uses the term *jahiliyya*, he means any people who have not yet been enlightened by the Koran and are therefore still living in darkness and acting blindly. When used by radicals the term usually denotes all other religions, including "moderate" Islam, since moderates are seen as looking to more than the Koran and *sunna* for guidance.

3. The two Arabic words rendered here as "partnership" (*shirk*) and "monotheocracy" (*tawhid*) are highly important and convey a major antithesis in Islamic theology. *Shirk* (partnership) is the greatest and only unpardonable sin in Islam—associating something, whether a physical thing or an abstract concept, with Allah. "Allah will not forgive those who set up partners with Him; but He will forgive whom He will for other sins. He that serves other gods besides Him is guilty of a heinous sin" (4:48). In fact, *shirk* is the fundamental state of being in rebellion against Allah. Conversely, the word *tawhid* (a conjugate of the word

"one") in a theological sense refers to the sovereign unity and oneness of Allah. When Muslims profess the faith—that there is no god but Allah—they are, in fact, professing the unity of Allah. Since *tawhid* is being used here in a judicial context, I have chosen the admittedly cumbersome "monotheocracy" to best convey the idea of divine rule rooted in the indivisible oneness of Allah.

4. The sixty-sixth article in full: "There shall be no crime or penalty except by virtue of the law. No penalty shall be inflicted except by a judicial sentence. Penalty shall be inflicted only for acts committed subsequent to the promulgation of the law proscribing them."

5. See p. 290, n. 11.

6. The pagan Mongol conquerors of Islamic lands all eventually embraced Islam and assimilated into the *umma*.

7. Along with denoting a theological conviction, the Arabic word for "religion" (*deen*) also connotes a way of life. Thus the "Islamic religion" is a way of living, not just spiritual conviction.

8. The eighty-sixth article in full: "The People's Assembly shall exercise the legislative power and approve the general policy of the State, the general plan of economic and social development and the general budget of the State. It shall exercise control over the work of the executive authority in the manner prescribed by the Constitution."

9. Letters A through D following this assertion—*jihad* against both apostates and infidels, subordination of non-Muslims and women—are, in fact, all firmly grounded in both the Koran and *sunna* while rejected by the Egyptian Constitution.

10. See p. 288, n. 24.

11. Article 2 of the Egyptian Constitution states that "Islam is the Religion of the State. Arabic is its official language, and Islamic Jurisprudence (*sharia*) is a principal source of legislation."

12. Zawahiri is using sarcasm to make his point, by showing that democracy contradicts the most fundamental concept in Islam, the "shahada," or profession of faith. "I witness that there is no god but Allah and Muhammad is the Messenger of Allah" in a democracy is little better than saying "I witness that Allah is *no* god and *the* Messenger [Muhammad] has a co-equal, in the true spirit of democracy": none other than the seventh-century false prophet and archenemy of Muhammad, Musailima "the Liar."

4. "*JIHAD*, MARTYRDOM, AND THE KILLING OF INNOCENTS"

1. The centrality of this *hadith* to the question of martyrdom operations is so that almost every proponent of suicide bombings quotes it at one time or another—including bin Laden (see, for example, http://www.qern.org/node/80).

2. The original title of this treatise is "*Jihad* and the Superiority of Martyrdom." However, since a significant portion of it revolves around the question of killing innocents, the title has been recast to make it reflect the treatise's contents more accurately.

3. See pp. 124–25 for Ibn Kathir's famous exegesis regarding the duty of deposing whoever does not govern according to the *sharia*.

4. Seized from the Visigoths in 711, Spain was part of the Islamic *umma* until 1492, when the final Muslim stronghold, Granada, was recaptured by the Christians. Under Islamic jurisprudence, once a land is "opened" by Islam (the Arabic word used for Islamic conquests), it permanently belongs to Islam and Muslims. Under this interpretation, modern-day Spain is occupied Muslim territory no less than Palestine.

5. The common phrase "May Allah have mercy on him/her" is usually uttered after evoking the name of a deceased Muslim. Since readers are here addressed with "May Allah have mercy on you," this treatise may have been primarily written for *mujahidin* who were on the verge of conducting "martyrdom operations"—perhaps even the nineteen hijackers of 9/11.

6. Waged in the year 636 by the river Yarmuk in Syria, the battle is considered by many to be early Islam's most pivotal victory—indeed, some historians have gone so far as to consider it to be history's most decisive battle. The Muslim forces, led by Khalid bin al-Walid—also known as the "Sword of Allah"—encountered the Byzantine forces, which outnumbered them by at least four to one. After the Muslim armies began encroaching on and invading Byzantine territories, and after they defeated the Byzantines in some skirmishes and battles (the most notable among these being the battle of Ajnadin in 634), the emperor Heraclius put together a massive force consisting of subjects from all around the empire to put an end once and for all to the desert upstarts. (Muslim sources make out the Byzantines' numbers to exceed their own by as much as ten to one, although most modern historians are content with a four-to-one ratio.) The unexpected Muslim victory opened a floodgate of Islamic conquests against both their Byzantine and Persian foes: less than five years after this victory, besides Syria, all of Mesopotamia to the east, and Egypt and its prized city of Alexandria to the west, fell to the sword of Islam permanently. Aside from the historical repercussions of this battle, Yarmuk became most symbolic—then and now—of how Allah always fights beside his faithful servants, defeating their foes, who often outnumber and outmatch them.

7. The four schools of jurisprudence (or *madhhabs*) of Sunni Islam are Hanafi, Maliki, Shafi'i, and Hanbali (named after their founders). All four are agreed to the main points of Islamic theology and differ only over finer details. Moreover, all four are considered valid by Muslims. Since support from at least one of

these schools is mandatory to establish legitimacy especially regarding controversial points, Zawahiri spends more time in this treatise than his others delin-
eating the various schools' perspectives regarding "martyrdom operations" and
bombarding infidels when women, children, and Muslims are among them.

8. Waged in 625, the battle of Uhud pitted Muhammad and a small band of Medinan followers (the "Ansar") against a larger force from Mecca. The Meccans defeated Muhammad at this battle, although they did not pursue Muhammad
and his followers when they fled.

9. The Algerian War of Independence against the French colonizers (1954–1962). Algeria is one of the last Arab countries to gain independence from the colonial
powers.

10. After fleeing Mecca (622), Muhammad sought refuge at the city of Ta'if but was
later ejected. Many have opined that he authorized the use of catapults during
the siege of Ta'if in 630 in particular due to this affront. Either way, after the city
was subdued, all of western Arabia belonged to Islam.

PART II: PROPAGANDA

5. AYMAN AL-ZAWAHIRI INTERVIEW FOUR YEARS AFTER 9/11

1. A reference to the March 31, 2005, Zimbabwean parliamentary elections, in
which the ruling party won but was accused of electoral fraud as well as threat-
ening the populace with starvation and violence if they did not vote for them.
U.N. secretary-general Kofi Annan expressed "concern" over the elections, calling on the ruling party to establish an atmosphere of confidence and to engage
in constructive dialogue.

2. Since July 2003, the Sudanese government of Khartoum (which is more ethnically "Arab") has been accused of genocide, mass murder, and rape in the Darfur region (which is ethnically more African). While the U.S. government has
referred to this humanitarian crisis as genocide, the U.N. has not. Approximately 400,000 have thus far been killed and 2.5 million displaced. In fact, as
opposed to Zawahiri's complaint, the U.N. usually comes under fire for not
properly responding to the deepening crisis of Darfur.

3. See p. 296, n. 2.

4. A reference to the U.N.'s oil-for-food program initiated on behalf of the Iraqis,
which was tainted with scandal.

5. See p. 299, n. 15.

6. See p. 301, n. 2.

7. By suggesting that Saladin, a Muslim ruler renowned for his magnanimity toward
the defeated Crusaders, would put the Americans to the sword, Zawahiri is saying
that even a forgiving ruler would have no choice but to execute them.

8. Since 2004 Pakistani and U.S. forces have focused on the mountainous region of Waziristan in Pakistan in their search for al-Qaeda.

9. Salman Rushdie is the Indian-born author who wrote the controversial novel *The Satanic Verses*. Some viewed the book as mocking Islam and its Prophet. A *fatwa* calling for his execution was issued by Iran's then-supreme leader, the Ayatollah Khomeini, in 1989, and it is still in effect.

10. After receiving political asylum in Britain in 1993, Abu Qatada, who is wanted for terrorist links in Jordan, was arrested and examined in England in 2001 for charges that he was committing or funding acts of terror. It is believed that the United Kingdom is trying to extradite him back to Jordan.

11. See p. 297, n. 7.

12. Sheikh Omar Abd al-Rahman is an Egyptian radical scholar who was indicted for the 1993 World Trade Center bombings and is currently serving a life sentence in a maximum-security penitentiary hospital in Colorado. He is also wanted in Egypt for the 1997 Luxor massacre, where some fifty-eight foreign tourists were slain by members of his terrorist organization, the Islamic Group, which is affiliated with al-Qaeda, especially through the Egyptian Ayman Zawahiri.

MESSAGES TO THE AMERICANS

6. "OSAMA BIN LADEN'S OATH TO AMERICA"

1. Since the colonial powers of the West partitioned the lands of Islam after World War I.

2. The issue of child mortality rates in Iraq during the sanction years (1991–1999) is a much contested one, from those who lay the blame entirely at Saddam Hussein's feet to those, such as bin Laden, who blame the United States directly. Moreover, the figures cited regarding these deaths vary considerably—between five- and seven-digit numbers. Indeed, bin Laden and Zawahiri quote various numbers throughout their speeches and writings. Most experts, however, seem to be agreed that some 500,000 children died as a result of UN-imposed economic sanctions against Iraq.

3. A reference to the atomic bombs the United States dropped on Japan during World War II. At least 120,000 people died immediately from the two attacks combined, and many more would die in years to come from the effects of nuclear radiation. About 95 percent of the casualties were civilians.

4. In August 1998 al-Qaeda carried out near-simultaneous suicide bombings against the U.S. embassies in Nairobi, Kenya, and Dar al-Salam, Tanzania. More than three hundred people were killed and nearly five thousand injured.

5. Housed with some 360 other idols in the Ka'ba, the supreme Muslim shrine in Mecca, Hubal the moon god was the chief deity of pre-Islamic Arabia. Due to his

preeminence, he was also often seen as the "one god." With the coming of Islam, Muhammad purged the Ka'ba by smashing all the idols, including that of Hubal.

7. " 'WHY WE ARE FIGHTING YOU': OSAMA BIN LADEN'S LETTER TO AMERICANS"

1. In 1916 the soon-to-be-destroyed Muslim Ottoman empire lost control over Palestine to the British. One year later the British government declared its intention of founding a new Jewish homeland in Palestine. The state of Israel received formal recognition in 1948, hence the "fifty years."

2. Other Muslims, including Shi'as, have used the same uncompromising language regarding Israel. The current president of Iran, Mahmoud Ahmadinejad, once said: "As the Imam [Ayatollah Khomeini] said, Israel must be wiped off the map."

3. Such as Genesis 15:18, for example: "In the same day the LORD made a covenant with Abra[ha]m, saying, Unto thy seed have I given this land, from the [Nile] river of Egypt unto the great river, the river Euphrates [in Iraq].

4. Before Palestine was inhabited by either Jews (Hebrews) or Arabs, it was in fact home to a Semitic people commonly known by their biblical name, the Canaanites. The Hebrews conquered the Canaanites in the twelfth century B.C. Nearly two millennia later, in 638, the Arabs conquered Palestine from the Christian Byzantines. In between those two dates, the vicissitudes of history saw various peoples and empires rule Palestine at one time or another, including the Babylonians, Persians, Greeks (Macedonians), Romans; and in modern days, the Turks, French, and British.

5. "You did not show concern" is probably a reference to Secretary of State Madeleine Albright's response to the question of whether child mortality rates in Iraq were "worth it," to which she responded, "I think this is a very hard choice, but the price—we think the price is worth it." Al-Qaeda—indeed, many Arabs and Muslims—often point out this assertion by a former U.S. authority as proof of American indifference to the deaths of Iraqi children. See p. 296, n. 2, for more on the actual numbers of child mortality rates in Iraq.

6. The site of the Aqsa Mosque has been a scene of much controversy and violence, especially in recent years. Although it is the third holiest site in Islam, it is built atop the remains of Judaism's holiest site—the Temple Mount, where the first two Jewish Temples were originally erected. Moreover, Jewish tradition maintains that the Messiah shall appear when the Temple is made to stand for a third and final time. Against the backdrop of these prophecies, Ariel Sharon, then leader of the opposition in the Israeli parliament, paid a visit on September 28, 2000, to the Aqsa Mosque with several hundred Israeli security forces, declaring that the complex would remain under Israeli control indefinitely. The second Palestinian Intifada ("uprising") commenced the following day.

7. To Muslims, Islam is to Christianity and Judaism what Christianity sees itself to Judaism—a fulfillment and completion. But while Christians accept the Old Testament as it is, Muslims believe that both the Old and New Testaments have been corrupted and thus are no longer inspired: anything in the Bible that contradicts the Koran (such as Christ's divinity) is seen as evidence of this distortion.

8. Bin Laden here is referring to the so-called Franklin Prophecy, a speech attributed to American statesman Benjamin Franklin and supposedly delivered at the Constitutional Convention of 1787. First published in 1934, the popularity of the Franklin Prophecy has been second only to the Protocols of the Elders of Zion among anti-Semites. Among the many anti-Semitic remarks in the forgery, bin Laden is most probably referring to this: "If they [Jews] are not expelled from the United States by the Constitution within less than one hundred years, they will stream into this country in such numbers that they will rule and destroy us and change our form of Government for which we Americans shed our blood and sacrificed our life, property and personal freedom. If the Jews are not excluded within two hundred years, our children will be working in the field to feed Jews while they remain in the counting houses, gleefully rubbing their hands."

9. Former president Bill Clinton's sexual liaison with White House intern Monica Lewinsky—with a public confirmation that the latter performed fellatio on the former in the Oval Office—created a scandal that led to Clinton's impeachment, although he was finally acquitted in 1998. On the eve of his impeachment, Clinton ordered a cruise-missile attack against Iraqi targets, which triggered the serious accusation—both at home and abroad—that the president was producing international tensions merely in order to divert the impeachment process.

10. In fact, AIDS originated and spread from sub-Saharan Africa. Bin Laden is probably either evoking the many conspiracy theories that assert that AIDS was invented by Western scientists in order to eliminate undesirable segments of the world's population or voicing the religious conviction that AIDS is Allah's way of punishing an iniquitous world that follows the U.S.'s lead.

11. The Kyoto Protocol is an international treaty on climate change. Its objective is the "stabilization of greenhouse gas concentrations in the atmosphere at a level that would prevent dangerous anthropogenic interference with the climate system." As of September 2005, 156 countries had signed on. The United States is the only major country not to ratify the agreement.

12. This is, in fact, a contested point. Several high-ranking U.S. military commanders during World War II, including Dwight D. Eisenhower and Douglas MacArthur (the Supreme Allied Commander in the Southwest Pacific), believed that there was no military justification to drop atomic bombs on Japan.

Also, a report published in 1946 by the United States Strategic Bombing Survey concluded that Japan would in all probability have surrendered even if the bombs had not been dropped.

13. In 1991, Algeria held its first-ever parliamentary elections. The first-round results clearly revealed that the Islamist party (the Islamic Salvation Front) was in the lead and would win the overall elections. The government reacted by canceling all further elections, which plunged the nation into a bloody civil war that claimed some hundred thousand lives. The United States is often accused of turning a blind eye or even supporting the Algerian government's antidemocratic actions.

14. Between 1972 and 2004, the United Nations cast thirty-nine resolutions critical of Israel. The United States vetoed them all.

15. On November 25, 2001, Taliban fighters surrendered the town of Qunduz to the forces of the Northern Alliance. Hundreds of them subsequently died of asphyxiation in the shipping containers used to transport them to the Qali Jangi prison complex, where 230 prisoners and a CIA agent were also killed during an uprising.

16. Apparently a reference to the Patriot Act—an acronym for "Uniting and Strengthening America by Providing Appropriate Tools Required to Intercept and Obstruct Terrorism." Passed shortly after the events of 9/11, the Patriot Act has come under criticism particularly by civil liberty groups—especially section 215, which grants investigators the right to look into personal records (including financial, medical, phone, Internet, student, and library records) on the basis of being "relevant for an ongoing investigation concerning international terrorism or clandestine intelligence activities," as opposed to probable cause, as outlined in the Fourth Amendment of the U.S. Constitution.

17. Guantánamo Bay, Cuba, is the site of a U.S. prison camp where foreign militant combatants are detained. Many al-Qaeda and Taliban personnel captured in Afghanistan have been sent there, facing tactics that some organizations have characterized as abusive.

18. Bin Laden is probably thinking of the Zoroaster Sassanian and Christian Byzantine empires. The Sassanian empire was swept away in Islam's first wave of conquests (ca. 650), while the Byzantine empire—known as the Roman empire to Muslims—long seen as Europe's eastern bulwark against Islamic aggression, finally fell to the Muslim Turks in 1453.

8. "ISRAEL, OIL, AND IRAQ"

1. Founded in the year 762 by the Abbasid caliph al-Mansur, Baghdad became the official capital of the Islamic empire—which at that point in time stretched from northwest Africa to Persia—and marks the shift from the Umayyad pe-

riod (when the Islamic capital was Damascus, Syria, ca. 650–750) to the Abbasid period (ca. 750–1250). Within a generation of its founding, Baghdad would become a great center of learning and commerce, and its population is said to have been as high as 500,000—an extraordinary number in that day and age. It remained the unrivaled center of Islamic civilization until it was sacked and its caliph killed by the Mongols in 1258.

2. After this message was delivered, both England and Spain were attacked. The London attacks, a series of coordinated suicide bombings that struck London's public transport system, occurred on July 7, 2005, during rush hour. The bombings killed 52 civilians and injured over 700 people. The Madrid attacks, also a series of coordinated terrorist bombings against the commuter train system of Madrid, took place on the morning of March 11, 2004, killing 191 people and wounding 1,460.

9. "YOUR FATE IS IN YOUR HANDS ALONE"

1. In several public addresses, the president has often referred to al-Qaeda and its affiliates as "enemies of freedom" and "people who hate freedom." In his address to a joint session of Congress and the American people delivered nine days after the 9/11 attacks, the president remarked, "Americans are asking, why do they [perpetrators of 9/11] hate us? They hate what we see right here in this chamber—a democratically elected government. Their leaders are self-appointed. They hate our freedoms—our freedom of religion, our freedom of speech, our freedom to vote and assemble and disagree with each other."

2. In fact, this is the first time bin Laden publicly acknowledges al-Qaeda's role in the events of 9/11. He had denied it previously.

3. On June 6, 1982, Israel invaded southern Lebanon in an attempt to eradicate the Palestine Liberation Organization. In the ensuing struggle, Israeli forces besieged Beirut for some seventy days, culminating in a bombing campaign. During the heavy bombardment, an estimated eighteen thousand Arabs, mostly civilians, died. Here bin Laden recalls the Israeli bombardment against West Beirut's high-rise apartment buildings as a precursor to the U.S. twin-tower attack.

4. As of October 2004—a year and a half after the war in Iraq was declared over—the civilian death toll there was popularly believed to be around 100,000, per the *Lancet* medical journal. According to the *Washington Post*, "The analysis, an extrapolation based on a relatively small number of documented deaths, indicated that many of the excess deaths have occurred due to aerial attacks by coalition forces, with women and children being frequent victims, wrote the international team of public health researchers making the calculations" (October 29, 2004). Other estimates, however, have been as low as 16,000.

5. See p. 296, n. 4.

6.   See p. 299, n. 16.

7.   President Bush served as governor of Texas in 1994 and was reelected in 1998. His brother, John Ellis ("Jeb"), was also elected governor of Florida in 1998. The role of Jeb Bush and his secretary of state, Katherine Harris, in the Florida elections of the presidential election of 2000, where his brother narrowly won the presidency, has been a point of controversy.

8.   Four days prior to this message the Pentagon had announced that the Bush administration would seek roughly $70 billion in emergency funding for the wars in Afghanistan and Iraq. The amount spent since the September 11, 2001, attacks has been approximately $230 billion, most of which has been spent on Iraq.

9.   Halliburton Energy Services and its subsidiary Kellogg, Brown, and Root (KBR) have had contracts in Iraq up to $18 billion, including a single no-bid contract known as Restore Iraqi Oil worth approximately $7 billion. Vice President Dick Cheney was chief executive officer of Halliburton (1995–2000) prior to becoming vice president. Controversies have arisen due to Cheney's close ties to the contractor.

10. During the attacks of 9/11, President Bush, as part of a photo-op, was reading a children's book about a girl's pet goat to a class of children in Florida.

10. "BIN LADEN'S TRUCE OFFER TO THE AMERICANS"

1.   A reference to a secret memo that leaked out, stating that only on the urging of U.K. prime minister Tony Blair did President Bush relent from his plan to bomb al-Jazeera's headquarters in Qatar (a U.S. ally). Al-Jazeera's offices in both Kabul (Afghanistan) and Baghdad (Iraq) have been destroyed by U.S. cruise missiles during U.S. campaigns, bringing the allegation that they were intentionally targeted by the U.S. military. Al-Jazeera, of course, is famous for airing al-Qaeda messages—such as this one. And though it often comes under heavy fire for doing so—it is often accused of being in cahoots with al-Qaeda— interestingly, here bin Laden accuses al-Jazeera of being a Western puppet.

2.   These three U.S.-controlled prison complexes have been the subject of much controversy regarding the ill treatment of their prisoners. Most notorious is Abu Ghraib; photographs of sexual abuse and torture of Iraqi prisoners there by U.S. soldiers have been published worldwide.

3.   On May 1, 2003, some six weeks after the U.S. invasion of Iraq, President Bush gave a speech on Iraq aboard a U.S. aircraft carrier where he declared that "major combat operations in Iraq have ended." The vast majority of the U.S. military death toll in Iraq has taken place after that assertion.

4.   See pp. 72–75 and 142–43, which treat the subject of *taqiyya* and deceit in Islam.

MESSAGES TO THE EUROPEANS

12. "TO THE ALLIES OF THE UNITED STATES"

1.   *Germans in Tunisia*: On April 11, 2002, a twenty-four-year-old Tunisian man, who is suspected of spending some time in Afghanistan between 2000 and 2001, carried out a suicide operation in the Tunisian island and popular tourist destination Djerba: fourteen German tourists, one Frenchman, and six Tunisians were killed and thirty were wounded.

  French in Karachi: On May 8, 2002, a suicide bomber detonated a car bomb alongside a crowded bus in Karachi, killing eleven Frenchmen and two Pakistanis. Fifty others were wounded.

  French tanker in Yemen: On October 6, 2002, the *Limburg*, a French oil tanker carrying 397,000 gallons of crude oil stationed in the Gulf of Amen off the Yemeni coast, was rammed by an explosive-laden boat. One Bulgarian crewman died, twelve were injured, and nearly 100,000 barrels of oil leaked out.

  Marines in Failaka: On October 8, 2002, while U.S. marines were conducting war games on the Kuwaiti island of Failaka, two Kuwaiti nationals walked up to the troops and opened fire, killing one American and wounding two.

  British and Australians in Bali: On October 12, 2002, three bombs were detonated in the town of Kuta on the Indonesian island of Bali, killing 202 people and injuring a further 209. It is considered the deadliest act of terrorism in Indonesian history. The majority of the dead were foreign tourists, including some 88 Australians, 26 British, and 38 Indonesians.

  Operation in Moscow: On October 23, 2002, 40 armed Chechen rebels seized a crowded Moscow theater, taking over 700 hostages and demanding the withdrawal of Russian forces from Chechnya. After a siege of two and a half days, Russian special forces stormed the building after firing in some sort of anesthetic gas. All of the Chechen rebels were killed, along with 130 of the hostages.

2.   Grandson of Genghis Khan, Hulegu (1217–1265) the Conqueror played a negative role in Muslim history. During his reign, he conquered most of southwest Asia (which was then already predominantly Muslim) and Egypt. However, he is most renowned for sacking Baghdad (1258), then the Muslim world's capital, and putting to death some 250,000 people. He is said to have had the last caliph wrapped in a carpet and beaten to a pulp. After the sack of Baghdad and with the fall of the Abbasid empire, leadership of the Islamic world would fall into the hands of non-Arabs—mostly Mongols and Turks—until the twentieth century, when it became leaderless, as it remains to this day.

3.   Khost, Afghanistan, where an alleged terrorist training camp was annihilated under a hail of U.S. cruise missiles in 1999.

On July 1, 2002, 48 people at a wedding party in an Afghani village were killed in a U.S. bombing raid; 117 were injured. Apparently the U.S. military mistook gunfire, which is traditionally used to celebrate Afghani weddings, for hostile gunfire. A B-52 bomber and AC-130 helicopter were both involved in the incident, which reportedly went on for over an hour. The victims included women and children.

13. "OSAMA BIN LADEN'S PEACE TREATY OFFER TO THE EUROPEANS"

1. The Arabic words used for the cease-fire proposals that bin Laden offered Europe differed from those he used in his offer to the United States. To the Europeans he offered a *mudabarat sulh* (essentially a long-lasting peace treaty); to the Americans, on the other hand, he offered only a *hudna*, a temporary and easily abrogated truce.

2. Spiritual leader Ahmad Yassin (ca. 1937–2004) cofounded the Islamic Palestinian party Hamas in 1987. In 1989 he was convicted and sentenced to life in prison for ordering the kidnapping and killing of two Israeli soldiers. Released in 1997, Yassin resumed his role as leader of Hamas. In March 2004, as Yassin was being wheeled out of a mosque after morning prayers, an Israeli helicopter gunship fired Hellfire missiles at him, killing him as well as eight other bystanders.

3. See p. 301, n. 9.

4. See, for example, http://people-press.org/reports/display.php3?ReportID=206 for statistics. The study finds an increasing shift in European public opinion regarding the United States between the years 2002 and 2004—that is, between the events of 9/11 and one year after the war in Iraq.

5. In 1982, during the Lebanese civil war, while Israel occupied Beirut, Maronite Lebanese militia, under the guidance of Israeli forces, entered the refugee camps of Sabra and Shatila in search of Palestine Liberation Organization members. A massacre ensued, with 700 to 3,500 refugees being killed. Ariel Sharon was Israel's defense minister at the time.

6. See p. 300, n. 1.

7. Aimed at averting a growing humanitarian crisis in lawless Somalia, Operation Restore Hope, a U.S. operation conducted under the auspices of the United Nations, began in March 1993. During the battle of Mogadishu in August 1993, approximately one thousand Somalis and eighteen U.S. servicemen were killed.

14. "AYMAN AL-ZAWAHIRI BERATES THE QUEEN OF ENGLAND"

1. The "blessed raid" on London occurred on July 7, 2005, during rush hour and consisted of a series of coordinated suicide bombings that struck the city's pub-

lic transport system. The bombings killed fifty-two civilians and injured over seven hundred people.

2. See "Osama bin Laden's Peace Treaty Offer to the Europeans," p. 234. On April 15 Jack Straw said, "One has to treat such claims, such proposals, by al-Qaeda with the contempt they deserve."

3. See note 2 in "Osama bin Laden's Peace Treaty Offer to the Europeans," above.

4. In April 2005 *Newsweek* published an article stating that U.S. personnel at the Guantánamo Bay prison camp had desecrated a copy of the Koran and flushed it down the toilet in front of Muslim prisoners.

5. Probably a reference to Britain's Sir Edmund Allenby's proclamation to the inhabitants of Jerusalem after the Holy City was taken from the Ottoman empire toward the end of 1917. Among other things, Allenby said to the inhabitants of Jerusalem that "since your city is regarded with affection by the adherents of three of the great religions of mankind [Judaism, Christianity, Islam] and its soil has been consecrated by the prayers and pilgrimages of multitudes of devout people of these three religions for many centuries, therefore, do I make it known to you that every sacred building, monument, holy spot, shrine, traditional site, endowment, pious bequest, or customary place of prayer of whatsoever form of the three religions will be maintained and protected according to the existing customs and beliefs of those to whose faith they are sacred."

6. See p. 296, n. 2.

MESSAGES TO THE IRAQIS

15. "TO THE MUSLIMS OF IRAQ"

1. See p. 299, n. 1.

2. See p. 292, n. 25, for "Greater Israel."

3. See Ayman Zawahiri's "*Jihad*, Martyrdom, and the Killing of Innocents," p. 141.

4. A possible reference to the first Gulf War (1991) and the alleged assassination attempt on George Bush Sr.'s life by Saddam Hussein (1993).

5. After the United States launched its military attack on Taliban and al-Qaeda forces throughout Afghanistan, most of al-Qaeda's members fled to Tora Bora (i.e., the "black dust" region), where a vast network of caves and trenches, built in the 1980s during the *mujahidin jihad* against the Soviets, was located. It was popularly believed that bin Laden, after finding nowhere to run from the heavy American bombardment, ultimately retreated to these caves as a final stronghold.

6. Most U.S. intelligence reports list between 1,000 and 1,500 al-Qaeda operatives present at Tora Bora.

7. All these countries are ruled either by monarchies or military dictatorships. It's unclear why bin Laden does not include Egypt, itself one of the most strategic Muslim countries, and its government, a longtime nemesis and target of al-Qaeda's number-two man, Ayman al-Zawahiri.

8. The former Socialist party in Iraq, known as the Baath party (which means, among other things, "resurrection"), was founded in 1945 as a secular, left-wing, Arab nationalist political party. Originally conceived as a pan-Arabist movement, Baathists ultimately came to power in both Syria and Iraq in 1963. By 1966, however, the party fractured, and Syria and Iraq, though following the same ideologies and maintaining parallel structures, became rival forces in the region. Iraq's Baathist regime reigned for forty years, until it was overthrown by the United States; Syria's Baathist party is currently still in power.

9. In June 1969 a radical and secular Marxist political party in Yemen gained power, changing the country's name to the People's Democratic Republic of Yemen (PDRY). Its seat of power was in Aden, then the capital of Yemen. Soon thereafter, all political parties were assimilated into the Yemeni Socialist party, which became the only legal party. The PDRY maintained close ties with Communist nations such as the Soviet Union and Red China.

10. See p. 294, n. 6.

11. In fact, decapitations have been notorious aspects of the war in Iraq—most notably U.S. contractor Nicholas Berg's decapitation at the hands of Abu Mussab al-Zarqawi, photographs of which were widely disseminated on the Internet.

16. "TO THE MUSLIMS OF IRAQ II"

1. These are names of various heroes from Islamic history who are somehow associated with Iraq. The renowned Muslim general Khalid bin al-Walid started the conquest of Iraq against the Sassanian empire (ca. 634); Sa'id ibn Abi Waqqas finished it. Al-Muthani was a fierce Muslim warrior renowned for great acts of prowess during these wars for Mesopotamia. Most familiar to the West, however, is Saladin, a Kurd born in Tikrit, Iraq (the same region Saddam Hussein hails from). After establishing his seat of power in Egypt, he went on to reconquer Jerusalem from the Crusaders, delivering them a major blow at the battle of Hattin (1187).

2. Another reference to the early warriors who, having converted to Islam and based in the then easternmost portion of early Islam's conquests, Mesopotamia (ca. 650), went on to launch more campaigns of conquests in all the lands between Iraq and China.

3. Bin Laden's father, Muhammad, was a Yemeni. Bin Laden probably singled out Yemen by name in an effort to evoke the tribal loyalties he no doubt enjoys there.

4. See Ayman Zawahiri's treatise "*Sharia* and Democracy," p. 120, for more on the subject of democracy and Islam.

5. After the overthrow of Taliban forces in Afghanistan, on December 7, 2004, Hamid Karzai (b. 1957) became Afghanistan's first democratically elected leader. A longtime and influential politician in the Fatah movement in Palestine, Mahmoud Abbas (b. 1935) was elected president of the Palestinian National Authority on January 9, 2005.

6. First outlined by President George W. Bush in a speech delivered on June 24, 2002, the "Road Map" for peace is a long-term plan whose ultimate goal is to resolve the Palestinian-Israeli conflict.

7. Along with the general meaning of "supporters of Islam" there is also a specific Islamist group in Iraq that goes by that name (in Arabic, Ansar al-Islam). An ultraconservative Kurdish Sunni organization formed around 2001, Ansar has maintained a strong presence in northern Iraq along the Iranian border. The United States has accused it of being a safe haven for terrorist groups and al-Qaeda associates, such as now deceased Abu Mussab al-Zarqawi, who in bin Laden's final message in December 2004 was appointed al-Qaeda's representative in Iraq. The "Ansar" are also the early inhabitants of Medina, who hold a prominent place in Islamic history for providing refuge and aid to Muhammad in 622 when he fled Mecca.

8. Fifty miles north of Baghdad and in the vicinity of the Sunni triangle, Baquba was the scene of heavy fighting during the 2003 U.S. invasion of Iraq. Mosul is Iraq's third largest city, populated by both Arabs and Kurds. Al-Anbar is Iraq's largest province, bordering Saudi Arabia, Jordan, and Syria. Containing the cities of Falluja and Ramadi, the insurgency is considered strongest in this province.

9. An allusion to the early years of Islam's militant expansion when the primary and longtime resisters were European Christians (which in the Arabic sources are always referred to as "Romans").

10. The battle of the Trench (627) was waged when a large coalition of Meccan-led forces attacked Muhammad and his followers in the city of Medina. The Muslims fortified the city by digging trenches along its barriers and, though greatly outnumbered, the Muslims triumphed. (Most sources say there were only 3,000 Muslims to the coalition's 10,000 men.) In the wake of this decisive Islamic victory, after surrendering, the 600 to 900 male members of the Jewish Qurayza tribe—who did not participate in the battle but were accused of secretly being allied to the Meccan forces—were summarily put to death by decapitation on the orders of Sa'id ibn Mu'adh, whose poetry bin Laden quotes.

11. All Muslim countries warring with either the United States or their non-Muslim neighbors: Palestine with Israel; Chechnya with Russia; Kashmir with

India; and the Muslim minority (5 percent) in the Philippines with the Catholic majority (80 percent).

12. See p. 299, n. 17.

THEMES

1. In fact, bin Laden does find the opportunity to go into this in detail in his first message to the Iraqis. See p. 245.

2. See p. 146 for the complete *hadith*.

3. In November 1998, an Israeli-owned hotel in Mombasa, Kenya, was targeted by terrorists and claimed by al-Qaeda. Sixteen people, mostly Kenyans, as well as the two suicide bombers, died in the attack. A nearly simultaneous attempt to down an Israeli civil airliner carrying more than 240 people from the Mombasa airport failed.

4. See p. 298, n. 9.

INDEX

Raymond Ibrahim is a historian and writer of the Arab world and Islam. He was educated at California State University–Fresno (B.A. and M.A. in history) and has done graduate work at Georgetown University. His essays, op-eds, analyses, and translations have been published widely (New York Times Syndicate, *Los Angeles Times*, *Washington Times*, United Press International, *Financial Times*, *National Review*, as well as in papers published in Europe, Asia, and South America). He works at the Near East Section of the African and Middle Eastern Division of the Library of Congress.